Showing West

Showing West

Three Prairie Docu-Dramas

Edited by Diane Bessai and Don Kerr

Prairie Play Series 5

NeWest Press
Edmonton

Number 5 in the Prairie Play Series, Diane Bessai, Series Editor.

The editors gratefully acknowledge assistance in the preparation of the
manuscript by The University of Saskatchewan and the Department of
English, University of Alberta, and give special thanks to Diane Lipsett.

Performance permissions:

The West Show and *Far As the Eye Can See*
Theatre Passe Muraille
16 Ryerson Avenue, Toronto, Ontario M5T 2P3

Medicare!
Playwrights Canada
8 York Street, Toronto, Ontario M5J 1R2

Canadian Cataloguing in Publication Data

Main entry under title:
Showing west

(Prairie plays series ; 5)
Bibliography: p.
Contents: Medicare! / Rex Deverell — The west show / Theatre Passe
Muraille — Far as the eye can see / Rudy Wiebe & Theatre Passe
Muraille
ISBN 0-920316-60-3 (bound). — ISBN 0-920316-58-1 (pbk.)

1. Canadian drama (English) - 20th century. I. Deverell, Rex, 1941-
Medicare! II. Theatre Passe Muraille. The west show. III. Wiebe,
Rudy, 1934-   Far as the eye can see. IV. Bessai, Diane, 1931-
V. Kerr, Donald C. VI. Series.
PS8315.5.P73S56   C812'.5408   C83-091060-3
PR9196.6.S56

Financial Assistance:

Alberta Culture
The Canada Council
Nova: An Alberta Corporation
Saskatchewan Arts Board

NeWest Publishers Limited
204-10711-107 Avenue, Edmonton
Alberta, Canada   T5H 0W6

Contents

Foreword

Some future historian of the Canadian theatre of the 1970's is bound to notice the two generally defining and often opposing theatrical trends of the era. One trend is towards the performance of established, internationally focused drama; it is the type of theatre requiring large, well-equipped, comfortable buildings located in major regional centres; such, for example, are Manitoba Theatre Centre, Winnipeg, St. Lawrence Centre, Toronto, and Citadel Theatre, Edmonton. The other trend expresses the impulse to develop new plays and new native talent, both the governing principles of the so-called alternate theatre movement. For this type of theatre, space demands are modest: a converted factory, an abandoned church, or a renovated city hall serve companies such as Tarragon and Theatre Passe Muraille in Toronto and the Globe Theatre in Regina. Playwright-composer John Gray once remarked that Canadian plays are apt to flop on large proscenium stages because they have been originally created for the intimate, open spaces of these improvised venues: it would be well for the reader of such plays to remember that the challenge of the unconventional space is itself an influence on their structuring and performance techniques.

The plays of *Showing West* are each specific examples of contemporary Canadian experimental dramaturgy of a particular kind: they are all historical documentary plays, dramatic instruments for the theatrical exploration of particular regional issues—social, political and ultimately cultural—drawn from both the recent and the more distant past of prairie life. They are basically presentational rather than naturalistic in style, which is to say that they draw attention to the play as a performance rather than as the simulation of actuality. But they also illustrate an interesting range of difference in their specific methods of dramatization and in their specific approach to the factual sources of the subject matter.

Theatre Passe Muraille's *The West Show* (1975) is a collective creation developed by director Paul Thompson and the eight members of his troupe; at the time of its performance (in the fall

7

of 1975, at many Saskatchewan centres with several stop-overs in Alberta and Ontario), it was not written down as a definitive text, but later compiled and edited for publication purposes by a member of the company. As a text it is actually a series of notations for performance; as Thompson once said of an earlier collective work by the same company of actors, the "real experience" of the play "is sitting through the show." Although the company did not work from a formal script for *The West Show*, once the performance plan was established (after several weeks of on-location research and improvisational acting techniques, or 'jamming'), there was no further improvisation before the audience; at most, actors might occasionally switch roles for the fun of it.

Readers familiar with Theatre Passe Muraille's earlier work, specifically *The Farm Show*, premiered in 1972 and *1837: The Farmers' Revolt* (with writer Rich Salutin), premiered in 1973, will notice that in a general way *The West Show* combines certain techniques from these plays: for example, the organization of contrasting scenes, each built around representative character portrayals, as in *The Farm Show*; the structuring of the play as a whole through recurring stage images that evoke and reinforce particular themes, as in *1837*. In so far as *1837* is an improvisation on historical events, the technique is also operative in certain sections of *The West Show* as well: the "Madame Tourond" section, for example, is broken into a sequence of roughly sequential scenes (a continuing technique in all the sections) that refer to the two Riel Rebellions from the perspective of a fictionalized character based on an historically documented name. As always, Passe Muraille is more interested in "mythologizing" history than just investigating it. Even the "Louis Lucas" and "Tractor Demonstration" sections, dealing with more recent memories, reflect the same improvisational freedom. In contrast, the one contemporary section, "Janet Rietz," set in Lac La Ronge, an Indian and Metis and administrative community in Northern Saskatchewan, is offered as closely observed investigative theatrical journalism.

Over all, the "myth" of Saskatchewan reflected in *The West Show* is two-fold; in his introduction Thompson speaks of *islets de bois*, while Ted Johns, one of the actors, has referred to the West as "islands of people on the prairie sea", imagery which is symbolically reinforced in performance by the fracturing of Joe Fafard's set. The other part of the myth, paradoxically, offers as an alternative to isolated individualists (e.g. "Tom Sukanen") and fragmented societies (e.g. "Janet Reitz") a vision of social cohesion through collective action, and that is the counter thrust of *The West Show*, vividly presented in the depiction of energetic Louise Lucas in her work with co-operatives in the early days of the CCF, and comically mythologized in the inventive body language of the 1969 tractor demonstration of the farmers. More precise versions of

Saskatchewan co-operative life were to be later developed by other companies in other shows: in particular in *Paper Wheat* (1977) by 25th Street Theatre, a troupe which learned much from Passe Muraille during its residence in Saskatoon during the creation of *The West Show*, and in Deverell's carefully particularized documentary reconstruction of the medicare issue. But the visitors from Ontario were important catalysts . in the development of audiences, performers and creators for this modern form of prairie theatrical regionalism.

By no means the least fruitful of Passe Muraille's contact with Western Canada was their encounter with Rudy Wiebe. The novelist's brief association with the company for the dramatization of the "Sam Reimer" section of *The West Show*, an episode drawn from Wiebe's novel *The Blue Mountains of China* (1970), led to plans for further co-operation in 1977, resulting in *Far As the Eye Can See*. The inclusion of the play (for the past two years out of print) in *Showing West* serves as an important illustration of the collective process of play-making in collaboration with a writer, in this case one relatively inexperienced in writing for the theatre, but as a novelist intensely absorbed in the particularities of prairie life and tradition.

In *Far As the Eye Can See*, the story-maker is given full reign to his inventiveness; thus the Passe Muraille habit of mythologizing history is unequivocally evident in Wiebe's creation of the three symbolic figures representing Alberta's history: Crowfoot, Princess Louise Alberta and William Aberhart. These, amazingly and unexpectedly, interact with the contemporary events realistically fictionalized from an actual public controversy between the farmers of Dodds-Roundhill and Calgary Power during the years 1973-1976. While the unghostly ghosts appropriately convey something of the spirit rather than the events of Alberta's history from Indian to colonial to progressive agricultural society, they also throw into ironic relief the contemporary fight to preserve the land from strip-mining. Yet, even though the play challenges the present-day Albertan ideals of technological progress, ultimately *Far As the Eye Can See* does not take sides as strongly as some observers have wished. Perhaps this is because Passe Muraille eschews political theatre as such; Paul Thompson once noted that in Canada it is a "political act to discover about yourself," and so "discovery theatre" is this company's particular *forte* for which political questions may serve as catalyst.

This play probably represents Passe Muraille's most sustained attempt to structure a whole show through plot, perhaps in part reflecting a novelist's participation in the project: actually there are four plots, some more loosely related to the main controversy than others, and others better sustained through their focal characters. Nevertheless, the remarkable ability of certain of the

9

actors to improvise and develop character vividly and convincingly has seldom shown to better advantage in a collective play. Outstanding examples are Janet Amos's Betty Mitchell, the gentle but firm-minded wife out to save her home and community; Ted John's brilliant satiric study of William Aberhart; David Fox's grumpy old prairie patriarch, Anton Kalicz. Passe Muraille's "texture work", the evocation of the particularities of local voice, tone and accent, is in itself a contribution to the contemporary Canadian drama.

Rex Deverell's play *Medicare!* is a dramatisation of events leading to the 1962 strike of Saskatchewan's physicians in response to legislation proposed by the provincial government, under the leadership of Tommy Douglas, which would introduce universal medical insurance in the province. As it turned out, the eventual outcome of the issue was a foreshadowing of the federal government's medical health program which came into effect for all of Canada in 1969; but at the time it appeared to the medical profession of Saskatchewan that its professional integrity was under governmental seige. This play is not a collective creation, but in its documentary format it does reflect Deverell's own particular kind of experience with this type of investigative play-making (as he discusses in his introduction); as a dramatist he has written many types of play in his long-standing association with the Globe Theatre of Regina, including collaboration in the documentary collective. Theoretically *Medicare!* could have been a collective with all the members of the cast contributing to its research and dramatization, as was the case with the Globe Theatre's 1978 production of *No. 1 Hard*. That he chose to research and write *Medicare!* himself perhaps accounts for the clarity with which complex public events are recovered and shaped into tripartite dramatic structure (initiation of action, crisis and resolution) that makes an intelligible pattern of essential events and issues without apparent distortion.

Among the plays of *Showing West*, Deverell's *Medicare!* represents documentary drama in its purest form, which is to say that it offers history as a dramatized record in a manner that serves the subject, not the personal or subjective responses of either writer or actor. While probably there can be no absolute objectivity in a dramatic rendering of controversial public matters, the documentary dramatist aims for that effect. Deverell draws precisely on records: of political speeches, committee debates, correspondence and public opinion. He reinforces their authenticity by a strict refusal to fictionalize. Only for the sake of compression and continuity does he allow himself a modicum of creative freedom: for example, in his characterization of two typical and opposing opinions of medicare as represented by Drs. Wilson and Scott, or in the brief vignettes that humourously note the arrival in Regina of the national press. But always the intention of the playwright's inventiveness is clear to the audience. Essentially, *Medicare!* gives dramatic shape to history as history, not mythology, and for that reason the play has a double textual value: as a type of theatre and as a type of historical presentation.

As theatre it offers particular challenges to both playwright and actor. Together they must make the show lively and at the same time keep the information flowing, well aware that audiences might include participants in the historical action itself. The impersonation of well-known public figures is a delicate matter; it cannot and should not try to be total, nor should it be caricature. There is a special pleasure for the audience in recognising the roles *actors* are playing, even the occasional portrayal of someone by an actor of the opposite sex (as in the case of actress Linda Huffman's Ross Thatcher). There is an intellectual distancing inherent in this type of performance (Brecht called it "estrangement") reminding the audience that this is theatre, not a mirror image of life; at the same time it allows them to refresh their memories and perhaps even re-think the issues that still affect them now. Or, if they are younger than the events on stage, the presentation provides an entertaining way of discovering the meaning of their own present in relation to the play's past.

All three regional plays celebrate western radical or populist politics but do so in complex ways. *Far As the Eye Can See* and *The West Show* obviously champion the battles of ordinary people against great powers. *Medicare!* documents the culmination of years of popular campaigning for state health care, though the play itself is primarily organized around a battle between two elites, government and doctors, and when the people make their entrance they are more often the right wing populists of the Keep Our Doctor campaign. There are ambivalences like that in all these populist plays. Deverell says how much energy he gave to imagining the doctors' point of view so that his play should not be one-sided. In *Far As the Eye Can See* John Siemens argues his case for a developed future with poetic intensity and in the end victory is tempered with the losses that go with it. In both plays the 'enemy' is presented sympathetically—from their own view of themselves—so the plays are as much plays of reconciliation as plays of protest. *The West Show* stays more resolutely on one side, partly because it only barely imagines the opposition. Yet if the theme we remember from the play is the struggle of the dispossessed for greater power, then there is an almost unconscious second theme running alongside that main one—the theme of defeat. In Act 1 the Metis at Batoche, Sam Reimer and Tom Sukanen all struggle in their individual or collective ways and lose. Act 2 seems more positive with Louise Lucas and the tractor demonstration surrounding the sequence of the man whose town has vanished, but the tractor demonstration of 1969 runs down into the prosperity and apathy of the mid-seventies, and if the Janet

11

Reitz sequence were placed in its chronological position and so ended the play, then the energy of Louise Lucas and the founding of the CCF and the energy of the agrarian protest that helped re-elect the NDP in 1971 would be replaced by an image of bureaucratic government that forces the Metis woman again into exile—and so the story has come full circle. The sub-theme to regional protest in *The West Show* is defeat. Not the least of the values of these three plays is their rich theatrical treatment of one of the great themes of western regional history: radical and populist politics.

The collective creation is a major dramatic form in the western Canadian theatre of the 1970's, lending itself to an indigenous expression of increasingly popular appeal over the decade. Passe Muraille's arrival in Saskatoon in the summer of 1975 encouraged Andy Tahn's 25th Street Theatre to work on its first collective creation, *If You're So Good Why are You in Saskatoon?* (1975) and the Saskatoon Theatre soon developed other such shows both for home presentation and tour. For a time 25th Street also enjoyed a useful exchange with Edmonton's Theatre Network, a company that developed its first collective creation, *Two Miles Off*, in the fall of 1976 under the direction of Mark Manson. For several years, the work of both these companies became well-known on the prairie touring circuits and beyond, particularly Twenty-Fifth Street's *Paper Wheat* (1977) and Network's *Hard Hats and Stolen Hearts* (1977). *Far As the Eye Can See*, after its premiere at Edmonton's Theatre Three, was remounted by Passe Muraille at Tarragon Theatre the following season, with a further production in 1978 by The Great Canadian Theatre Company of Ottawa. Rex Deverell's work with *Medicare!* in 1980 at the Globe Theatre in Regina marked an important stage along the way of that theatre's long interest in documentary style plays, dating back to *Next Year Country* with Carol Bolt in 1971 (revised as *Buffalo Jump* with theatre Passe Muraille in 1972); *Tales from a Prairie Drifter* by Rod Langley, 1973; *Davin: the Politician*, by Ken Mitchell, 1978. Deverell's success with *Medicare!* led him the following year to write his docu-drama *Black Powder*, a play about the Estevan miners' strike in 1931 that recalls and develops from a major episode in the earlier *Next Year Country*. The researching of local stories for the stage has become almost a standard mode of dramatic expression in the prairie theatres that most care to reflect the indigenous life of the region. These plays are major examples of that mode.

Diane Bessai
University of Alberta
Don Kerr
University of Saskatchewan
Dec. 1982

Further Reading

Plays

Deverell, Rex, *Black Powder*, in *Grain*, Feb., 1982; *Black Powder*, Moose Jaw, Thunder Creek Publishing Co-Op, 1982.

Bolt, Carol, *Buffalo Jump, Gabe, Red Emma*, Toronto Playwrights Canada, 1976.

Langley, Rod, *Tales from a Prairie Drifter*, Toronto, Playwrights Canada, 1974.

Mitchell, Ken, *Davin: The Politician*, Edmonton, NeWest Press, 1978.
— *The Shipbuilder*, in *Canadian Theatre Review*, #21, Winter 1979.

Salutin, Rick, *1837: The Farmers' Revolt*, Toronto, James Lorimer, 1976.

Theatre Passe Muraille, *The Farm Show*, Toronto, Coach House Press, 1976.

Twenty-Fifth Street Theatre, *Paper Wheat*, in *Canadian Theatre Review*, #17, Winter 1978; *Paper Wheat: the Book*, Saskatoon, Western Producer Prairie Books, 1982.

Background

Bessai, Diane, "Canadian Docu-Drama," *Canadian Theatre Review*, #16, Fall 1977, 7-10.
— "Documentary Theatre in Canada: An Investigation into Questions and Backgrounds," *Canadian Drama*, Spring 1980, 9-21.
—. "The Regionalism of Canadian Drama", *Canadian Literature, No. 85, Summer 1980, 7-20.*

Johns, Ted, "An Interview with Paul Thompson," Performing Arts Magazine, Winter 1973, 30-32.

Kerr, Don, "Paper Wheat: Epic Theatre in Saskatchewan," *Paper Wheat: the Book*, 15-30.
— "The West Show", *Next Year Country*, Jan.—Feb. 1976, 21-25.
— "Three Plays: *Farm Show, Ten Lost Years, Almighty Voice,*" *Next Year Country*, April 1975, 41-48.

Melnyk, George, "Theatre from the People, From the Land," *Radical Regionalism*, Edmonton, NeWest Press, 1981, 22-26.

Nunn, Robert C., "The Meeting of Actuality and Theatricality in The Farm Show," *Canadian Drama*, Spring 1982, 42-52.

Wallace, Robert, "Paul Thompson at Theatre Passe-Muraille: Bits and Pieces," *Open Letter*, Second Series, Spring 1974, 49-71.

Wallace, Robert, "Rex Deverell: Framing the Mysteries," *Canadian Theatre Review*, Spring 1982, 165-171.

Wallace, Robert and Cynthia Zimmerman, *The Work: Conversations with English Canadian Playwrights*, Toronto, Coach House Press, 1982; Rex Deverell, 127-141; Paul Thompson, 237-251.

Actors and the set. L. to R. Connie Kaldor, Anne Anglin, Eric Peterson, Miles Potter, and Janet Amos

The West Show

Theatre Passe Muraille

The West Show was first performed at Rosthern Junior College, Rosthern, Sask., Oct. 6, 1975, conceived, directed and produced by Paul Thompson of Theatre Passe Muraille with the following cast:

Janet Amos   *Mme. Tourond, Sam's Grandmother, Psychiatrist, the Pregnant Girl, Farmer's Wife, Anna.*

Anne Anglin   *Marie, Janet Rietz, Myrtle, Trudeau, Winnie.*

David Fox   *Tom Sukanen, Celeste, Priest, Sam's Father, God, Katrina's Father, Constable, Morris, Hitchhiker, Walter, Angus.*

Paula Jardine   *Metis Woman, Emily, Simon Linklater, Flo, Lilian.*

Ted Johns   *Cochrane, Riel, Bandit, Mr. Dorion, Second Son, Farmer, John.*

Connie Kaldor   *Louise, Student Radical, Louise Lucas, Carol, Bessborough Hotel.*

Eric Peterson   *Baptiste, Wandering Spirit, Patrice, Pastor, Reporter, Neighbour, Eric, Judge Fafard, Percy, Henry Lucas, George.*

Miles Potter   *Stenner, Dumont, Sam Reimer, First Son, Manager, Probation Officer, Brian, Andrew, Lorne.*

Set painting and ceramic sculpture of Louis Riel *(stolen during rehearsal)*: Joe Fafard

Set design and construction: Bob Pearson

Research assistance: Maria Campbell *Halfbreed*; Rudy Wiebe *The Blue Mountains of China, Peace Shall Destroy Many*; Juliet and Napoleon Perret of Duck Lake, Saskatchewan; Joe Fafard of Pense, Saskatchewan; Andy Tahn of 25th Street Theatre, Saskatoon; Ronald MacDonald of Rosthern College

Text transcribed and edited by Ted Johns with the assistance of Paul Thompson and Don Kerr

Drawings: Anne Anglin

Introduction

Paul Thompson

I think there are two ways to read *The West Show*: first as a guide to what is sometimes called the Passe Muraille house style, mainly associated with my direction, and secondly, from an acting point of view, as a key for actors and others to enter into the landscape and characters that help define "the west."

The actors who were involved with this production were for the most part quite experienced in the collective mode and the novelty of the form had long worn off. They were therefore looking for other rewards in making this play. For Eric Peterson and Connie Kaldor, it was an opportunity to bring their acting skills back to their original province and attempt to rediscover characters and situations familiar to them. For the rest of us, it was a challenge to explore and finally name some of the elements of the "western" psyche and also come up with a show that would make sense to both a local audience and the folks back east. Janet Amos would probably call that an example of my penchant for "high risk theatre." Others, more objective, preferred words like impossible.

This was 1975 and we were lodged in Saskatoon at the Queens Hotel at $65 per week, where a sympathetic lady desk clerk had decided to put us on the fourth floor out of regards for our children. The third seemed relegated to a more transient activity that gave strong hints of semi-pro hooking. And the first floor bar held promise of all sorts of exotic "material" for the play. We of course never got a bar scene in the final version, but this bar played an important role in the making of our show. For some reason, we as a nomadic band of actors were accepted here—no more unusual than a lot of the regulars. The place had a local reputation as an Indian bar and I remember having to give my word to Andy Tahn that no one would beat him up before he would drink with us there. The atmosphere was exhilarating and just a little dangerous. By the seventh or eighth beer anything seemed possible—even connecting together a play with Mennonites, Indians and socialists. Rudy Wiebe got drunk there one night—on ginger ale. Our generating station had been found, we needed only a rehearsal space. Enter 25th Street

17

House Theatre—a lovely space alas no more—a former church on 8th Street—and a company of people—wonderful talents, with Tahn over-producing enthusiasm and optimism like some uncapped well. Could we help each other? An idea came forth—don't tell the Touring Office but we'll shift some of our production money over to 25th, say something like $2500 or $3000. A board member said "watch out, these guys from the east are pretty tricky with money." He had been an administrator for a theater in St. Catharines. But a trade was effected. We were given a base of operations, and 25th Street would try this collective method with Layne Coleman, Andy Tahn, Bob Collins, Karen Weins, Christopher Covert, and Linda Griffiths in a play that ended up being called *If You're So Good Why Are You in Saskatoon?*

The West Show rehearsed for five weeks: the Saskatoon show rehearsed for four. I attempted to work with both. *The West Show*'s dilemma loomed large—in fact as large as the mileage gauge on the cars or trucks we'd use to come. Bob and Anne had been as far as Lac La Ronge and had copped an airplane ride to Pelican Narrows, David snooped around Moose Jaw, and Eric had this farm organizer from Indian Head whose character kept popping into rehearsals. Ted kept leaving rehearsals early to nip back around Duck Lake, Batoche, and the odd point south of Saskatoon. He came up with an inventor whose inventions, although true, couldn't make it past an early rehearsal—nobody would believe him. Joe Fafard came to play with us. Could we make characters out of his statues? We try and he works with Bob on our touring set. Our set becomes a rarity—a Fafard painting. We work with three statues— his aunt, his uncle, and Louis Riel—the characters are enigmatic— their gestures say all, their words come hard—we can't go back to farm show portraits, but Louis' voice starts to come. Suddenly, SOMEBODY HAS STOLEN LOUIS RIEL—his statue is gone. Louis the captive has been kidnapped again. Is history working on us or are we working on history? Joe is philosophical; the rest of us feel rotten. Does whoever stole it even know what he's done? It becomes harder to make the play. But the acting gets stronger and stronger. The women characters push forward, Connie's Louise, Janet's Mme. Tourond and Anne's Metis Woman. They grab for a means to show themselves. Could they ever meet? Can we invent a meeting point? No, they have their own frame, and the eventual shape of the play emerges. When I read Kroetsch's *Badlands*, later on, I felt very much like the photographer—beautiful pictures but how much of the journey will we be able to bring out?

The parts and the whole are one, and we are both. Even though the characters ignore each other, even though they lock themselves into their own cultural coulees, their *ilets de bois*, there is a thematic unity to the play and it comes *through* the characters, and through their particular sense of self. The form must be direct and the

18

care, the concern and the skills of the acting are the key. This is an actor's show. It must all go through them. Miles takes us into Sam Reimer, the words are sparse, the situation at best an indication, but he is full of *The Blue Mountains of China* and *Peace Shall Destroy Many*. The moral dimension transcends. David grabs hold of the set and tears it apart, putting it on its end. It rises above us maybe ten feet high. Can we go much higher? Some of the halls we're booked into have a twelve foot ceiling. How else can we make people imagine a twenty-five foot high boat in the middle of the prairies? Tom Sukanen's dream takes shape. David's character becomes a meditation on impossible dreams. The language is banal, the dialogue is, to say the least, cryptic. But look at his hands as he wrestles his dream into place. They know what they're doing. Thorough, practical, dependable. What do they know of the passion for the untried? Between the head and the hand stands the actor.

And the set becomes our accomplice. It is both trampoline and backdrop. We act on it. We act in it. It serves to isolate or protect. It will become transformed like the actors to present this everchanging face of experience. A boat, sure—a tractor, no problem. Narrow road to the deep north, turn the pieces on end to form a Canadian Stonehenge. And cannot the whole story of Louis Riel be told on a Red River cart? Take off the frame, and the wheels form a gatling gun, put the frame on its side and you have a courtroom, turn it once more and there's a gallows. Riel is hanged by the cart of flight.

I describe all this only to evoke the passions aroused by the making and the playing of this show. Some plays come out clean and a little like a stranger. They start to have their own life once they've been played. Others, like *The West Show*, continue to haunt the people who made it. Pieces of Louis, Louise, Sam, Tom, Mme. Tourond and Anne's Metis Woman keep coming back. Why? I don't know. Maybe to remind me they're still out there. I still need to know who stole Louis Riel?

The Set

The set consisted of two main elements. The first was a steeply raked, curved stage, about twelve feet wide at the front and fourteen feet wide at the back and ten feet deep, on which was painted a Saskatchewan farm landscape in winter. This stage could be taken apart into five independent pieces like a jigsaw puzzle. There was also a three-quarter scale Red River cart which disassembled into body, axle, and wheel elements. During the play all these pieces were manipulated and manoeuvred to represent a large range of visual metaphors.

Act I   Section I   Tom Sukanen

Scene i

The play begins when the concealed actor playing Tom begins to rise, slowly heaving one of the sections on its side and then lifting another section onto its side and, in the course of his slow relentless labour, moving them into place to create an image of Tom Sukanen's boat.

STENNER: Tom! Tom?

TOM: That you Stenner?

STENNER: Yah, I come round every day Tom. Tom, there's a man come round. He says he wants to talk to you—but I wouldn't let him come round till you said it was all right. *Tom labours without comment.* It's alright, Mr. Cochrane—you can come down now. *Cochrane enters in an attitude of dubious curiosity.* Tom? This is Mr. Cochrane.

COCHRANE: I see you're quite an engineer, Mr. Suka'nen.

TOM: Su'kanen. *Pause. Tom continues his relentless toil.* This is the keel of my boat. Nine feet high! Lap-planked. Tarred and caulked. And then what did we put over that Stenner?

STENNER: Horseblood!

TOM: And why did we do that, Stenner?

STENNER: Cause—cause it don't corrode!

TOM: So the salt water won't corrode the planking.

STENNER: So the salt water won't corrode the planking.

TOM: On top of that—sixteenth inch steel plate! Squared. Sewn together with steel wire—like fish scales to give it flexibility in heavy seas. The hull—forty-three feet long, ten feet high, lap-planked—I shaped every plank and every rib. A superstructure of two cabins. When you put it all together—a boat twenty-nine feet high. *Stenner, as always, is entranced and delighted with this description. Cochrane is intrigued but unconvinced.*

COCHRANE: Kind of far from the water—isn't it?

TOM: With a winch—and a horse—and log rollers—and poles, I can move it a few feet a day and launch it on the Saskatchewan River!

COCHRANE: *Takes this in and then observes another blunt fact.* The average depth of the Saskatchewan is somewhere around . . . five feet.

TOM: Have you ever heard of rafts Mr. . . . ?

COCHRANE: Cochrane.

TOM: Did you ever see an ice cream cone Mr. Cochrane? I float it to the deeper part of the river on rafts. When it's deep enough the hull fits inside the keel like ice cream into a cone. The keel's going to be flooded—water ballast—to keep it upright. I bolt the superstructure on top, and then . . . I'm going to sail down the Saskatchewan, to Hudson Bay, to Greenland, to Iceland—to Finland!

STENNER: Did you ever see anything like it Mr. Cochrane?

TOM: *Sits.* I had an uncle in Minnesoda. He was ninety-two when he died. Right up to the last he always wanted to get to Finland but he never got there. I'm going to get there. And the hull of my boat is going to be filled with wheat to feed the starving people of Finland.

COCHRANE: *Takes this in and then tries a new tack.* What would you say if I . . . *gave* you a steamship ticket to Finland?

TOM: Stenner? Why didn't we think of a steamship ticket?

STENNER: I don't know, Tom. Why didn't we?

TOM: Because you have to rely on so many other people! Somebody's got to take your bags when you get on the train. And then somebody's got to put you on the steamship. And a pilot and a captain's got to be at the controls. And if you hit an iceberg!—you're helpless.

A man's got to stand by himself—how did I get here from Minnesoda, Stenner?

STENNER: Tom walked.

TOM: And how long did it take me?

STENNER: It took him forty-one days. It would have taken him forty but he went lame the last day.

TOM: Do you understand what he means? How did you get here Mr.?

COCHRANE: I drove in my car.

TOM: What kind of car is it, Stenner?

STENNER: It's a chevy, Tom.

TOM: And do you know how to turn a piston or a cam shaft?

STENNER: I don't think so, Tom. It run pretty rough.

TOM: I feel sorry for you Mr. Cochrane. There's a thing called "the human spirit." And it's got to be moulded and refined and shaped to perfection. When you've been out on the prairies for so long you'll discover that you've got nothing else you can rely on.

STENNER: Do you want to know something else Mr. Cochrane? Tom had a dream. You see all this prairie here? It's going to be under water. There's going to be another flood, Mr. Cochrane. Tom dreamed it.

COCHRANE: *Gazing about the horizon somewhat baffled by this logic.* If all this land is going to be under water . . . you're going to need a boat. *Starts to exit.*

TOM: Where's yours?

STENNER: He ain't got one Tom.

TOM: I don't want to talk to him any more, Stenner.

STENNER: What're you going to do now, Tom?

TOM: It's time, Stenner. We've waited too long now.

STENNER: Are you going to move it, Tom? I'll get the horse and the winch!

TOM: We don't need it!

STENNER: Course we need the horse and the winch, Tom. How else are we going to move it?

TOM: Don't need it, Stenner.

STENNER: Look. I know some men in town, Tom. They don't hardly do nothing. We could give them some money. They'd come out and . . .

TOM: Where were they fourteen years ago when the idea first came for my boat? Where were they when I first started building? *Starts working himself into imaginary shoulder harness.*

STENNER: Come on, Tom. You can't do it all by yourself!

TOM: Stand back, Stenner.

STENNER: Tom, you can't do it yourself!

TOM: Stand back, Stenner. You watch. And you remember!

STENNER: Tom, you can't pull the boat all by yurself! Tom, you can't pull . . . *Tom collapses and Stenner takes him in his arms.* Tom.

Enter actor who will play Mme. Tourond.

ACTOR: What happened?

STENNER: Tom pulled too hard. He said he didn't need nobody and he pulled too hard.

ACTOR: *Who plays Stenner, to audience.* South of Moose Jaw, the land is very flat. And right in the middle of this flat prairie, just off the highway, this boat stands—rising thirty feet into the air.

The place where that boat was built is now under Diefenbaker Lake.

Actors playing Tom and Stenner break into neutral characters and reassemble the stage.

Section II   Mme. Tourond

Scene i

Actress who will play Mme. Tourond addresses the audience.
The west is full of enormous individual and enormous collective
efforts. That was a true story about a man. The next story is about a
woman. That's not me so I'll show you what she looks like. *Turns
around into character, perhaps with a slight costume change.*

Allo? My name is Mme. Tourond. You've never heard of me, have
you? You've heard of Louis Riel? Sure. You've heard of Gabriel
Dumont too, eh? And do you know why you've heard of them?
Because the men write the history books—that's why. They don't
write about the women so I'm going to tell you about me.

I'm four feet high and four feet wide. I have black eyes with circles
round them like a racoon. And I have big ears that hang down like
my grandfather's. And I'm smart like him. I have a big family with
lots of children—so many I can't count them anymore. And I have a
husband.

I have lived here in Red River all my life. You know where that is?
Well, Fort Garry, you've heard of that. We've got everything here—
we've got farms, we've got buffalo, we've got friends, we've got
people. But things are bad here and I don't know why.

I have lived in Red River all my life and now there is strange people
coming here and they want to live on my farm. Well, why is that?
There is a lot of room here, or there? Why my farm? I don't know and
still they keep coming.

And the next thing you know my friends, the farmers that are here,
the friends that I know are worried and they get together. And they
talk and they talk and they talk with this man Louis Riel. You know
him? He's only twenty-five years old but he can talk the ears off the
devil that one.

And they get together and they form a ... a ... "government." Well
what is that I don't know—but the next thing you know we got
soldiers here and everyone is running around, a man is killed, and
Louis Riel is gone I don't know where.

Janet Amos as Madame Tourond

Enter soldiers carrying body on overturned rack of a Red River cart.

FIRST SOLDIER: Mme. Tourond?

MME. TOUROND: There! You see? The Henglish soldiers I was telling you about.

FIRST SOLDIER: *Sets down the cart rack.* We've brought your husband.

MME. TOUROND: My husband? *Takes him in her arms.*

FIRST SOLDIER: Yes, m'am. He's dead. Some of the soldiers got a little out of hand. Somebody said he had something to do with killing Thomas Scott and all and . . . well, anyway they got out of hand and they chased him and I'm afraid he's killed.

MME. TOUROND: *Weeping.* He's dead—how can that be? I sent him for some water just an hour ago. How can he be dead?

FIRST SOLDIER: There'll be an inquiry, m'am.

Enter Louise.

LOUISE: Ma Mere! Ma Mere! I saw it! They chased him into the river. He started to swim. They threw stones at him until they killed him!

FIRST SOLDIER: There'll be an inquiry, m'am. *Begins to exit.*

26

LOUISE: You! You were there. You could have stopped them. You just stood there! You did nothing! *Both soldiers stop, whirl and face her.* Maudit anglais! *They pause and then continue out. Louise turns to her mother.*

MME. TOUROND: *Kneeling by the body.* Smile... where is your beautiful smile . . . your face is all broken . . . you . . .

Enter Celeste, Mme. Tourond's daughter, followed by Marie, an old woman.

CELESTE: Ma Mere! *Pause.* Give him to me. Give him to me, Ma Mere! *They struggle over the body.* Give him to me. There are others outside. We are going to carry him down the street. We will get our rifles. There will be trouble now!

MME. TOUROND: No, give him to me!

CELESTE: You will lead the procession!

MME. TOUROND: No! Give him to me. He is mine. You will not carry his body like a flag! *Tears the body back.*

CELESTE: Ma Mere.

MME. TOUROND: *Cradles him and begins with Louise and Marie to wrap the body in a buffalo robe and to moan their death chant.* He is dead.

CELESTE: But *we!*—are not dead!

Scene ii

The funeral ceremony is crossed by the fleeing figure of Riel who races to the cart top and struggles to raise it upright so that he appears trapped.

CELESTE: *Seizes him by the hair and pulls him to his feet.* Louis Riel! He is in trouble in Canada everywhere he goes. Five thousand dollars on that head—whether it's attached to the rest of his body— or not. *Reaches through the bars of the cart, takes his head in her hands and whispers.* Louis?—Run!

LOUIS: *Breaks free and runs to another portion of the stage, turns and addresses the audience while two other figures approach him.* After I founded the provisional government of Red River. After I wrote the constitution of Manitoba. For fifteen years I was hunted— like an elk! *The two figures converge on the spot where he was. He continues from another area of the stage as they continue their pursuit.*

By priests. And politicians. And doctors. And "friends." Three times

I was elected to the parliament at Ottawa—as bait! *Escapes again.*

To bring me into the light with promises and knives. *Begins to fade to backstage area.* Finally, I chose a quiet life. I became an exile, a teacher. I married. I lived a long way away but I remember. *Kneels in prayers and remains on stage as a retentive image during the following two scenes.*

Scene iii

MME. TOUROND: *Enters with a hearty cry organizing the assembling of the Red River cart which she loads up with her sons among other things.* We are going from here! Celeste, get this cart together and we will go. Louise, get the little ones! Colette, give away everything that we don't want. Get the pictures. Get the Bible.

OULETTE: Maybe I will see you there.

MME. TOUROND: Maybe, if you can make it!

They say I can't go alone.

I put my nine children on my back.

Takes the cart in her hands and pulls herself upright. Ohh—that's heavy.

I put my beds and my buffalo robes on my back. Ohh . . .

I put food enough for two years on my back and I started to move. *Begins to pull the creaking cart in a circle which, when it is completed, will signify her arrival at Fish Creek.*

Away from this river which is red with blood. And I begin to move out—away from this small place where there is not enough room for us people.

And at night I dream and my dream takes me across the prairie. It takes me through mud up to my hips. For days and months I move. It takes me through the heat and my fears until I reach a place where there is so much room I can see so far and the sky is so big. And I look down and the river is clear and fresh and I say, "I am going to stay here in Fish Creek!"

Music begins, cart is unloaded and is taken apart as more people gather. The rack forms a wall/seat with a buffalo robe spread over it. A wheel with its upright axle forms the cooking area as the Metis begin to dance.

I am going to build the biggest barn that you have ever seen with my children! We are going to have the finest farm . . . *Continues but is*

28

drowned out by the commotion during which among other things she discovers Oulette who has made it ahead of her.

Scene iv

DUMONT: *To audience.* She's talking about the banks of the Saskatchewan where Metis halfbreeds came from all over because here there was a community and had been for many years—St Laurent, Batoche.

Here we had our own community, our own laws, our own churches, our own priests. We haul freight on the Carlton Trial. We farm—a little bit—not too much. And we hunt—buffalo! *Dance crescendo rises and falls.*

There were many good years here. 1871: that was a very good year. *Spins the upright suspended cart wheel with his rifle butt.*

1875: that was not such a good year. The mounted police came. But they leave us alone—we leave them alone.

1879: listen! *Music halts.* We looked everywhere. We shot two buffalo. There is no more.

OULETTE: *Annoyed that Dumont is raining on the parade, coaxes him.* Ehh . . . Gabriel?

DUMONT: You'll have to learn to be a better farmer Oulette! *Music resumes.*

1880: you can't farm. Dust so thick you choke on it. The government from the east is coming west. The mounted police say we have to live by their laws but they won't give us any legal papers for our land.

1884: hey! *Music halts.* This new government has already formed their own "Council of the Northwest." Is there one Metis on that council?

OULETTE: No!

DUMONT: Our brothers the Indians are starving on their reservations. It makes me wonder, "Who is going to starve next?" I think we need help. *Turns and moves toward the kneeling figure of Riel.*

Scene v

DUMONT: Louis Riel?

RIEL: *Startled, turns and rises.* You look like a man who has come a long journey.

DUMONT: Seven hundred miles. To get you.

RIEL: You seem to know me. But I don't know you.

DUMONT: Gabriel Dumont. *Shakes hands.* I've come to ask you to come back with me to the Saskatchewan. It's starting again.

RIEL: Go to my house, sit down, have something to eat, rest, we'll have a visit.

DUMONT: Riel, I've come seven hundred miles. Can't we . . .

RIEL: *Returns to prayer.* I must finish mass first. *Both fade offstage during the following.*

Scene vi

MARIE: What a mess—I don't know! But your boys are there— that I know. They're trying to catch a pig but they can't catch it.

MME. TOUROND: They can't catch it because they know when they catch it they will have to work.

MARIE: Ahhh . . . too bad.

MME. TOUROND: Tell me, do you know where Louise is?

MARIE: Ehhh? I haven't seen her. Ehhh? Louise? She's down by the river. She's going to have a big belly someday—ehh?

I was down by the river too. I had some bread. And you know what? Somebody was following me. You know who that was?

MME. TOUROND: Who?

MARIE: *Mysteriously.* Mr. Raven. All the way from his place here. I turned around to him and I said, "Why are you following me?"

He turned around and he said, "Ohhh . . . I'm just waiting around for the red sun and then I'm going to fly right into it!"

MME. TOUROND: What does that mean?

MARIE: I don't know. *Enter priest.* Ahh . . .

MME. TOUROND: Ahah, come in. Would you like some stew too?

PRIEST: Not to-day.

MME. TOUROND: Ahah, not to-day.

PRIEST: Ma Mere, I am constantly surprised. Every time I come here I expect to see a giant.

MME. TOUROND: And you see only me, ehh?

PRIEST: Yes. When I go about the village and I want something done, they say, "Don't ask me. Ask Ma Mere Tourond." When they want to do something, they don't ask me—they ask Ma Mere Tourond first.

MME. TOUROND: That's because I'm smart you know.

PRIEST: You have almost the power of your priests.

MME. TOUROND: Oh, I wouldn't want that. I . . .

PRIEST: On the contrary, I must tell you . . .

MME. TOUROND: Well? Did you come here to talk to me or to give me a sermon? *Hands him some stew.*

PRIEST: We have very much to thank God for.

MARIE/MME. TOUROND: Yes, we have very much to thank God for.

PRIEST: And we must be very careful to leave what we have in the protection of God and of those who follow God.

MME. TOUROND: So you want to talk about Gabriel Dumont.

PRIEST: Yes, Gabriel. He is . . . a . . . "good leader" Ma Mere. But he is given to violence. If we are to keep what we have, we must guard it with skill and patience, not with the impatience and violence of Gabriel Dumont.

MME. TOUROND: Well, I'll tell him if I see him.

PRIEST: You understand what I am saying to you, Ma Mere?

MME. TOUROND: Yes, I understand, thank you very much, that's good. *Priest begins to exit.* I'll tell him.

Enter Dumont.

DUMONT: Good-day Father.

PRIEST: Gabriel. *Exit.*

DUMONT: See you at mass.

MME. TOUROND: Ehhh you! I'm in trouble with the priest because of you again.

DUMONT: You're not going to welcome me back?

MME. TOUROND: Oh welcome back. Welcome back.

MARIE: What's the matter with him, eh?

DUMONT: Don't worry about it. He is a priest Ma Mere—let him concern himself with God. Me, I am concerned with Louis Riel.

MARIE: Ahhh.

MME. TOUROND: You have brought him back?

DUMONT: I have brought him back. Now the English will have to listen to us.

MME. TOUROND: I don't like this man. I don't like him at all.

DUMONT: He is a very good man.

MME. TOUROND: Mmmm.

DUMONT: You should have seen the men when they brought him up. They were cheering and singing.

MME. TOUROND: I have seen that "cheering" before. I am telling you I don't want to see him.

DUMONT: Ma Mere, we need him. We need his voice. *Crowd noises rising in the background, "Riel! Riel!".* He is coming Ma Mere.

Enter Riel.

MME. TOUROND: I don't want to see him. I don't want him in this house.

RIEL: Mme. Tourond. I have come to ask for your support.

MME. TOUROND: It is fifteen years since I have seen that face. It fills me with fear.

RIEL: Do you remember your husband Baptiste?

MME. TOUROND: *Stung.* Do I remember Baptiste! Do you think I have forgotten!

RIEL: Do you think I have forgotten! Baptiste and I rode together at Red River and we put our foot on the surveyor's chain and we said, "You go no further!"

MME. TOUROND: I remember. I remember too much. And you! Where were you!

RIEL: Ma Mere, I can go no further without your support. ·

MME. TOUROND: You come to me? After Red River, still you come to me and you . . .

RIEL: Ma Mere. I remember too. What shall I tell them?

MME. TOUROND: Tell them! Tell them that . . . you . . . have the support of Mme. Tourond.

RIEL: Ma Mere, it is an honour to . . .

MA MERE: Tell them! *Returns to work.*

RIEL: *Returns to the crowd.* Ca commence!

Scene vii

DUMONT: *To audience.* Things move fast now. Riel, he talks, he writes letters. Me, I work better on a horse. I ride from Prince Albert to Duck Lake talking to anyone I can—English, Indians, Half-breeds, French. Say, "Come to Batoche. Riel is going to declare a provisional government. Come to Batoche! Come to church on Sunday. And bring a gun!"

Service is set up on the overturned Red River cart and with a simple cross.

PRIEST: My people. It is a seeming blessing to see you all united as one.

RIEL: Pray for us father.

PRIEST: You would ask me to pray for you even though you know it is a crime and a sin to raise arms against a tyrant no matter how unjust.

Know that, if you choose to follow this man, I will deny you holy sacraments.

Confusion in congregation.

DUMONT: Father, we must have a priest.

RIEL: *Rushes forward and seizes the cross.* Look!

This is your faith. This is your truth. This is your nation. Look at it. Look at it!

Touch it. Hold it!

Lift it. Show them your faith. Show them your truth. Show them your nation! Qu'est-ce que c'est Fort Carlton? Qu'est-ce que c'est Prince Albert?

Aux armes mes amis. Aux armes!

Scene viii

This is a montage scene, first of all a series of battle scenes using the entire cast. The battle scene freezes for the actors playing Marie and Mme. Tourond, and then Wandering Spirit and the Priest, to emerge for their scenes.

DUMONT: March! *To audience.* It is very cold. You can see your breath. There is plenty of supplies here at Duck Lake. I want them. So does one hundred police and volunteers. I got here first.

I am waiting for you Crozier, with your mounted police and your little cannon. I have men there and I have men there and I have men there. All very good shots.

I can hear you Crozier. Your horses. Your little sleighs. Come a little nearer. And I'll show you how we fight on the prairies!

Battle.

Off to the left! Keep firing from the left!

Battle.

Don't be afraid my friends. You see they die just like we do. You see that little one there—

Battle.

You think you can get away from me in your little sleighs, Crozier? I'll cut you to pieces!

Battle, Dumont is slightly wounded.

RIEL: Stop!

DUMONT: I can kill a lot of them Louis.

RIEL: We are Christians! Christians in war. Christians in peace.

We have a victory. Look at our victory. Look at your leader. Look at his terrible wounds. Look at the victory which God has given us. God has given us a victory. God has given us time. Time.

Actors freeze.

MARIE: Ma Mere? Why are we waiting?

MME. TOUROND: I don't know.

WANDERING SPIRIT: April second, Frog Lake—an Indian reserve between Battleford and Edmonton. Father Fafard says mass to the assembled whites.

MME. TOUROND: We wait too long.

WANDERING SPIRIT: Wandering Spirit! War chief of Big Bear's band. *Miming.* War paint. Rifle!

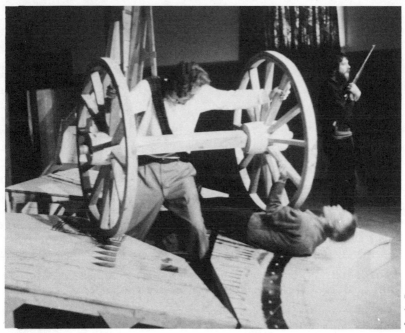

Batoche

Ritual slaying of the Priest. He cuts his throat. Hi yi yi yi! Hi yi yi!

DUMONT: Riel. You call me "oncle" but you don't trust me. It's been too long we've been waiting here.

RIEL: We need you here.

DUMONT: No, you need me out there. The English are just eighteen miles from here. They walk around Fish Creek like they own the prairie. Well they don't, and we do!

RIEL: Wait. Wait my friend.

DUMONT: Listen. It's like . . . when you lead the buffalo hunt. You are at the top of a rise and you have all the men behind you. And they all want to rush down there and kill the buffalo.

But you are the leader! *Flattering him, while accelerating "drum" beat from Metis arranged in battle positions behind them begins.*

So you raise your hand to give the signal. And those men behind you are very anxious. But you are the leader. So maybe you play with them a bit. You look like you're going to drop your hand but you don't.

But. Once you raise your hand in the air Louis! Sooner or later—you're going to have to drop it!

RIEL: No!

DUMONT: Tell me, Louis.

RIEL: Wait.

DUMONT: Whether you tell me to or not, Louis, I'm going.

RIEL: Wait!

DUMONT: Too late!

RIEL: Now!

Battle. In this case the wheels and axle of the Red River cart form a British cannon for which Dumont and a soldier wrestle for control. The three part action is punctuated by the Metis "drums." Dumont wins when he tricks the soldier into a false advance, kicks the axle upright leaving the free wheel racing in the air. Cheers, then silence.

OULETTE: *To audience.* There is nothing left at Fish Creek now. Bits of wood and shattered glass. Even the grass is burned at Fish Creek.

DUMONT: Ehhh! Ma Mere.

MME. TOUROND: What? What happened?

DUMONT: You know your house at Fish Creek?

MME. TOUROND: Yes, I know my house at Fish Creek.

DUMONT: Well, you wouldn't know it now.

MME. TOUROND: What's the matter?

DUMONT: I wanted to build a prairie fire—you know, to hide behind the smoke?

MME. TOUROND: And you burned down my house!

DUMONT: Well, the wind shifted—I'll build you another one.

MME. TOUROND: But what happened?

DUMONT: Ma Mere! We won! Your boy Patrice—the English took one look at his face and they ran like rabbits.

RIEL: Gabriel. I have reached a decision—fortify Batoche.

DUMONT: *Takes him by the arm and leads him to the front of the stage.* Tell me what you see out there.

RIEL: I see the prairie . . . the cemetery. I see our church—and behind, the Saskatchewan and old Batoche's store.

DUMONT: Do you know what I see? *Behind them the stage is taken apart as the Metis prepare their final battle positions.* I see the only place in two hundred miles where I can't win. Don't ask me to defend Batoche, Louis. I can build barricades. I can dig rifle pits. But, if we stay in one place, Louis, sooner or later they're going to come right down our throats. We've got to keep moving, Louis . . .

RIEL: No. Here. Here on the rise of the hill . . .

DUMONT: Louis, give me . . .

RIEL: That leads to Batoche. We shall meet our enemies . . .

DUMONT: You're wrong, Louis.

RIEL: And we shall break them!

Battle. Centred on Metis women using stones and scrap iron as bullets until the cannon shatters their placement. Patrice attempts another cannon wrestling match but is crushed by it.

DUMONT: *To audience.* For three days we held Batoche. The English had more men than we did, a cannon, and a gatling gun they brought from the States to try on us.

But our priests told them that we had not enough food or ammunition—and that made the difference.

On the third day they got up their courage. They broke through the rifle pits. We fought them hand to hand.

When it was all over those that were left had to flee. *Riel joins him.* There are people all along the river bank. Women and children. I brought them some food and blankets.

RIEL: Gabriel . . .

DUMONT: My friend, I have a horse. They will never see us . . .

RIEL: No, I . . .

DUMONT: Louis, there are English all over.

RIEL: I came here to negotiate the same status as Manitoba.

DUMONT: All they want is you. Now, come on, we won't give them that.

RIEL: We are a civilized people. We are not criminals!

DUMONT: There are still men in the woods. You can ride with me.

RIEL: Our capital, Batoche. Something must last.

DUMONT: It is too late for that.

RIEL: I came to speak. And these words . . . must last longer than bullets.

DUMONT: That is not my way, Louis.

RIEL: Or stones, or violence, or the days of my Metis on this prairie.

PRIEST: *Approaches Riel from behind and loops his sash around his neck.* For thine is the kingdom, and the power, and the glory . . .

And deliver us from evil . . .

Riel hangs, dropping the large cross he has carried ever since he seized it from the priest. Mme. Tourond's scream of agony is heard as it falls.

MME. TOUROND: *Kneeling over Patrice.* He's dead.

DUMONT: Come on. There are English all over. I will hide you.

MME. TOUROND: My son Patrice is dead.

DUMONT: Ma Mere, there is not enough time.

MME. TOUROND: Help me. *She lifts the body onto her shoulders and slowly begins to carry him off.*

Sings—to the melody of an old Metis love song.

> Ah mon fils, quand je te regarde,
> Les larmes amers coula les yeux.
> Ah mon fils, quand je te regarde,

DUMONT: *To audience.* You tell General Middleton . . .

MME. TOUROND: Quand je te regarde!

DUMONT: That I'm still in the woods.

MME. TOUROND: Les larmes amers—

DUMONT: And I have ninety cartridges to use on his men. *Exit.*

MME. TOUROND: Coula les yeux! *Exit.*

Riel and the priest remain in a freeze until the actor introducing the next section of the play begins to speak.

Section III   Sam Reimer

As the Actor speaks the stage is re-arranged and the characters in the next section take their place. For this entire sequence one part of the landscape is isolated at the centre of the stage, the other parts drawn back to form a kind of background. Actors use the central segment as a focus and playing area, sometimes sitting on it, sometimes standing on it.

ACTOR: We had a lot of help with this from western novelist Rudy Wiebe. This next story is taken from *The Blue Mountains of China* from the chapter entitled "The Vietnam Call of Samuel U. Reimer."*

Scene i

FATHER: Sam, I want to tell you about Russia.

We were landowners there. And we were so rich that when the revolution came, we had nothing.

The communists came and took everything that we had. They said, "We are all equal now."

They tore our furniture out, our clothing, our bedding.

And neighbour turned against neighbour.

And the vans came at night and in the morning we awoke never to see our fathers again, or our neighbours, or our brothers.

But there were bandits too, anarchists who took advantage of the situation. They rode from village to village killing and robbing.

My father knew in advance that they were coming and he prepared for them.

*Published by McClelland and Stewart, Toronto, 1970.

My brother David and I—we were young then—we crept up and hid behind a fence and watched them ride up shooting into the air and waving their swords.

Bandit begins slow entrance.

And my father went up to the leader and offered him food—borscht!

And they got down off their horses and went into the house.

They left behind them a man who was half dead—his face shot away. And my father came out to him and fed him like a child.

Enter Sam's grandmother as a young woman carrying a tiny baby.

GRANDMOTHER: *Protesting about the bandit molesting her house.* No . . .

FATHER: And when they had finished, they took what little we had and headed out to their horses. *Sam has become so entranced with the story that he has begun as early as the bandit's entrance to enact the role of his grandfather.* And my father had to preach to them!

GRANDFATHER: God said, "Thou shalt not kill." He said, "It is an abomination to shed the blood of another man." In the last village you left one hundred and eighty-seven dead. If I had that much blood on my hands, I would kneel down and . . .

FATHER: The leader drew his sword and already I could see my father's head rolling down the hill. And then my mother . . .

GRANDMOTHER: Before you kill this man, you must first kill this child and me.

BANDIT: *Feigns a thrust, laughs when she does not flinch.* Let him live! Let him live to preach again. *Exit.*

FATHER: You should have known my father Sam.

Grandmother exits.

SAM: They must have been very great people.

Scene ii

EMILY: *Who has been listening untouched by the story now begins bustling about.* Sam?

SAM: What?

EMILY: Sam, are you going into town to-day?

SAM: Yes, I have to pick up some more lumber for the pig barn.

EMILY: Could you pick up some things for me?

SAM: Yes. Only just don't send me all over town. I want to get back and . . .

EMILY: Do you have a pencil?

SAM: No, I . . .

EMILY: Here.

SAM: Thanks.

EMILY: Three rolls of tinfoil, the big kind, I . . .

SAM: Emily, I was looking into the kids' room on the way down— it's a mess. Do you think you could speak to them or something?

EMILY: Why don't you?

SAM: Well, yes, I suppose I could. Tinfoil . . .

EMILY: Toilet paper, light bulbs, sixty watt and hundred watt . . .

GOD: *Actor who played the father is transformed into this higher authority.* Sam!

EMILY: Construction paper, coloured . . .

SAM: Construction paper . . .

GOD: Samuel!

EMILY: And laundry soap, the big kind . . .

GOD: Sam. I am the God of your fathers, the Lord your God. Go and proclaim peace in Vietnam.

EMILY: Sam?

SAM: Sorry, construction paper . . .

GOD: Samuel! I am the God of your fathers, the Lord your God. Go and proclaim peace in Vietnam.

EMILY: Laundry soap and rubber gloves, size medium.

SAM: Would you repeat that?

GOD: Of course. I am the God of your fathers, the Lord your God. Go and proclaim peace in Vietnam.

EMILY: . . . rubber gloves, size medium.

SAM: Listen, Emily, don't worry about lunch for me, I don't know when I'll be back.

Exit Emily, enter Pastor.

Scene iii

SAM: It was very clear, Pastor. It was a voice.

PASTOR: *In swivel chair.* A "voice." This "voice," Samuel—you heard it while you were taking down the grocery list?

SAM: I wrote it down, Pastor. It's right there after tinfoil.

PASTOR: What kind of a voice was it Sam? Was it a woman's voice, a man's voice, a child's voice? Was it a voice like mine, Sam?

SAM: No, it definitely wasn't your voice. It wasn't like any voice I've ever heard.

PASTOR: Well, I suppose you've been reading a lot about Vietnam, seeing it on the television . . .

SAM: No, I didn't even know where Vietnam is. I had to look it up. I don't watch much television, the kids . . .

PASTOR: Well, in my sermon last Sunday in church I dealt with Vietnam, Sam.

SAM: You did?

PASTOR: Yes Sam, I did. It's a small country in Southeast Asia. There's roughly two hundred and fifty thousand Americans there fighting Communists—or Viet Cong. There are no Canadians involved officially. I spoke of the role of the Mennonite Church, its historic role as a peace moderator, and how we must strive to uplift and give solace to a people so terribly downtrodden, so brutally . . .

SAM: Pastor, what am I going to do?

PASTOR: Why not forget it, Sam?

SAM: I don't think I can do that—suppose I hear it again?

PASTOR: Well, Sam, there *are* some things we can do. Yes, there's three things we can do.

First of all—here's my file on Southeast Asia. I want you to read through that. Now there are articles for and against and in the middle—you should know what's going on in the world Sam.

Secondly Sam, I want you to read your Bible. I think you should read your Bible.

And thirdly, Sam, I think you should hear it again.

SAM: You want me to hear it again?

PASTOR: I want you to take this tape-recorder. Now this tape-recorder belongs to the church, Sam—you helped pay for it so you might as well use it. This way we'll get scientific proof. We'll hear the voice and we'll . . .

SAM: I'm not sure I understand, sir. You want me to tape the voice of God?

PASTOR: Yes.

SAM: Well somehow that doesn't seem quite right.

PASTOR: Oh yes, Sam—it's Biblical.

SAM: Biblical?

PASTOR: Gideon, when he doubted that he had received the command of God, put a sheepskin on the ground to test it. In the morning the sheepskin was dry while all else was covered with dew. Well, this is a kind of modern-day sheepskin.

SAM: Well, I'll try it. *Sam turns around and meets Emily.*

Scene iv

SAM: *Has a tape recorder that emits no sound.* Emily, take that. Now, that's me . . . now . . . here.

GOD: Samuel. I am the God of your fathers, the Lord your God. Go and proclaim peace in Vietnam. *Long pause while pastor stares intently at the recorder.*

SAM: There it is, Pastor. There's your sheepskin.

PASTOR: Sam, I only hear your voice.

GOD: I am the God of your fathers, the Lord your God. Go and proclaim pcacc in Vietnam.

SAM: There! Look! Emily, don't you hear anything. Here.

GOD: . . . Go and proclaim peace in Vietnam.

PASTOR: Sam . . .

SAM: Then why is that needle moving. It only moves when it is registering a sound.

GOD: Samuel!

PASTOR: It's some kind of electrical malfunction! Sam, I only hear your voice on that tape.

SAM: That's because the voice is meant for me. It's not meant for you. It's not meant for Emily. It's only meant for me. God can put anything he wants on a tape-recorder, can't he? He's saying very clearly what I should do.

PASTOR: What you should do, Sam?

SAM: Yes. I'm going to go to Vietnam and proclaim peace. *Exit Pastor.*

43

Scene v

EMILY: Sam, I can't stand this any longer. Nobody understands you. The kids won't talk to you anymore.

I've arranged for you to meet some people in Winnipeg. Perhaps they can talk to you.

SAM: Talk to me? Doctors?

EMILY: *Weeping.* Yes.

SAM: Sure. Yes, I'll go and talk to them—if you think that's best Emily.

Exit Emily.

Enter psychiatrist, in this case, a woman.

Scene vi

DOCTOR: Mr. Reamer . . .

SAM: Reimer. *As in rhyme.*

DOCTOR: Yes. Well, what we have here is a kind of misplaced guilt.

SAM: Yes. Well, I've seen pictures of burned homes, dead children, torture—I feel very guilty about that.

DOCTOR: Well, we all feel guilty—guilt is something we experience, but in the case of Vietnam it's not something we can do very much about.

SAM: But I *can* do something, can't I.

DOCTOR: But not in any practical . . .

SAM: Do you believe in God?

DOCTOR: Well, it's not a question of whether *I* believe in God or not. It's a question of . . .

SAM: Doctor, if we're going to sit and discuss my feelings, I think whether or not you believe in God is going to lend a pretty important bias to your opinions!

DOCTOR: *Stung, but rides our her desire to reply to this challenge with professional dignity.* I'm going to prescribe some valium. Now, that's a sedative. It will help you relax.

SAM: Drugs . . .

44

GOD: Samuel.

SAM: No. I don't think it will help. I don't think you can help me doctor.

Exit psychiatrist.

Scene vii

NEIGHBOUR: So you want to sell your farm, Sam? Well, what do you want to sell it for?

SAM: I need the money.

NEIGHBOUR: What do you need the money for, Sam?

SAM: I'm going to Vietnam.

NEIGHBOUR: That's what Emily told me. Sam, what about your wife and kids?

SAM: They'll be looked after.

NEIGHBOUR: By who!

SAM: The community. *Enter Official.*

NEIGHBOUR: The community! That's baloney, Sam. Your responsibility is to look after your wife and . . .

SAM: My responsibility is to go to Vietnam.

NEIGHBOUR: You have no responsibility to Vietnam! Your responsibility is to . . .

SAM: I have a call.

NEIGHBOUR: That's crazy, Sam.

SAM: Then you won't buy my farm?

NEIGHBOUR: No! *Exit Neighbour.*

Scene viii

OFFICIAL: Mr. Reimer, your visa has been refused. If you had some sort of sponsoring group—the Quakers, the Red Cross, the UN . . .

SAM: I want to go as an individual.

OFFICIAL: Mr. Reimer, there are no tourist facilities in Vietnam.

SAM: I don't want to be a tourist.

OFFICIAL: Look, Sam, this is a sensitive mattter. Canada is in a very delicate position regarding the American role in that area.

What you *could* do is test your theories on a more limited scale. There's a war in Bolivia, in the Sudan—not as impressive perhaps— but you could go there and . . .

SAM: You put that application through again! Please. It's very important.

OFFICIAL: *Shrugs in consent, exit.*

SAM: Thank you.

Enter reporter.

Scene ix

REPORTER: O.K. now, Mr. Reimer. I think we've got everything here. We've got your statement, the picture . . .

SAM: I'd appreciate it if you could . . .

REPORTER: I'll give it my best, Sam!

Exits as student radical enters and spins Sam around in the opposite direction.

RADICAL: Far out, man, you should teach a course at the university—talk about raising their consciousness—that was too much.

SAM: There weren't very many people there. I'd hoped that . . .

RADICAL: Student apathy, man, the place is crawling with pigs.

SAM: There were only six people.

RADICAL: Yeah, well, maybe. But that was something else, man. See ya . . . *Exit.*

Enter Pastor.

SAM: Well, sir, I don't think it was very fair to make up a petition to keep me from leaving.

PASTOR: Well, it hardly just concerns you, Sam. You've involved the papers. You've involved radical groups.

SAM: I couldn't get a visa, Pastor. I couldn't get help anywhere. I had to go where I thought I could . . .

PASTOR: Sam. God does not speak to people in this day and age. In the old days, in the time of the Old Testament—maybe God did. But right now, God does not.

SAM: How can you say that? How can you sit there with your books and your sermons and tell me that God does not speak to people? Do you think God only speaks through your sermons on Sunday?

I've been reading my Bible, Pastor, as you told me to. And I read where God said, "My servant, Nebuchadnezzar." Now this Nebuchadnezzar was a heathen, wasn't he?

PASTOR: Yes, he was.

SAM: Yes he was. And God sent "his servant Nebuchadnezzar" to slay Jews. Because they were getting too fat, too comfortable, too content.

Did it ever occur to you, Pastor, that "in this day and age" God just might say, "My servant Ho Chi Minh." Or, "My servant Mao Tse Tung!"

PASTOR: Sam, what would you do in Vietnam? Where would you go? Would you talk to the Communists? Would you talk to the Americans? Would you go up into the mountains? Would you go down to the sea? I mean—what, exactly, would you do?

SAM: You're the Devil.

PASTOR: Sam . . . You could have at least said I was an "agent" of the Devil.

SAM: No. You're the Devil. Otherwise you wouldn't have been so helpful when I first came to you. Pastor, I think you'll have to agree that was the work of the Devil.

Exit Pastor. Enter Emily weeping, and on stage right a chorus of girls in Central European folk costume.

Scene x

GOD: Samuel.

SAM: Emily. I made a mistake.

GOD: Sam. *Singing begins.*

SAM: I just should have gone. *Begins putting his life in order, here expressed by reassembling the stage.* God does not care about visas or tape-recorders or student apathy.

I just should have left a note and gone.

47

I made a mistake. God told me what to do—and I didn't do it.

I made a mistake. *Lies down on his back centre stage and dies.*

GOD: Samuel . . . *Exits.*

Enter Neighbour.

NEIGHBOUR: I know it's hard, Emily—but with the farm, the insurance, and one thing and another—it came to a little more than we thought. About a hundred and fifty thousand.

Maybe we'll sell that old Ford—buy a Chrysler—eh? Something like that. *Emily and neighbour exit.*

SONG:

> Way up in heaven there's a place
> That is free from all care.

Section IV   Norwegian Love Song

Scene i

A scene front stage and without props.

ERIC: Holy smokes!

Exit Sam.

Was it ever gloomy on the prairie! Sure! People dropping like flies!

It was hard there. The people came from all over and it was hard there.

The winters were hard. The summers were hard. The spring was hard. And you usually had a hard fall too.

The weather and the land were very hard. But that's not what I found the hardest. What I found the hardest was—there wasn't any girls.

So I was so fed up you know that I was going to head back to where I came from—when suddenly I saw her—the girl of my dreams—Katrina Johannsen!

Enter Katrina.

Holy Smokes! Was she good looking!

She could cook. And she could sew. And she could sing.

Katrina illustrates his first two compliments and concludes by singing the first few lines of the Norwegian national anthem.

ERIC: Golly!

Oh, and she could laugh too.

Katrina laughs.

And right away I gave my heart to her—along with about ten other fellas in that community in Manitoba.

And I determined that I would go over and I would declare my love to her. I would tell her exactly how I felt. Our hearts would beat as one. Nothing would come between us.

Enter Father.

Except her father.

How do you do, Mr. Johannsen?

He was a sour old prune of a fella but of course I didn't say that to his face.

Mr. Johannsen? I just came over to introduce myself. My name is Eric Peterson.

FATHER: Uhhh.

ERIC: And I also came over to tell you that I was just going—to Saskatchewan, where it's cold and bleak and hard—who knows if I'll ever come back!

FATHER: Yorty florty fjords and fish gebullan!

ERIC: And we went to Saskatchewan! My brother and me, we had a homestead near Melfort at Granley.

And in the summer we broke the ground and we broke our ploughs and we broke our backs. And there was grasshoppers and there was drought and there was dust. It was hard! hard! hard!

But all I kept thinking about was Katrina. Katrina! Katrina! Katrina! Golly, I was in love!

And I determined that I would go back and get her for my wife. So back I went!

FATHER: So you've come back! Who do we see more than you?

ERIC: You've only seen me twice, sir.

FATHER: Enough is enough.

ERIC: I came to ask for the hand of your daughter Katrina in marriage.

FATHER: Do you have any money?

ERIC: No.

FATHER: Do you have a farm?

ERIC: I have a homestead. We've cleared fourteen acres. I have a pig, and a cow, and a poplar pole shack for two.

FATHER: Are you sound of mind and body?

ERIC: I can't speak for my mind—but my body sure is sound.

FATHER: It's time she was married.

ERIC: Well, I thought I'd come to you first as is right and proper.

FATHER: It is right and proper.

ERIC: *To audience.* I knew that one would get him.

FATHER: You'll have to ask her yourself—if you're man enough.

ERIC: *To audience.* I hadn't thought about that part of it. But I went in—golly, my heart was pounding—and there she was—a picture of nordic beauty!

Her blonde hair. Her flashing blue eyes. Hello Katr—Katrina.

KATRINA: Hello, Eric.

ERIC: I was just wondering, if . . .

KATRINA: Yah? *Moves one step closer.*

ERIC: Well, I thought maybe if . . .

KATRINA: Yah? *Moves one step closer.*

ERIC: Well, just on the long shot you know . . .

KATRINA: Yah? *Steps beside him.*

ERIC: Will you marry me?

KATRINA: Yah! *Shakes his hand vigorously.*

ERIC: *To audience.* We had fourteen children, fifty grandchildren, a hundred and five great-grandchildren.

You know, they wanted us to retire in Victoria.

KATRINA: Sure. All that rock and rain.

ERIC: We might as well go back to the old country. It took us this long to get used to the prairies.

Well, we're just going up to the house now, so you might as well go out and have an intermission.

KATRINA: Yah. Fifteen minutes. *Exit hand in hand*

The audience is invited to look at the set between acts.

Act II   Section V   Janet Reitz

All but two of the stage sections are in a vertical position and twisted about to form an abstract design. The characters loiter about on these as the audience enters. One upturned section forms the judge's desk.

Scene i

ACTOR: *To audience.* To the outside visitor perhaps the most dramatic difference the west can display is the difference between the north and the south. Two of us went north as part of the research for the play and we became involved in the idea of justice in the north. One difficulty is the gap between legal jargon and sentencing.

There is a new young judge up at La Ronge called Judge Fafard. I don't think he sees himself as a radical idealist but I think he'd like to try to bridge this gap a little bit.

He flies out of La Ronge by float plane to hold courts about every other day. He's also learning to speak Cree and to try to make the punishment fit the crime.

We're going to show you one of his cases in Pelican Narrows—that's about thirty miles east of La Ronge—and see what *you* think.

CONSTABLE: All rise please!

I declare the court now open: God save the Queen!

No smoking. You may be seated.

JUDGE: Simon Linklater? And Leonard Dorion.

PROBATION OFFICER: Leonard Dorion is in Southend, your honour. This is Mr. Dorion, he'll be standing in.

JUDGE: You're standing in for your son? If you'll just come up here Mr. Dorion . . .

52

This is the information of Constable William Blanchard of Pelican Narrows, a police officer.

He says that he has reasonable and probable grounds to believe and does believe that Simon Linklater of Pelican Narrows and Leonard Dorion of Pelican Narrows on or about the third of August, 1975 in Jan Lake, Saskatchewan, did commit mischief by wilfully damaging without legal right the windshield of the vehicle of Val Cliff by throwing rocks and cracking the windshield which damage did exceed $50.00 in value contrary to section 387 of the criminal code.

Simon, do you understand the charge?

SIMON: *Giggles, nods.*

JUDGE: Do you plead guilty or not guilty?

SIMON: I'm guilty. *Giggles, looks at his friends watching with amusement this bizarre ritual.*

JUDGE: And Mr. Dorion? You're pleading for your son? You understand the charge against him? How do you plead—guilty or not guilty?

MR. DORION: We're going to plead guilty.

JUDGE: These were the only two involved, constable?

CONSTABLE: Yes, your honour.

Apparently at about 1:40 a.m. on the third of August, the complainant, Mr. Cliff, who operates a gas station, came to the office and stated that when he was driving he was approached by a native person who asked to purchase some gas for his car. He went to one end of the road, turned around, and as he was coming back several rocks were thrown at his truck. The rocks caused considerable damage to the windshield. One of the rocks went through the passenger window striking the rear window and cracking it. The complainant came immediately to my office and subsequent investigations showed the responsible persons to be Leonard Dorion and Simon Linklater.

JUDGE: Fine. Was there any estimate of damage?

CONSTABLE: I have no estimate of damage in my report your honour. The complainant does not want restitution. He simply wishes that the responsible persons be brought to trial.

JUDGE: He's probably got insurance in that case.

Mr. Dorion, I wonder if you could tell me something about your son. How old is he?

MR. DORION: He's twenty.

JUDGE: Is he working?

MR. DORION: Yes.

JUDGE: Does he intend to go back to school?

MR. DORION: No.

JUDGE: Is he married?

MR. DORION: Yes.

JUDGE: A family?

MR. DORION: Yes, he has one child.

JUDGE: And he supports the wife and child, does he?

MR. DORION: Yes.

JUDGE: What about you, Simon? How old are you?

SIMON: I'm fourteen.

JUDGE: And what are you doing with yourself?

SIMON: Oh, I got a job. I work at the Bay.

JUDGE: And is this your first job?

SIMON: Yes.

JUDGE: And are you thinking of going back to school?

SIMON: Oh, no.

JUDGE: What grade did you get to?

SIMON: Grade six.

JUDGE: And you think that's far enough, do you?

SIMON: Yeah.

JUDGE: There's no criminal record on either of these two, Constable?

CONSTABLE: No, your honour.

JUDGE: I'm curious about why you did it? Did you think he had some gas and wasn't going to sell it to you? Is that why you threw the rocks?

SIMON: I don't know—we just went crazy.

JUDGE: Mr. Dorion, did your son talk this over with you at all?

MR. DORION: He didn't say why.

JUDGE: Do you have any recommendations about what I should do. Now I can send him to jail. I can fine him. Or I can place him on probation.

MR. DORION: I don't see jail.

JUDGE: Does your son drink?

MR. DORION: Yes.

JUDGE: Does he have a drinking problem?

MR. DORION: Yes.

JUDGE: I'll tell you what I'm going to do. I'm going to place him on probation. Simon? What about you? Do you have a drinking problem?

PROBATION OFFICER: Simon is all right in that department, your honour.

JUDGE: Well, I'm placing you both on probation for a period of one year. Now that means that you're going to have to report if and when required to the chief probation officer here. He's going to make suggestions about what you should do and I think you should follow his instructions because they'll be for your own good and to keep you out of trouble. If you don't, you'll be in breach of probation and you'll be brought back to me.

Now the reason I'm putting you on probation is that neither of you has a criminal record. I don't like to send people to jail for the first time unless it's a very serious offence. I think jail has a bad effect on some people and they come out worse than when they went in. And so, unless I feel the public needs some kind of protection, I don't like to send people to jail for the first time.

Now in the course of this year you're going to have to mend your ways and to keep out of trouble. Being on probation means that you keep the peace and are in breach of no law in the land. That means drinking in a vehicle, drinking in a public place, drinking in a pub under age, throwing stones, assault—these are all breaches of the law. If that happens you will be brought back to me and I will sentence you on those charges as well as this one. This is just a conditional discharge.

At the end of the year, if you both behave yourselves, you will have no criminal record. Now, that's very important. My feeling about probation orders is that I don't give them out with reckless abandon and I only give you that break once. Now you bear that in mind.

In the case of your son, Mr. Dorion, I'm adding on to his probation order that for the period of a year he cannot abuse liquor. That doesn't mean that he can't have a drink. But he can't be drunk. If that happens, it's breach of his probation order and he'll be brought back to me.

PROBATION OFFICER: Excuse me, your honour, if Leonard Dorion remains in Southend he'll be outside of my jurisdiction.

JUDGE: Well, we can do the order in your office and I'll take it over myself when I fly over.

PROBATION OFFICER: Fine.

JUDGE: If the two of you can come over to my office with Jim and me, we can make out the probation order.

I guess that's it. We can close up now. *Exit.*

CONSTABLE: All rise please! The court is now closed. God save the Queen.

The Indians and Metis begin to drift lethargically out but until the final scene in this section there are always at least two figures lounging in the upstage area, retentive images not only of the trial but of the boredom and generally low expectations which seem to be common in small northern settlements administered by whites.

Scene ii

JANET REITZ: *Usually the actor who made the opening remarks because in a sense she is continuing to lead the audience on a guided tour of her life. She addresses the audience.*

Allo?

This is La Ronge.

You see that pink house there? That's where I live with my two boys. My name is right beside the door—Rietz. That's me.

You know, there used to be swings over there. They put them up and in one week they were all broken. The kids around here—they do that.

When I was young, I lived on an island way out there. Now there's a mine there. Nickel, I think. We used to go over and look at the pigeons.

I've got one long braid goes all the way down my back. To there.

These are my rose bushes. I brought them in from the bush. The government says I can't do that.

This is my kitchen. My radio—I have it going all the time. I take it with me to my cabin when I go out to the trapline. I'd like to have a transistor but it costs ninety dollars—that's as much as I pay for rent on this house. But if the children want to put a message for me on the radio, they can go down to the station and do that—so that's good.

My sink here has no taps so I get water from the bay. I think they're going to put in pipes but I hope they don't break the whole lawn.

Her son, who has been lying reading behind her loudly slaps his book shut.

56

Oh? What's the matter?

SON: Listen! French and English in 1763 . . .

JANET: Ohhh? That's very expensive . . .

SON: No, that's a date. *Shrugs.* I don't understand it.

JANET: Well you have a teacher. She can help you.

SON: I don't think she understands it either. I don't think I'm learning anything. I'm going to quit and get a job—make some money.

JANET: Ohhh?

SON: What's the matter? That's what lots of people do.

JANET: You know nothing now. You must do homework.

SON: I can't do it! It doesn't make any sense.

JANET: You've got to learn these. *Indicating books.* And you've got to learn enought to get grade twelve. I know that. Then you can get a good job—now you can get nothing. Then—it's magic. You don't have to understand the books—you just have to get your grade twelve. You go for a job then—the door opens and you walk right in.

Enter her second son with a coat pulled over his head, drunk, laughing.

SECOND SON: Heeey! Turn on the lights! Turn on the lights!

Sits awkwardly overwhelmed by his own joke. I was down at the bar and I said, "Turn on the lights!"

The guy looks at me and says, "Don't bother. I'm blind." Ha! Ha! Ha! *Turns to the girl who has been peeling potatoes in the background, usually on the upturned section of the stage which had formed the judge's desk. She is pregnant.*

Hey, you're worse than the Post Office—you can't deliver! No baby, no baby bonus! Both of you are just stin—owwh!

Janet leaps viciously at him, grabbing him and throwing him to the floor. She sits on him and punctuates the following speech by pounding his head on the floor.

JANET: I told you never to come in here like that—eh? I told you never to come here drunk like that!

You're such a "smart guy" aren't you? I'm going to tell you a story and you're going to *listen*—because it's about you! It's a story of a very smart man.

This man was so smart that he got drunk so many times and he fell down so many times and the police dragged him into court so many times—that pretty soon he didn't need a lawyer.

He'd say to the judge, "That woman can't put her hand on the Bible—she's not Christian!"

And the judge would say, "Very good." They respected him!

But one night they had a party. They were drinking and it wasn't just moose milk—no, it was hair spray. That makes you *real crazy*—doesn't it!

And he had one of his ladies there—I guess he had three or four and she was pretty jealous—eh? Because she took her big gun and she shot him—Bam! Bam!—right there.

But he's so crazy that he just sat there rocking back and forth—laughing . . . and laughing . . .

Until he's dead. And then the police came and they arrested her—you know what for?

For drinking hair spray. They didn't care about him—they were glad to see him gone.

First son laughs.

That is the life of one smart man. *Releases his hair. His head drops to the floor. Still sitting on him, she turns and gives her full attention to her first son.*

You want a story too? You know the tourist booth down there?

FIRST SON: Sure, that's Al . . .

JANET: I knew him twenty years ago. He was a very good guide. He knew all the lakes around here.

Then he sees all these new government buildings going up around here and he thinks, "I'll go in—maybe they have a job for me."

And they say, "How much school do *you* have?"

"Grade seven."

And they say, "There's no job for you." So back he goes.

Then one day he's crossing the road and a car comes and—*Bam!*—it smashes his leg and he can't walk any more. He can't even go in the boat.

So he goes to them again and he says, "You've got to help me now—I can't even walk."

And they say, "Hoo kay . . . You can sit in that booth and tell tourists where to go on paper."

PREGNANT GIRL: *Passing remark as she exits.* You see? You have an accident and you get a job—pretty smart—eh?

SONG:

> All my little sons
> You're growing so tall now.
> You're laughing with the sun
> But that's not all
>
> Now look—
> Where the road is coming through.
> Here comes a new kind of man you must talk to
> Just like the beaver you must swim
> And walk on the land and then
> You win—

The tune is an old Metis love song. The song is directed at her boys who react in character and then either exit or drift into the background images depending on the balance of the cast.

Scene iii

Enter Morris and Percy.

MORRIS: Three years ago, when I first joined the Metis Society, I thought it would take ten years to get where we are now. We have one of the strongest societies in the country—a hundred and ten locals! We have political power.

PERCY: Morris, my partner, is always talking about "political power." He thinks we have political power because we can fill out application forms.

MORRIS: We have to learn the white man's game! He is a man just like us. We have to find his soft spot and work on it and that's . . . politics.

PERCY: "The white man's game"—he thinks he's going to be the next premier of the province.

MORRIS: Well I'm talking sense—aren't I?

PERCY: Morris, they're not going to give us that land.

MORRIS: We're going to get the land! This time we're going to break the DNS. [*Department of Northern Saskatchewan.*]

PERCY: No, it isn't going to happen.

MORRIS: It is—we've got the highest offer!

PERCY: That doesn't matter. It matters who you are and who put it in and they won't give it to us.

MORRIS: Well you can take my word for it.

PERCY: I won't.

MORRIS: Well, you'll take Jay Rietz's word for it—Jay!

JANET: Yes?

MORRIS: Come on!

They start walking together.

PERCY: Morris thinks we're going to get the land.

JANET: Well? We are.

PERCY: We're not getting it.

JANET: You've got to be positive.

PERCY: I am positive. I'm positive we're not going to get it.

MORRIS: Come on—you can see.

PERCY: I can watch your faces when you lose.

JANET: I work there you know.

PERCY: Sure—but nothing's going to happen.

MORRIS: If I had my way—we'd all come up here and draw a line right across the province and stay here.

PERCY: That's right, Morris—you draw a line.

JANET: We're here.

MORRIS: *To Percy.* Put on your hat!

PERCY: You don't wear a hat in a building!

JANET: There it is—Land Office, right down there.

SECRETARY: *Sitting on the edge of one piece of stage.* Oh, I'm sorry. The Native Friendship Society is three doors along.

JANET: My name is Janet Rietz.

SECRETARY: Yes?

JANET: I work for social work here.

SECRETARY: Oh, I'm Mrs. Campbell.

JANET: How do you do. We represent the Metis Association.

We made a bid on the land for sale north of the Eagle Wing Reserve. They told us to come here in three weeks—that's to-day—and get an answer.

SECRETARY: Oh? Oh, yes. Just a minute, please, I'll pull your file.

That decision hasn't come through yet. I'll have to phone Mr. Broderick—pink, pank, pink, pank. [*Push button phone.*]

PERCY: She has to call all the way to Ottawa.

JANET: No. She's calling next door.

PERCY: She should yell.

SECRETARY: Hello? Mr. Broderick?

Hi, this is Mrs. Campbell.

Have you got a decision on that Eagle Wing property yet?

Yes . . . Well, there are three members of the Metis Association here and they . . .

Yes . . . Sure . . . Fine. See you for coffee then.

To Janet. I'm sorry, your tender has been refused.

JANET: We made the highest offer—I know that.

SECRETARY: Well, money isn't the only consideration.

MORRIS: We made the highest offer—what other considerations are there?

SECRETARY: If you plan a housing project, the government has to provide sanitation facilities, roads, water . . .

JANET: If we buy the land—it's ours, not the government's.

SECRETARY: But the government has to maintain certain standards.

JANET: We have "certain standards" too.

SECRETARY: Yes . . . I'm sure you do.

Well, anyway, I didn't make the decision. Obviously the DNS has long range plans for the area.

MORRIS: Can we ask who got it?

SECRETARY: Yes, I suppose so. It will be made public shortly anyway.

It was a lumber company. They're going to develop that area.

PERCY: I told you so. Come on, I'll buy both of you a beer. *All exit except Janet.*

SONG:

> The DNS is
> Government for the north here.
> I took their job to see
> What I could see
>
> Up high—
> From a plane the water's brown here
> I tell them it's much too dirty for one to drink

They frown—
And turn their other ear.
No mouthing off around here.

During the song the stage section representing her house is lifted into a vertical position and the manager enters for Scene IV following.

Scene iv

MANAGER: I think the quality of the drinking water is one of the least of our worries, Jay.

JANET: Oh? They have petitions all over town.

MANAGER: Yes, I know. I've seen every damn sign in town.

Look. I've pulled this report you brought me on the Andre family.

JANET: Oh yes? I put it in about four weeks ago.

MANAGER: Yes, I know. But it's not relevant.

JANET: Ohh you know it is because he has a job and his wife works but she gets welfare. And then they have three others who live with them and one of the girls had a baby and she . . .

MANAGER: And so your recommendation is that we take welfare *away* from them.

JANET: Yes, it's too easy.

MANAGER: Jay, this department is not set up to take welfare *away* from people.

JANET: Well, you know, when I was a girl there was maybe just three old men who got welfare and that was for flour and tea.

MANAGER: Jay, I really don't want to get into the whole welfare thing right now.

Look. I'm getting a lot of flack.

JANET: Flack?

MANAGER: Static.

JANET: Oh?

MANAGER: Feedback?

Look. My head is on the chopping block and so is yours. Jay, you're in trouble!

JANET: Ohhh?

MANAGER: They've been complaining to me that you've been complaining too much.

JANET: Complaining?

MANAGER: Yes. You go into anybody's office around here, you hound whoever happens to be in there—and we've heard that you've been criticizing the department to the community.

JANET: Oh, no. I talk about my work and the things I know.

MANAGER: And the things we're doing "wrong"?

JANET: Well, I . . .

MANAGER: Yeah, well people don't appreciate that, Jay. We're here to try to solve problems. We have channels.

JANET: I follow channels. I write on the pieces of paper . . .

MANAGER: I know. You bring me problems about the Reserve. Now you know that the Reserve is a federal problem—right? So why do you bring those problems to me?

JANET: Well, you could give the papers to the federals.

MANAGER: Don't get me wrong, Jay. I think your work here, your liaison with the community, is fantastic. But all I can say is that they said to ask her . . .

JANET: To stop talking.

MANAGER: To work in the department in a constructive manner. Now, would you like to do that or would you like to stop working?

JANET: I say . . . what . . . I think.

MANAGER: I can't take that answer back. *Pause.*

I'm sorry, Jay, I have no other choice. *Exit.*

SONG:

> The wind comes from the south
> It's blowing stronger.
> We simply live
> But can we live much longer.
>
> I've tried—
> All the learning that I know
> It's pushing me to take the plunge in Lac La Ronge
> And swim to my cabin in the trees
> And walk with the wolf and they
> With me—

During the song, the last section of the stage is thrown up vertically revealing a rifle which Morris hands to her. She is alone on stage for this last scene.

63

JANET: *Cocks her rifle.* Since my husband died, I've worked his trapline.

See his cabin there? I put a roof on it. I like to stand up straight.

I put a kitchen on it too. I like to cook and keep warm.

Steps inside vertical piece and rocks it gently.

I love it out here. When we canoed the water was so clean you could see right down.

I walk ten miles to set my traps in the snow. I catch beaver, fox, lynx, mink.

One winter we were walking along the edge of the lake and we came around a corner and there were five wolves just sitting there—tak! tak! tak! tak! tak!

They had their heads on their side like that and they were whining, "Mmh . . . Mmh?" As if they were saying, "What are you doing here?"

Then more wolves came round and my son was with me and he said, "Ohhh, I'm going to shoot them—we can make lots of money!"

And I said, "No—they're so beautiful!"

He shot—but he didn't hit them.

We went on to the lynx traps and you could hear them calling to each other there . . . and there . . . and there.

I love it out here. Last year I came out in September, I went back December twenty-first. This year I'm going to stay longer.

And when my boys get their grade twelve? I don't know . . . *Turns and walks off. Full cadence of a wolf howl.*

Section VI Louise Lucas

Scene i

ACTOR: There'll be a moment for another set change.

Stage is reassembled.

Several decades ago, Saskatchewan elected the first socialist government in North America.

In spite of the immense distances between people, or perhaps because of them, the west in Canada has been the centre of collective activity and the origin of a lot of co-operative reforms.

It is this co-operative activity which is the subject of the next section.

MYRTLE: *To actor.* So you want to talk about politics, d'ya? Well you know there's nothing gets me going more than politics—here kitty, kitty—meowh!

Sit down and have some tea. Now where d'ya start, eh? Oh—I know where—the Conservatives. You know what they did before that depression? They just took our money and ran! And then of course during the depression the Liberals got in and they were going to do us a lot of good—eh? They were going to give us money—relief! Of course the inspectors had a pretty good idea of how you voted and you stood a much better chance of getting relief if you happened to be liberal.

So what were the farming people going to do? Well, what could they do? The government couldn't do anything for them so they had to unite! And they did! And they discussed issues and they got some action!

You know—you've seen these pools and co-operative stores and health insurance—well that's their doing! They finally got a co-operative party—the CCF! And it's the only party to-day that can still do anything for the farming people.

ACTOR: Excuse me, did you ever meet Louise Lucas?

MYRTLE: Who?

ACTOR: She's called the "Mother of the CCF."

MYRTLE: Is that a fact? No, I can't say that . . .

Trails off into silent mime as they're overlapped by, and exit during, the following.

Scene ii

HENRY: Louise may have been the "Mother of the CCF Party" but before that she was my wife. And that doesn't make me the "Father of the CCF Party" either.

No, she was a good hard-working woman. We had six kids together. We shared the farm and the responsibility and what I've got to tell her now, I don't think she's going to be too keen about.

LOUISE: What's that? It can't be too bad—the crops are so good this year that it can't be anything that we can't handle.

HENRY: I think we should sell. I know it's rough and it's taken us eighteen years to get to the position where we just about own the place. We've got a good crop out there and we should get a good price for it so I can see that all in all we could put away a nice chunk of money.

It's going to get tough here, Louise, and well, I want that insurance so we can roll with the punches a bit.

LOUISE: We've got a home and neighbours and now—we're just going to pick up and throw it away!

HENRY: I don't want to "throw it away." I've given this a lot of thought and I think it's the best course.

LOUISE: Well, I'm not going to move.

HENRY: Louise, if I go and the kids go, then you've got to come too. It's love, honour, and obey or whatever.

LOUISE: It doesn't say I've got to love, honour and obey some fool notion. I'm going to stay here if I have to work this farm with my one good arm.

HENRY: Now look, I'm not the only one who's talking about selling out!

LOUISE: Well, sometimes there are some things more important than money.

HENRY: Well, things could get tough you know.

LOUISE: Oh, we've been through tough times before.

HENRY: I'm talking about tough, tough, tough! times.

LOUISE: Well, the Good Lord will provide, I suppose—He always has.

SONG: *By Louise.*

> It's not easy to introduce a farm wife
> There are so many of them around
> And you see them in the good times and the depression
> Trying to make a garden grow in that dry old ground
>
> And Louise, she was one
> With a house and family
> And she stood up and spoke
> For humanity.

Scene iii

LOUISE: Well, I don't really know how I got started in all this. I hadn't planned anything.

I guess it was a grain growers' meeting. Henry was going out and I thought it was about time I found out where some of our wheat was going.

Politician mounts platform composed of upended Red River cart rack trimmed with bunting.

There was a fellow up there from Saskatoon and he was talking about old age pensions . . .

Politican mimes his speech.

LOUISE: . . . and it didn't rub right with me. So after he finished his talk . . .

Pardon me? I'd like to thank you for coming out to-night. But I don't agree with that example you gave. I think that if that old fellow came over here and worked so hard and then gave everything he had to his sons—then they should help take care of him too. I don't think we should encourage our sons to leave it up to the government.

POLITICIAN: Well! If you disagree with the policies sent down from the central office, then you'll just have to get yourself elected as a delegate from your own local so you can go to the next conference and voice your own opinion. *Exit.*

LOUISE: Well, after the meeting, people said, "Louise, why don't you do it. We'll elect you. You can go up there. You like to talk."

But I said, "Hold on a minute. I've got my family to think of. I'll let you know after I talk it over with Henry."

Well, that evening the car had broken down again.

HENRY: *Working with the Red River cart wheels.* Louise, can you hand me that jack?

LOUISE: What do you think of me going down to Saskatoon to that meeting now? They want me to go as a delegate.

HENRY: They want *you* to go as a delegate? You sure they didn't mean *me*?

LOUISE: I suppose you could come along and all that Henry. I'm sorry . . .

HENRY: Of course they want you as a delegate, Louise. I couldn't talk my way out of a bag. It's a dandy idea. It's a good idea. You go. *Exit.*

LOUISE: Well that settled it—I was going to Saskatoon.

At first I thought it was going to be a business meeting and all that— but then they started talking about how we could change things and better the world if we could work together and if—well, I got some wonderful ideas!

SONG: *By Louise, as if addressing a political gathering from the platform.*

> Co-operation!
> That word sends chills
> Up and down my spine.
>
> Co-operation!
> I see it as salvation
> For the whole of mankind.
>
> It seems like practical
> Christianity
> And a chance to work for
> Humanity.

Angus and Brian, etc., applaud.

ANGUS: Louise! Louise! Get down over here!

BRIAN: Whoop! Whoop! Whoop! Louise!

ANGUS: That was a very fine speech, Louise.

BRIAN: It was rough but it could be polished.

ANGUS: Yes, indeed. Yes, indeed. You come very very close indeed to filling the bill for what we need on tour.

LOUISE: Well, I'm not sure, but I . . .

ANGUS: Oh, I *know* you'd *love* to do it!

BRIAN: You'd *like* to do it, wouldn't you?

ANGUS: Oh, there's many that'd *like* to do it, but there's many that can't . . . hack it!

They're not all your Saskatoon audiences!

BRIAN: No, sir!

ANGUS: They're not all your shirts and ties.

BRIAN: City people are easy, Louise.

ANGUS: Go out into the small towns if you dare! You know where you're going to have to speak?

BRIAN: Tell her, Angus!

ANGUS: Ice-rinks!

BRIAN: Yep. Pig-barns!

ANGUS: Auction barns!

BRIAN: Schools!

ANGUS: Churches! And they're tough as nails—they'll tear you limb from limb!

BRIAN: Tell her what she'll have to deal with, Angus.

ANGUS: Let's give it to her both barrels, Brian!

Hecklers!

BRIAN: Can you handle hecklers!

LOUISE: I don't know.

ANGUS: You don't know, do you? You watch and I'll show you exactly what hecklers can do. *Gets up on the platform and addresses the audience, which the actors have filtered into.*

HECKLERS: I don't like your hat! Can't hear you! Speak up! Drop dead! *Etc.*

ANGUS: I'd like to speak to you to-day . . .

HECKLERS: Boo! How long have you been dead! *Etc.*

ANGUS: Concerning section 3b of the Regina Manifesto.

HECKLERS: What do you know about it! *Etc.*

ANGUS: So's your old lady! *Gets down.*

BRIAN: Now you see, Louise, fortunately Angus there is a master of the whip lash reply. But when you get up there you have to face . . . *Gets on platform.*

HECKLERS: Boo! Sit down! *Etc.*

BRIAN: Hostile audiences! Sheer hostility!

HECKLERS: Boo! Throw him out! *Etc.*

BRIAN: Let me give you some statistics!

HECKLERS: Boo! Fool! *Etc.*

BRIAN: Let me give you some facts and figures!

HECKLERS: Finish it off! Make up some more! Get out! *Etc.*

BRIAN: Let me give you some examples from history!

HECKLERS: Boo! We've heard it! Get lost! *Etc.*

BRIAN: *Gets down.* It's no piece of cake, Louise.

ANGUS: Can you handle that kind of audience? If you can, why then maybe we'll think about lettin' you come along on the speakin' tour.

LOUISE: Why, I don't know, but I'll try.

BRIAN: Whoop! Whoop! Louise. Get up on the box.

LOUISE: Oh I don't need any box.

BRIAN: It's the only protection you've got!

LOUISE: I'm not a politician, you know. *Gets on platform.*

HECKLERS: It's a woman!

LOUISE: Why yes, you're very observant.

HECKLER: Then why aren't you home looking after your kids the way any woman your age should be!

LOUISE: Well I'd *be* home looking after those kids if I thought the struggle here could be won without the help of you women.

I think it's important to try to get a *future* for those kids.

HECKLER: Now you're talkin'!

LOUISE: I don't need to tell you that something's the matter.

HECKLER: You bet it is!

LOUISE: There's fruit farmers in B.C. who can't sell their fruit to go down and buy the flour that's milled from our wheat.

HECKLER: What about us!

LOUISE: And we can't sell our wheat to go down and buy their apples.

HECKLER: Well, why's that!

LOUISE: Somebody in the middle doesn't care about human need. They just care about profits!

HECKLERS: *Go wild.* Man-in-the middle! Profits! *Etc.*

LOUISE: I think that it's time we got together.

I think that it's time we stopped leaving the fate of our homes and families in the hands of men who are not concerned with homes or families!

HECKLERS: 'Ray! Give it to them! *Etc. They pour onstage ignoring Brian and Angus in their desire to congratulate her.*

BRIAN: Grab her, Angus—she's a hot one!

ANGUS: There's just one last thing, Louise. Do you think you can stand the sheer grueling strain of it all?

BRIAN: The late nights, the early mornings, the back seat of a bus, the heat, the cold, the endless ridin', stoppin', goin', comin'.

ANGUS: Brian! *Hits him with his hat.* Brian here gets the odd relapse of "tour fever," Louise.

LOUISE: Well, I don't know if I can. But I've done one thing neither of you boys has done.

BRIAN/ANGUS: What's that?

LOUISE: I've had six kids. And if that doesn't prepare me for grueling strain, late nights, and early mornings—I don't know what will.

ANGUS: It's a deal, Louise!

SONG: *By Louise.*

> We headed out in a broken down Ford
> I'm sure you know the kind—
> We headed out of Milden with a half tank of gas
> And I think we left the muffler behind—
> We headed for the towns across the prairie, saying
> "Farmer, there's one thing that you lack—
> A little rain, and co-operation
> To help you get those bankers off your back!"
>
> We hit Delisle, Pense, and Biggar
> Moose Jaw, Craik, and Davidson
> Elbow, Hague, and Eyebrow
> Nipawin . . .

ANGUS: *Falters.* It's my heart!

BRIAN: Louise, Angus here has run out of poop. I gotta take him back to Delisle. Do you think you could carry on by yourself for a few days?

LOUISE: Well, I'll try.

BRIAN: Oh, you're a corker, Louise.

LOUISE:

Well I headed on to Kerrobert, Candiac, and Unity
Saying, "I'll give my vote to the CCF
Cause it stands for humanity!"

Scene iv

Farmer and Louise seated for this scene.

FARMER: So you're Mrs. Lucas.

LOUISE: Yes, I'm Louise, I'm . . .

FARMER: A real, live, socialist.

LOUISE: Well, no, I'm . . .

FARMER: Now, let's not argue about it. I'd just like to invite you to my home for supper.

LOUISE: I'd love to, I'd . . .

FARMER: Cause, if there's any way to catch a socialist—it's to *feed* him.

LOUISE: *To his wife.* Hello? How are you down there? The dinner smells lovely. *The wife is on her knees behind the handle of the upturned Red River cart, cleaning an imaginary window.*

WIFE: Oh, it'll be on in a minute—I'm terribly busy—I'll be right back.

FARMER: She sometimes gets a little excited.

Now, I should warn you—I eat socialists for breakfast.

LOUISE: Well, it's a good thing I came for supper then, isn't it?

FARMER: Socialism is a bankrupt economic policy—are you a socialist?

LOUISE: Well, I don't really know.

FARMER: You "don't really know"—eh?

LOUISE: I'm just a person who cares about people.

Take your wife, for instance. I'd like to know why she's working in the kitchen while we're out here.

Are you comfortable down there?

WIFE: Well, no. I'm not.

LOUISE: Well, if there's anything I can do.

FARMER: Now there's an old socialist trick! You get off into some sentimental slosh about "people" and you don't answer the question!

Money! Money is what we're really talking about—right?

Now, money is the root of all human dignity—who said that?

LOUISE: I don't know.

FARMER: George Bernard Shaw said that! And if you don't know that how are you going to argue socialism?

LOUISE: Well, I think that is a wonderful idea and you should develop that.

Now, more than ever, people seem to lose their human dignity when they haven't a penny in their pockets or enough money to clothe themselves and feed their children. People should be paid for the work they do—don't you agree?

FARMER: And take it away from them if they don't work!

LOUISE: Take your wife, for instance—she's working so hard. *To her.*

Do you have any money?

WIFE: I don't know. I can tell you one thing, though. There isn't enough money to buy soap!

FARMER: Now let's not get into soap! Let's get on with the next question. This is something which no socialist has *ever* been able to answer.

Since the Garden of Eden, every time you give somebody something for nothing—his backbone turns to mush.

LOUISE: Well that may be true if you give people something they don't deserve. But I think there *are* certain things which we can give each other and I'd like to give a few to your wife here.

FARMER: Like what?

LOUISE: Well, I'd like to give her a little self-confidence for one thing. *To her.* You're down there working all the time.

WIFE: Ohhh?

LOUISE: And I'd like you to realize that what you're doing is very important.

WIFE: Ohhh. *Stands up.*

LOUISE: And we need your help to make a change in this world.

WIFE: Ohhh—I don't think anyone has ever said that to me before.

LOUISE: I'd like you to get out and meet the people. We've got to work together, you know.

WIFE: Well, I don't have time, I can't afford it, and I haven't got a babysitter.

LOUISE: I'm sure we can work something out. *Glancing at farmer.* Come on out and meet some of the other women in the community.

FARMER: Well, once a year's all right, I guess.

WIFE: *To audience.* Ohhh! Hello out there, hahhh! *Turns and starts to run back into her kitchen.*

LOUISE: Oh, you're not through yet. Tell them your ideas.

WIFE: Well . . . I think . . . what we need around here more than anything else is a hospital and I think we should start organizing for that. *Starts to run back home again.*

LOUISE: What about that "human dignity" stuff. What have you got to say about that?

WIFE: Oh. *To husband.* I look after the chickens and clean the eggs and sell them. And I look after the cattle and you look after your crops.

Well, why is it that you have all the money?

FARMER: Well, Marjorie, that's because I'm here to love and protect you.

I could pay you a salary if you like but that would introduce a master-servant relationship. The only bond between us would be the cash nexus.

And all the love would go out of our life.

WIFE: All right, then, you look after the cows and the chickens. *Pauses in triumph, then realising the effrontery of her retort, starts to run for her kitchen.*

FARMER: *Double take on his retreating wife and on Louise.*

LOUISE: Now, hold on! There's more. We've got to make a better world too.

WIFE: You want me to stand up there? *The platform.*

To husband. You don't mind giving me a hand, do you?

FARMER: Now, careful when you're talking to strangers.

WIFE: Thank you. *On podium now.*

I'd just like to say that . . .

I'm very proud to accept the presidency . . .

Of this district in our farmers' union. Thank you very much.

Clap! Clap! Clap!

LOUISE:

> By this time tomorrow, I—
> Could be gone.
> But I'm counting on you ladies.
> To carry on.
>
> Work strong together and make sure—
> They always see
> That they've got to think first
> Of humanity.

Section VII   Homecoming

Scene entirely mimed by actors.

Scene i

Wind sounds. A man and a woman in winter clothes centre stage. Man mimes difficult driving. They converse slowly, putting in time.

FLO: And I said, "If I carry anything on that ice I'll break my neck." And do you know what she was telling me? She said that they put water in the sand first and freeze it into steps and they last all winter.

ANDREW: That's smart.

FLO: It's going to be drifting tonight . . .

ANDREW: They're going to pile up. They're really going to pile up.

FLO: We should have left earlier . . .

Enter hitchhiker lightly clad for winter hunched against the cold.

ANDREW: Is that a—my god, it is!

FLO: We'll have to stop.

HITCHHIKER: Are you going to Genesis?

ANDREW: I don't know where that is.

HITCHHIKER: It's about seven miles straight down this road.

ANDREW: Get in! Get in! We're going that way.

On a night like to-night we'd have to pick you up even if we were going in the other direction!

HITCHHIKER: Thank you. *Gets in the car. Wind noise stops.*

FLO: Bad weather for hitchhiking—eh?

HITCHHIKER: Yes. I'm not used to prairie winters any more.

FLO: Oh? Where're you from?

HITCHHIKER: I'm *from* Genesis—about twenty years ago.

ANDREW: Well, the winter's haven't changed much.

FLO: Where have you been?

HITCHHIKER: Oh I've been around. Been in the Air Force.

ANDREW: Were you a pilot?

HITCHHIKER: No, I was just a navigator.

FLO: Oh.

HITCHHIKER: I left Genesis when I was about sixteen, joined the Air Force a little while later.

ANDREW: Armed Forces now—eh?

HITCHHIKER: Yeah.

FLO: That Menzies boy is in the Air Force.

ANDREW: Menzies boy?

HITCHHIKER: *Ignoring them.* Yeah, that's why I got out.

ANDREW: New uniform?

HITCHHIKER: Yeah, yeah. The spirit's gone, you know.

ANDREW: Yeah, I know what you mean. A lot of men got out I think.

HITCHHIKER: Now that's Kootchmer's farm.

This is called Kootchmer's Road.

ANDREW: Oh yeah? *To Flo.* You what?

FLO: There's a turn off here.

HITCHHIKER: You see that crossing there? I'll close my eyes—I used to do this when I was a kid. Now I'll tell you exactly when . . . the poplar bluff comes up on the left. Heh, heh, you ride these roads so much, you know—right there!

FLO: Ohhh!

HITCHHIKER: I didn't forget after twenty years!

ANDREW: Are you heading home for a visit?

HITCHHIKER: Yep. I've had enough of Halifax, Paris . . .

ANDREW: Paris!

HITCHHIKER: Yep. I've put in my time.

77

There's a house, a stucco house—it was boarded up when I was still living there. It was a tall two story thing. A beautiful place, a beautiful place.

ANDREW: Gonna spend some of that Air Force money—eh? Get yourself a home—that's real nice.

HITCHHIKER: It's just around this bend.

Well, I want to thank you very much. *Gets out. Wind sound starts up again.*

FLO: I don't see anything.

ANDREW: It's not blowing *that* much. You sure you got the right road?

HITCHHIKER: *Retreating back to the car.* Was that a Texaco? Yeah, it was—eh? A Texaco station at the corner—eh? Where you picked me up?

ANDREW: Yeah, that was a Texaco. Maybe it's further down.

HITCHHIKER: No, it's around here! There should be a Catholic church . . .

ANDREW: Don't see it!

HITCHHIKER: Byegrad's store. He had the Post Office and an old black model T car. There—you can see it when the wind drops. The trees there—that's where the school is.

ANDREW: I see the trees. I don't see any school.

Look—I'm getting cold.

HITCHHIKER: *Digging in the snow.* There's a house here!

ANDREW: You've found a foundation?

HITCHHIKER: That's the house I was going to buy!

ANDREW: Listen, can we take you on down the road? There's a motel a couple of miles on. It's real nice—colour T.V.

We'll be in the car.

FLO: Is he coming?

ANDREW: Yep. He's got to.

HITCHHIKER: *Returns to the car. Wind sound stops.*

FLO: Too bad.

ANDREW: That happens you know. People die and, well . . . people die and the buildings—they move them away.

HITCHHIKER: *Still glancing back incredulous.* Even the grain elevator's gone!

Section VIII   The Tractor Demonstration

Scene i

GEORGE: Morning! *Homecoming characters exit.* See that red behind that bluff off in the east there? The sun will be up in five minutes—it's going to be a lovely July day. *Cart wheel slowly raised upright against the back of the stage forms a half circle of spokes representing the rising sun.*

Yup.

I'm just opening the door to my shed here. *Pulls section of the stage out, turns it on its side and pulls it around.*

There we go. That's my tractor!

Now I'm going to start that tractor up and I'm going to drive it and, well you're probably wondering what's so odd about that? Why waste valuable stage time showing us a farmer driving his tractor?

Well, I'm not going out to the field. I'm taking it down the lane, I'm turning right and I'm going two miles east to the highway.

I could be going to help a neighbour. I could be taking it to the city to get some repairs. But I'm not.

You see, when I get to the highway, I'm going to drive my tractor very slowly up and down the highway so people can read the signs on it. I got a couple of signs on it.

One of them says, "This tractor belongs to me and the bank."

The other sign says, "The United States has President Nixon and Bob Hope. We've got Prime Minister Trudeau and no hope."

It might help a bit if I were to explain that this is July, 1969. Now that was a good and a bad time.

It was a good time because I had more grain than I knew what to do with.

It was a bad time because I couldn't get rid of it. I couldn't sell it. Grain sales had slumped and my initial payment went down to about 20¢ on the bushel—so I was in trouble.

And like anybody in trouble, I started to squawk. Nobody wanted to meet with us. Everybody seemed to think it was my fault. They expected me to store it and nobody seemed to want to do anything about selling it.

I got to the point where I said, "I'm *tired* of making resolutions that nobody listens to. I'm *tired* of giving suggestions and being given a deaf ear." What you have to do is draw a little attention to yourself.

It's like you have to go out into the middle of the road and take your shirt off, take your pants off, stand there and say, "This is happening to me!"

So that's why this morning I'm getting on my tractor and—now I'll be perfectly frank with you—just you and me and the morning here—if nobody else shows up . . . I'm gonna look awfully foolish.

But, you know, you've got to do something. We can't talk any more and I helped organize this corner so I'm going! But if nobody else shows up . . .

Rroarrrh!

SECOND TRACTOR: Rroarrrh!

GEORGE: Rroarrrh!

SECOND TRACTOR: Rroarrrh!

GEORGE: An answering call! Somebody as crazy as I am is out here this morning!

JOHN: *Enters driving the second tractor which he mimes.* Rroarrrh!

GEORGE: Morning John.

JOHN: Morning George.

80

GEORGE: John, you're the *last* person I expected to see out here. *To audience.* John is a conservative—big C, little c.

JOHN: What're you doing out here George?

GEORGE: John, I'm gonna make a stink. I'm gonna make a demonstration—public disobedience if you like. I'm gonna draw some attention to myself and our problems.

What're *you* gonna do?

JOHN: Well—you got *my* attention.

GEORGE: Uh huh.

JOHN: You've got the same problems I got.

GEORGE: Uh huh.

JOHN: We're sittin' on the same road.

GEORGE: So we may as well go the same direction and maybe we'll get something done! *Both roar, third tractor enters, again mimed.*

GEORGE: Walter! Good to see you!

To audience. Walter had everything organized like a crack military unit.

WALTER: You see this old tractor I'm pullin' behind me—that's for spare parts.

GEORGE: Never thought of that!

WALTER: You want to raise a stink, George—well jeezus!— you're going to need more organization than this!

I got spare parts, spare fuel, I got fifteen relief drivers waitin' fifteen miles down the road!

We're in radio contact with all units so we can all converge on Saskatoon all at the same time!

GEORGE: Walter, you're a wonder! *All three roar.*

CAROL: Rring! Rring!

Tractors freeze. The callers are each standing on a chair by one of the four stylized telephones ranged across the backstage area.

LILIAN: Hello?

CAROL: Hello Lilian—is Ted out there? I haven't seen him.

LILIAN: Yes, he's out there.

ANNA: Click! Click! Click! Excuse me! I've been trying to phone Winnie for two days. I know you're busy but could I just have the phone for five minutes?

81

CAROL: Oh, all right.

ANNA: Thanks a million. Rring! Rring!

WINNIE: Hello?

ANNA: Oh, Winnie. Hi.

WINNIE: Say, have you seen what's going on out there?

ANNA: Oh, I know. They're trying to talk my husband into it but I said, "Forget it!"

WINNIE: I don't know what they think they're going to achieve—I don't think the Good Lord is going to listen to that racket!

CAROL: Well, you never know *who* might be listening to it, you know!

I'm just run off my feet trying to get this thing organized.

ANNA: Well, I'll give you a hand if you'll let me use the phone for five minutes.

CAROL: You're on!

Tractors roar into life. Enter Lorne driving a popping, spitting old wreck. Other tractors gradually quiet down as he lurches into his place.

GEORGE: Morning Lorne.

LORNE: Hello George.

GEORGE: Lorne, are you taking that tractor to the Western Development Museum?

LORNE: Well, you never know, George. I thought there might be some of those income tax fellas just lurkin' around in Saskatoon.

GEORGE: And you didn't want them to know just what a big operator you really are?

LORNE: No sense in tippin' your hand, George.

GEORGE: Lorne, people are going to look at that tractor and they're going to say, "It's worn out, it's outdated, it's obsolete."

And they're going to say that the man *riding* that tractor is worn out, outdated, and obsolete.

Now you go home and you get that twenty-five thousand dollar tractor.

LORNE: The big one?

GEORGE: The big one. And you show them what kind of men they're *really* dealing with!

LORNE: Well, if you think it'd be the right thing to do?

GEORGE: I know it is!

All tractors roar into life moving in a slow circle.

ANNA: Rring! Rring!

Tractors freeze.

WINNIE: Hello?

ANNA: Hello Winnie? We're desperate—we've simply got more food than we can handle. We need your camper.

WINNIE: You do? Well, all right.

ANNA: You'll help us?

WINNIE: Sure. Say, why don't I drive it over?

ANNA: Oh, good. I'll see you in an hour!

ALL TRACTORS: Ppeeeepppp! Ppeeeepp!

GEORGE: *To audience.* It started to work! You can see how we backed up the traffic!

ALL TRACTORS: Ppeeeeppp! Ppeeeepp!

GEORGE: *To audience.* Once we backed up the traffic—pretty soon the cops came along—eh? *Transforms into cop by taking off his red peak cap and waving it about his head.* Whooo ooo oooo oooo! All right, you guys!

ALL TRACTORS: Rroarr! *Etc.*

GEORGE: You *know* you gotta get these things . . .

ALL TRACTORS: Rroarr! *Etc.*

GEORGE: *Replaces cap. To audience.* Finally he got so frustrated that he just got in his car and drove away!

ALL TRACTORS: Rroarr! *Etc.*

LADIES: *Heave the wheel of the Red River cart, representing the food, from upstage to downstage. Either the tractors or the women are in freeze during this sequence.* One thousand five hundred apple pies!

TRACTORS: Rroarr! *Etc.*

LADIES: Two thousand gallons of freshie!

TRACTORS: Rroarr!

LADIES: Thirty thousand ham sandwiches!

TRACTORS: Rroarr! *Etc.*

GEORGE: *To audience.* And that was the thing! In the course of a week, we went from being rabbits!—to being lions!

TRACTORS: Rroarr! *Etc.*

GEORGE: To audience. Till by the time we got to Saskatoon—we didn't *ask* them where we were going—we *told* them where we were going!

TRACTORS: Rroarr! *Etc.*

Enter Bessborough Hotel, actress with a fox fur. All freeze.

HOTEL: *Posh British accent. I* am the Bessborough! And *nobody* fools around with the Bessborough. And I'm certainly not going to be intimidated by your little machines.

GEORGE: We want to speak to the Prime Minister.

HOTEL: The Prime Minister is safe inside my gentle bosom and he's not coming out.

GEORGE: Well, get him out of your "gentle bosom"—we want to talk to him!

HOTEL: He can't be disturbed.

GEORGE: All right! Then we're coming in there after him!

TRACTORS: Rroarr! *Etc.*

Prime Minister emerges.

TRUDEAU: Might I remind you gentlemen that Canada has one of the highest living standards in the international world.

If the government grants the farmers special consideration—then the miners will want special consideration, the fishermen, the lumbermen, and then where would we be?

Since the beginning of civilization, history has had its "ups" and "downs" and right now we seem to be in a "down."

But if you people want to destroy civilization then just continue to carry on as you are doing.

Now, if you'll permit me—I have to get back to the business of government. *Exit.*

WALTER: I don't think he even knew who he was talking to.

ANNA: Did he say anything about Saskatchewan?

JOHN: No.

LORNE: Did he say anything about farming?

CAROL: No.

GEORGE: Did he say anything?

ALL: No! Rroarr! *Etc. Freeze.*

OFFICIAL: Now, you see, this is the kind of emotionalism that we in government have to deal with.

Now, I *love* Saskatchewan. I love the skyline and I don't want to see it disappear anymore than anyone else.

WALTER: *To audience.* These are the actual views expressed to us by the press assistant to Otto Lang.

OFFICIAL: The average education of the members of the Farmers Union is—now let's be realistic—between grade six and seven.

Now these are ignorant men. They are simply unaware of what is happening outside their narrow range of interests.

Roy Atkinson, for example, brought a coffin to one of our meetings—trying to suggest I suppose that farming is dying. Now how do you *deal* with that sort of mentality!

ALL: Ho! Heh! Did you see the look on his face! *Etc.*

LORNE: I told a reporter from the Globe and Mail that my name was Massey Harris—and he believed me!

ALL: Haw! Haw! *Etc.*

There is a passage of time here during the next two speeches and we are in the present, 1975.

WALTER: Don't anybody get away! We're going to set out from here and we're going to head down to Regina and right into the legislature!

GEORGE: Oh, I don't know Walter. Maybe next year! I've got to get back to the farm. I've got work to do.

WALTER: What about you Lorne! You're not going to stop now, are you? On to the legislature!

LORNE: Jeez, Walter, you better wake up—this is 1975! Do you know how much I'm gettin' for my wheat these days? I can't go foolin' off on some parade.

WALTER: John? You're not going to listen to him?

JOHN: The big fish eat the little fish, Walter. It's sunset city for a lot of farmers. It's all right if you're a big fish!

GEORGE: *To audience.* Well I don't know what's going on with these good years or whatever you want to call it—I guess nothing.

I guess times will have to get tough again before the people get moving. That's the way people are, I guess.

WALTER: George! We're rollin'—we're just gettin' rollin'.

JOHN: Now Walter, there's no law says you can't change your mind.

ACTOR: Well, we're going to wrap it up now. These fellows will go on all night.

We'd just like to say that we found the material for this play different from anything else we'd ever worked on.

And then, when we put it all together—it *looked* different from anything else we'd done.

So, just to get back to familiar territory, we decided we'd end it just the way you end a regular play.

So. This is how you end a regular play. *Bows.*

Far As the Eye Can See

Rudy Wiebe

Theatre Passe Muraille

Norman Yates

Far As the Eye Can See was first performed at Theatre 3 in Edmonton, Alberta on April 12, 1977 with the following cast:

Gordon Tootoosis	*Crowfoot*
Ted Johns	*William Aberhart, Henry Stutzman*
Beti Trauth	*Princess Louise, Agnes Reynolds*
David Fox	*Anton Kalicz*
Graham McPherson	*Wadu (Walter) Kalicz, Elton Preschuk, Don Ritz*
Connie Kaldor	*Caroline Kalicz*
Janet Amos	*Betty Mitchell*
Layne Coleman	*Roger Mitchell, Errol Hanks, Peter Lougheed*
Dennis Robinson	*Joe Nussbaumer, Orest Kusnik*
Eric Peterson	*John Siemens*

Director: Paul Thompson

Designer: Richard Roberts

Music: Allan Rae

Introduction

Rudy Wiebe

The play tries to tell a story that's being lived here right now. . . . People like to see themselves reflected, and that happens so rarely in drama staged in Alberta.[1]

Working with Paul Thompson and the actors of Theatre Passe Muraille on *The West Show* in 1975 was an imaginative jolt for me. Twenty years earlier I had written my first play; at a climactic moment in it the hero hurled a highly significant glass trinket to the floor, where it must needs smash to mirror his despair, but it never did smash, neither the first night nor the second; so the audience merely laughed, nervously. I had acted in plays since the second grade, my histrionic peak being the rake MacHeath (I still have the gilded pistols) in *The Beggar's Opera*. I had directed half a dozen plays, from *Job* to Kobo Abe's *Friends,* but sitting in an abandoned Saskatoon church and watching Thompson and troupe embody scenes from *Peace Shall Destroy Many* was a dramatic revelation. Eric Peterson lay carelessly on the floor while Janet Amos leaned over him, and suddenly I was aware of her body moving almost imperceptibly, and then he moved, barely, and like a stroke I recognised Louis Moosomin on his barn straw and Elizabeth Block: *she* was going to seduce *him*. And in my imagination exploded a whole new way of seeing what I had written sixteen years before, "—she had to have a man—she could not live—she had to have a man—"

So in the spring of 1976 Paul and I began working on a different idea. We wanted to make an entirely new play by means of a total collaboration between actors, director and writer. We talked to theatre directors in Edmonton and tried to persuade them to put us on their next winter's program, although no word had yet been written and we didn't even know the subject of the play. It must be about contemporary Alberta and it must premiere here, not Toronto. And Theatre 3—bless Mark Schoenberg and Stephen Gentles—agreed to reserve us one slot. Now all we had to do was do it: the obvious subject was glamourous oil. The drama of Eric

[1] "Rudy Wiebe—An interview with Chris Bullock," *Prairie Star,* Edmonton, 1977.

Harvie's discovery of the Leduc field in his "Moose Pasture" as he called it interested us, but dull coal proved more evocative. In early summer of 1976 the struggle of the Dodds-Round Hill farming community with Calgary Power over an enormous thermal power-plant development just outside Edmonton was reaching a climax; it seemed to act out much of what booming Alberta represented both to itself and the rest of Canada.

> *We wanted to create a picture of two forces, two good forces colliding with each other: one is the need for resource development and the other is for people not to have their livelihood and their life destroyed.*[2]

In Ottawa, Toronto and Edmonton Paul and I met all that year. We talked endlessly (he's a tremendous talker!), we visited Calgary Power officials and individual farm women and men active in The Agricultural Protective Society, and on November 24 we attended the society's annual meeting in the Round Hill high school gym. That was a triumphant gathering of over two hundred people who had forced big capitalism and big government to change their plans; people who had always considered themselves small, perhaps insignificant, now found within themselves a certain stature, a worthy pride. We wanted to tell their story and they, with a bit of apprehension, were excited to see what we would do with it.

The play was scheduled to open in Edmonton on April 12, 1977; on Monday, February 14 we began to work in Toronto with four actors: Janet Amos, Layne Coleman, David Fox and Connie Kaldor. We had discussed the ideas, concepts and general plans with them at length; I brought in a rough outline of what we thought could happen in the play and they began to 'jam', to use Passe Muraille parlance, various characters, scenes, possible new situations. Some days were great, some were terrible. We missed Eric Peterson (playing in *Les Canadiens* in Montreal) and Ted Johns (we did not try to create the character of Aberhart until he joined us during the last week), but those four actors were so strong that in a day or two whole characters and scenes emerged, new situations Paul and I had never thought of. Paul would throw out ideas: "What does Roger Mitchell do in the morning when he gets up?" and I would scribble down scraps of dialogue, and action as the actors fought to make a farm breakfast somehow dramatic. "Okay, Caroline—(she didn't have a last name yet) bursts in, desperate about her grandfather selling his farm—what happens?" and ten minutes later: "Anton's coming after her, what does he do?" My job was to make sure I noted down everything really good, invent names and suggest alternative situations, and when the actors lay around, exhausted in mind and body, hammer out something else with Paul, whose energy level was unbelievable. In the evening I typed up rough scenarios of some

2   Ibid.

scenes we thought we might use. It was like being boiled in a hothouse, six days a week, and when we started worrying about deadlines on Sunday afternoons too.

> *Paul: Rudy, you're ready to take over as director?*
> *Rudy: I probably should, but I doubt if either of us will*
> *live long enough to see that happen.*
> *Paul: I should become a pure Canadian director.*
> *Rudy: Pure?*
> *Paul: Just make applications to governments—raise*
> *money. Yeah.*[3]

A novelist spends his life working alone: this was like trying to write in a shopping mall—and for the company I loved it. Hanging onto every laugh, every strange twist of word or body that gave the flash of meaning to a character. Sometimes, out of actor despair at Paul's insatiable demand for 'More, More!', scenes flamed into absolute brilliance. I remember when Connie Kaldor vanished and Caroline incarnate suddenly seized the milk pail and dashed milk in her father's face so that old Anton could win in the arm-wrestling scene. Perhaps it would never have happened if the Passe Muraille space, where we had been working, had not been needed for something else that morning and we were jamming in the Thompson's narrow living room; as the two men strained, Connie suddenly ran into the kitchen and came back with a jug of water and threw it full in Layne's face. He was soaked, and swearing while we all roared with laughter.

To make a play this way is not for worriers, nor for tender egos. Five times a day you might feel yourself assaulted, your brilliant ideas ignored if not actually derided, but there was always the adrenalin of a marvelous discovery, or the gradual growing to necessity of a character's or a scene's demands, to pull you along and make you forget everything in a moment's magic. Sometimes the loveliness which happened at the moment of discovery was never quite captured again: there were scenes we worked on for hours, trying to get that exact instant again—and they didn't return even in the staged performances. At other times the scenes we most feared because they had never quite caught, though the play made them necessary, suddenly were alive on opening night. Sometimes for a whole day one actor or another was dead; fortunately Paul and I never had coincidental low days, so there was always someone to push or to pull. For four intense, crazy weeks we 'jammed' everything we could about this story; on the last day I wrote out the possible order of scenes on a huge sheet of gyproc (Passe Muraille was remodelling a warehouse into a theatre—this play wasn't for the tidy either), we re-argued them once more and then I took the night plane back to Edmonton with 350 pages of notes in my briefcase.

[3] Wiebe, Rudy, unpublished diary, March 5, 1977.

From March 7 to 17 (with two days off for a reading in Saskatoon) I worked blessedly alone, writing the complete script of *Far As The Eye Can See*. Paul arrived just as I was handing it over to the typist; we spent the weekend looking for an Indian actor to play Crowfoot, found him in Gordon Tootoosis, and on Monday, March 21 rehearsals began at Theatre 3.

> *The play is meaty because it is filled with ambiguities. The play is sneaky because its emotional impact is clear. Having been fair with the head, the audience feels morally freed for passionate partisanship with the heart. They leaped to their feet night after night to applaud the comfortable individual capitalist defending his private interest against the wealthy corporate capitalist speaking for the public interest. On reflection, the audience may feel they were had.[4]*

The script took three and a half hours to read through! Obviously a lot had to be done in three weeks, and the massive cuts and changes we made as the demands of stage and performance hammered the play into shape cannot be detailed here. On April 16, at the fourth performance, we were still making major cuts; some pages of my script are almost totally blacked out and re-written, and not one is untouched. I want to end this brief sketch by mentioning two matters.

The first relates to the Regal Dead. I got the idea for them from Hebrews chapter 12 verse one: "Therefore, since we are surrounded by so great a cloud of witnesses . . . let us run with perseverance the race that is set before us." I have always liked the notion (picture?) of the dead observing us, the living, and often wished they could (would?) give me the benefit of their long wisdom; when Paul told me that Brecht had used something similar I of course read *The Good Woman of Setzuan*. I was a little disappointed not to have been the first with the idea, but to have both the Bible and Brecht sanction a dramatic idea, who could pray for more? Actually, the Regal Dead became my favorite people in the play and, with old Anton, really carried it for me.

The second has to do with a persistent scene that made for a great deal of argument. I had declared from the very beginning that this was one play that would not have a drunk scene in it, so of course I was outvoted six, seven and eight to one. On the very last day before I left Toronto we 'jammed' a scene between the community drunk—Orville, invented solely for that purpose—and John Siemens because, as Paul insisted, "We have to see John truly in despair, speaking the truth, the unvarnished truth about himself." Bars have never done a thing for me; if you need wine to tell the truth, I believe you are basically a liar. However I succumbed to massive

---

4   Thorsell, William, *Edmonton Journal*, May 7, 1977.

pressure; the scene was 'jammed' with great relish and I wrote it in, but during rehearsals I kept hammering Paul until he agreed it was unnecessary. But then, several days later he came with a new idea: why not have John get drunk with his greatest enemy, Joe Nussbaumer? Now that made some interesting dramatic sense; Eric Peterson and Dennis Robinson went to it with a will. It was to be inserted into Act Three, between the present scenes four and five. But this scene, like several others, never made the stage. Paul agreed with me: it was unnecessary.

In a way, writing *Far As The Eye Can See* seemed easy. The euphoria of producing 160 pages of script in eight writing days made me note in my diary: " . . . it is possible Shakespeare wrote three plays a year for fifteen years. (If he had a good company of actors) it is *very* possible!" The creative 'trial and error' onslaught of the company allowed me to choose and polish what had already been made in various ways several times; there is only one major scene which I wrote entirely by myself. In writing fiction, experience gives you the great advantage of anticipating problems; that is even more true in writing for the stage. Working with Paul Thompson and Theatre Passe Muraille gave me the extraordinary benefit of their experienced, creative imagination, and helped us to produce, together, a play I am still happy about.

List of Characters

Crowfoot
William Aberhart
Princess Louise   *the Regal Dead*

Anton Kalicz   *Round Hill farmer*
Wadu (Walter) Kalicz   *his son, Edmonton businessman*
Caroline Kalicz   *his granddaughter*

Betty Mitchell
Roger Mitchell
Elton Preschuk
Joe Nussbaumer
Henry Stutzman   *farmers of Round Hill*

John Siemens
Don Ritz   *engineers for Calgary Power*

Orest Kusnik
Agnes Reynolds   *the townspeople of Round Hill*

Errol Hanks   *young city man*
Peter Lougheed

Setting

The Rocky Mountains, Edmonton, and the nearby farming community of Round Hill, Alberta, March—July 1976.

Act I

Scene i

The audience enters to a stage with no curtain. A wide sky of horizontal blues, below which an all-embracing ramp half-circles the stage: a suggestion of the wide levels of prairie, hills, mountains of Alberta, and the valleys or smaller particular places like farms, houses, rooms—enclosed within them.

The house lights fade to black: mountain music of wind, distance, rises. Stage lights come up on the Rocky Mountains, perhaps near Lake Louise: sound shifts to Regal Dead music. Above the ramp, center, the face, body of Crowfoot appear out of the darkness. He is searching, the light of distance in his eyes. Distant mutter of thunder.

CROWFOOT: The shining mountains, where the sun falls behind the sharp white teeth of the earth. From nowhere we came, to nowhere we go, we are the shadow that runs across the grass and is lost in the sunset . . .

ABERHART: *Calling off stage.* Crowfoot, Crowfoot, hey . . . *He emerges scratched, suit disheveled, but nonetheless robust and enthusiastic; Regal Dead music continues.* You set a mean pace there, chief, the Princess Louise, she's all . . . *He is clambering up.*

Crowfoot is obviously annoyed at the interruption.

PRINCESS LOUISE: *Off stage.* Yoo-hoo, yoo-hoo—oh— *She appears distantly in full court dress, very perturbed.* where . . . running ahead . . . like little boys. Rascals really. If you had so much as mentioned an entire mountain range, rocks upon rocks, rivers . . .

CROWFOOT: *Declarative.* I'm not going any further with this . . . *An ominous roll of thunder; he lifts both hands in conciliation.* Okay, I will, I will. But I don't like it.

ABERHART: *Quickly content.* Well if this is the place, we'll just stop and look at the beauties of . . .

CROWFOOT: *Muttering to himself.* It is not the place. *To Aberhart.* It's your turn to help her.

ABERHART: She's always getting lost, chief, she . . . *Concedes at Crowfoot's look and turns to the Princess.* If you'da wore a proper dress . . . you know, Princess, not this trailing . . . *Assists her.* The snow in the passes, it's not your cobblestone streets, you know, your . . .

The Princess becomes aware of where she is; the music has faded.

PRINCESS LOUISE: William, oh William! *They look about the stunning mountain vista.* That was almost worth . . . it. I can see . . . *so* far . . . what a *tremendous* landscape, so strikingly . . . virile, so balanced, the lake . . . the black bristle of pine . . . oh . . . oh . . . *She is near ecstasy.*

ABERHART: Yeah, it's pretty.

PRINCESS LOUISE: *Sings with reverence, elegance.*

Unto the hills around do I lift up

Aberhart comes to attention, sings also.

PRINCESS, ABERHART: My longing eyes.
                   Oh, whence for me shall my—

CROWFOOT: *Roars.* Quiet!

The other two are abashed as he goes off muttering angrily in Blackfoot.

ABERHART: *Confidentially to the Princess.* They're not like us, you know. This much nature, it rubs 'em a bit raw.

PRINCESS LOUISE: Lorne, of course, wrote that song.

ABERHART: Eh?

PRINCESS LOUISE: My husband, Lord Lorne, before he was Governor General of Canada. *Gradually her voice gathers bitterness.* He was always travelling, here, there, his poetic melancholy . . . here and there . . .

ABERHART: I sorta like that, unto the hills do I lift up my longing—

CROWFOOT: *Loud.* I said, this is *not* the place.

Aberhart starts, Princess Louise moans, clumps herself down on a convenient rock.

PRINCESS LOUISE: I wasn't informed of any of this—that there would be ice, poor little stunted trees, and I lost my sketch pad—

ABERHART: *Trying to comfort her.* Now Princess, it—

PRINCESS LOUISE: *She shrugs him off impatiently, rises.* Well, if it's not up in the mountains, it must be down lower, and to get there we have to go down. *She wheels.* I'm going back to that beautiful lake, and perhaps my sketch pad . . .

She strides off; Regal Dead exit music.

ABERHART: Out of the cold mountains, down to the simmering plains. Yes! *He trundles after her.*

Crowfoot looks majestic for a moment, then comprehends he is being left alone and goes quickly. Lights out as music shifts to "Ball and Chain".

Scene ii

In one part of the circle of the ramp emerges Caroline Kalicz's Edmonton pad. Pack sack, jacket heavy with buttons, some placards, revolutionary pictures are scattered about. Caroline in jeans, dark shirt and bare feet squats on the mattress, deep in depression; very heavy "Ball and Chain". Suddenly a thunderous banging on the door.

ERROL: *Outside.* Caroline, hey Caroline!

She grimaces, glances at the door, but otherwise does not move.

ERROL: *Singing outside.* O Caroline, hey Caroline, I'm the one you want to see! I'm the one, the one, the one. *Hammering to the rhythm, the door flies open; typically bearded, jeaned campus male.* Are you ever lucky, it's me bringing you something big and healthy before lunch and after lunch and for supper, with a whole flavour too.

CAROLINE: *Discouraging.* Oh, Errol, god I . . .

But he is already kneeling astride her, bending over her until he becomes aware of her resistance. Then abruptly he stops, leans back, looks.

ERROL: What's the matter?

CAROLINE: *Acidly.* You're kneeling on my hair.

ERROL: *Elaborately.* Sor-ry. *He moves off her and she pushes up.* You got something to drink? *He is buzzing around again.* Or smoke? You got some of that sweet stuff we had last night?

CAROLINE: *Distraught.* Look, Errol, there's nothing here, I haven't any time to get anything. I've got the Morganthaler Committee to organize, again, and there won't be anyone there, and there's another anti-Kraft article, their profits are *up!* I've got all these letters to write and I'm just so tired, so god-awful tired of it all I could—

ERROL: *Wheels on her.* You're pregnant!

CAROLINE: What!

ERROL: *Moving in on her again.* That's what's the matter, you're carrying my seed! Hey, you want to get married? It'd be—

CAROLINE: I just want to get sorted out—I—

ERROL: I've never been married before, it'd be a trip!

CAROLINE: *Exasperated.* I'm trying to think through my life!

ERROL: Well I'm in your life.

CAROLINE: No! It's nothing but meetings and stupid classes and essays and placards and I'm not even interested—political scene, California grape pickers . . . I would just love a grape, I can just taste—

ERROL: Look, don't think, open up to experience. Politic's the gig you do out there, in your pad you—

CAROLINE: The world is moving in on me; who am I? I'm so— wiped, I worked my guts out for that *Poundmaker* and it went belly up the minute the grant died . . .

ERROL: *All solicitude and flurry.* Let me give you a foot massage. I was reading this book; it has all the diagrams in it, positions . . . for hands . . . *He has her down again.* Everything passes through the foot, see, sooner or later everything goes through the foot, everything . . .

CAROLINE: Ugh. *But she submits.* I just wanta be alone.

ERROL: It's not good for you, not when you feel like this.

CAROLINE: *Relaxing.* Errol, I know what I want . . .

ERROL: You don't know what you want!

CAROLINE: But I just don't want it!

ERROL: *Busy.* Don't get discouraged kid. Lenin didn't.

CAROLINE: And my mother called again. *Her mother's whining tone.* 'Why do we never see you, Caroline? Are you staying clean? Really Caroline, the proper underclothes, it's not as if . . . ugh . . .

ERROL: *Working higher up her leg.* Why'd you talk to her? When you hear her on the phone just drop it, drop it . . .

CAROLINE: I had to talk to her, she's flying to Iran.

ERROL: Iran!

CAROLINE: To visit Uncle Henry. He's a computer for Imperial Oil, they plug him in here, there, he runs, bleep blip blip . . .

ERROL: *Stops, his hands high on her naked thigh.* Heavy! Your uncle works for the biggest capitalist rip-off in the whole world!

CAROLINE: He was doing it before I was born.

ERROL: O Caroline! *He embraces her; starts rolling up her shirt.* I didn't know, oh you poor baby, let me comfort you—

She gets her leg up; abruptly he goes flying.

CAROLINE: *Up on her feet.* That's twice! What do you think this is, Jump Time at the OK Corral?

ERROL: I'm just trying to help you sort out your life.

CAROLINE: You've never seen past the end of your cock! Now get out, I've had it with you, out.

ERROL: Caroline, we've been together for two weeks!

CAROLINE: That's thirteen days too long—now out, out!

ERROL: *Starting to go.* You better be careful, you start turning it off like this, it gets pretty hard to start turning it on.

He exits.

CAROLINE: Out! Out! My body's my own, my head's my own, my body, my . . . *She gasps, on the verge of tears.* This stinking room! *She kicks the mattress.* I have to get out of here, out, where's my knapsack . . . where . . . *She is hunting furiously, finds it, begins stuffing things into it.*

Regal Dead entrance music. Enter Crowfoot and Aberhart, exhausted, trudging up the ramp. They do not notice Caroline below them rushing about.

ABERHART: *Gasping a little.* This better be it, Crowfoot, the Princess, she can't handle another puddle.

CROWFOOT: She should watch where she's going.

ABERHART: They're not like us, Crowfoot, they're not used to seeing for themselves. She's royalty.

CROWFOOT: I too was a king. Once.

ABERHART: Oh sure, sure, as much king as Alberta ever had, sure, but you never had the red-carpet treatment now did you!

CROWFOOT: *Red* carpet?

ABERHART: *Guffaws, slapping Crowfoot on the shoulder.* Oh— red! Sorry there chief, you're a regular card.

The Princess enters, dishevelled and very nearly spent.

PRINCESS LOUISE: Endless, endless mountains and now a city, such a smelly, noisy city, spread everywhere, oh, I can't, I can't . . .

ABERHART: City! *He looks around; slowly his smile broadens.*

Caroline has finished throwing her things together in a knapsack and is scrambling for high workboots.

CAROLINE: I'm just going to run...run...anywhere...just run ... *Stops, remembering.* My pills, I have to take my ... *Flips up the mattress, seizes something, then hurls it away.* Screw the pill!

She flings herself out the door.

ABERHART: Of course, I recognize it, despite all those skyscrapers—that's what we call those. *He gestures and the Princess perks up a little.* High buildings, Princess, skyscrapers. They weren't there in my day but I knew they'd come. And they came. *The complete tour guide.* Yes, and that brown stone building, the dome and the cupola, you can hardly see it there among all the skyscrapers. It was there I stood; it was there my voice rolled. And when they said to me 'Social Credit is a hairbrained scheme,' I said.... *He bends forward.* 'Thank goodness I haven't got any hair.' Ha, ha. When they said, 'Where will you get the money to back your first dividend?' I said, 'Where do you get the money to issue the bonds you sell in Toronto and New York?' 'We don't need any money, we're backed by the resources of the country.' 'You've answered your own question, my friend! It is the resources of this province that will feed and clothe and shelter us.'

CROWFOOT: *Looking about while listening.* This is *not* the place.

PRINCESS LOUISE: Not the place!

She screams, faints backwards. Aberhart, startled, catches her in his arms at the last instant.

CROWFOOT: We're almost there now. Come.

He picks up the Princess's feet while Aberhart holds her shoulders; they begin to carry her off to exit music.

PRINCESS LOUISE: *Recovering a little, sobbing.* I have never been dragged so far to see so little.

ABERHART: I don't know ... it looked pretty good to me.

Lights out.

Scene iii

As the city-scape disappears, in the opposite curve of the ramp Orest Kushnik's cafe in Round Hill appears. Orest is sweeping the floor as Betty Mitchell enters dressed in an early spring coat.

BETTY: Orest, can I use your phone?

100

OREST:　It's behind the counter, Betty.

BETTY:　*Dialing.* I have to make a long distance call to Florida.

OREST:　*Refusing the joke.* Just put the money on the counter.

BETTY:　*Laughs into phone.* Hello, Agnes. Yes it's Betty. Sorry Agnes, I can't come today, I have to wait for Roger . . . it's the truck again, yes . . . I'm just having a coffee, just me and Orest . . . *She grins at him.* . . . . Did you miss a meeting last night. We haven't had so much excitement since the arena burned down. *She laughs a little.* Would you believe it, I said something at a public meeting? Yes, *laughs,* yes, in front of four hundred people, me! I was on my feet and the chairman—the man from Calgary Power, he was pretty puzzled by then and he asked me what I wanted to know and I, I just blurted out what I'd been wondering; it was all so confusing, the whole meeting. I couldn't understand anything; all those soil samples and overhead projections and strata in meters . . .

Roger Mitchell and Elton Preschuk enter.

ROGER:　That goddam truck, Elton, I can't believe it. Another 1100 dollars! I can't even afford to sell it. *He slumps down on a stool.*

ELTON:　*Straddling another stool.* If you leave it somewhere, maybe somebody'll at least drag it away.

Roger roars with laughter and Orest goes behind the counter to get coffee.

BETTY:　*On phone.* What? Oh, I can't hear, Roger and Elton just— what?—oh, I just blurted out . . .

ROGER:　Coffee, Orest, I can still afford coffee.

BETTY:　*On phone.* I said, 'When are you ripping up my farm? What day?' That's what I said, I just—

ELTON:　You sure did, Betty. And the high school auditorium was just ringing with your voice.

Orest slides up three coffees.

BETTY:　That P.A. was so loud, I never . . . heard . . .

ELTON:　And the whole auditorium was ringing with silence after.

ROGER:　Oh, the wife, she does all the public speaking you know.

BETTY:　*On phone.* What? Agnes? Oh, I can't talk here, these men clumping themselves down; I'll call you later. Yeah. Curling, Thursday. Bye. *She hangs up.*

ROGER:　You sure missed a hell of a hockey game, Elton, going to that meeting. The Leafs got hammered again.

ELTON:　*To Betty.* You think Joe Nussbaumer's gonna string up that handsome blond engineer?

101

BETTY: *Seating herself on the stool between them.* I hope so! *Laughs.* I've never been so embarrassed in my life; they were giving all that complicated information about coal seams, and faults and . . . oh . . . kilowatts and I just . . . what a night.

ROGER: The wife out on the town alone, feeling her spring oats.

ELTON: Oh it wasn't a bad question. It was a real good question. A lot of us were thinking it, just didn't have the nerve—I mean, if they're gonna tear up your farm, anywhere from ten to fifty feet down, you want to know when, eh?

ROGER: Nobody's gonna rip up nobody's farm.

BETTY: He won't listen to me.

Caroline enters the cafe, very tired. She takes the last stool beside Elton at the counter and, in city-fashion, she does not listen to the talk.

ELTON: They said a lot of real interesting stuff there. Now I figure my number one land should get at least $400 an acre and they were—

ROGER: You're crazy, four—

ELTON: Well, at least 350, and they were—

ROGER: You ever test it all out? Gordon Teske's got more number one than you.

ELTON: Maybe, maybe, but he's got more land than anybody, but all that higher stuff on the hill—

CAROLINE: *To Orest.* A chocolate milkshake, please.

ROGER: That ridge of yours on your east quarter? You'd be lucky if that run number four and—

BETTY: Oh stop comparing land, what will it matter if—

ROGER: Even if the number one was worth 350, and I don't think it is, but with all that other stuff in there you wouldn't average more'n 250, maybe 275.

ELTON: No, no, that's too low. But you know what Calgary Power was offering last night? Clear across the board? Fifty-five square miles? One hundred dollars an acre.

BETTY: *With him.* One hundred dollars an acre.

OREST: *Over the counter.* You want anything else?

ROGER: Eh?

BETTY: Yes, put something in his mouth, a piece of pie, anything.

ROGER: No—com'mon Betty, the cows— *He gets up.* Nobody's buying anything, nobody's selling anything. One hundred dollars cowshit. *Exit.*

CAROLINE: *Leaning across Elton to Betty.* Does the bus still run from Round Hill to Ryley?

BETTY: *Looking up.* Oh—no—that stopped. *Pause.* Oh, I know you!

ELTON: *Thoughtful.* Maybe they'll just strip the land, and let you keep the good stuff, you know, roll it up like they do them green lawns and put it . . . no, then you'd have to have some place to put it.

BETTY: You're Anton Kalicz's granddaughter; you used to come every summer—my, you've changed . . . *She laughs to cover up.*

ELTON: *To Orest.* You know that Calgary Power said last night they'd be spending between one and two billion dollars on this project.

CAROLINE: I don't remember—

Roger is coming back.

BETTY: I'm Betty Mitchell and . . . that's Roger.

ROGER: Com'mon, com'mon, Betty. Elton, the farmer's the foundation of this country.

OREST: *To them all.* You know how much money that is, two *billion* dollars?

ROGER: Eh?

OREST: You could cover 55 square miles with dollar bills, completely, three deep. *Everyone stares at him a moment.* The sooner they build that power plant, the better. This town needs something.

ELTON: Two billion . . . and they offer us a hundred dollars an acre!

OREST: I'd sell this cafe for that, right now.

ROGER: You must have all of a third of an acre here, Orest, 25-30 bucks worth anyway.

OREST: *Humourlessly.* Nobody's offered me that in five years. And I'd throw in the wife and three kids for nothing.

ELTON: You'd have to pay them, Orest, you'd pay them.

BETTY: *Taking Caroline by the arm.* You come with us, we drive right past old Anton's.

ROGER: *Paying.* There's two bits extra, just for you.

OREST: Look at that, a tip! That power project's paying off already!

ROGER: *As they go.* You come over tomorrow, Elton, watch the Canadiens clobber Washington.

ELTON: Slaughter's the word you want.

Lights out.

Scene iv

Old Anton Kalicz in his farm-house kitchen. He wears clothes worn white by many washings and sits rolling cigarettes, talking as it seems to the empty chair across the table from him.

ANTON: Somonabitch Anna! *He coughs deeply.* I remember, you have smile . . . white teeth . . . long hair . . . gold when you run through the blue flax . . . Anna! You never argue then, why do you argue now? I sell that Ruby. No goddam good, sell her to the knackers, buy two heifers. Goddam old cow. *Pause.* Always know better. You remember, you say leave the Mitchell's steers alone, they only the road, leave them alone, okay, okay, then they're in my barley, tramping, shitting—huragh! I send them through the fence with the dogs, shotgun! *Caroline is standing in the door, watching him.* You were wrong then, heh? What I tell you that time?

CAROLINE: *Coming forward.* Grandpa? Grandpa, it's me. Hi. *Anton looks up; stares.* It's me, Caroline. *She comes closer as he does not move, and her voice gets a bit anxious.* Come to see you. *He does not move.* How are you . . . Grandpa . . .

ANTON: Caroline?

CAROLINE: Yeah, it's me. *She laughs a little, self-consciously.*

ANTON: *Getting up slowly and enfolding her in his arms.* Caroline, oh, oh. *They embrace with real emotion.* My Car-o-line. *He holds her at arm's length.*

CAROLINE: Hi.

ANTON: Laugh. Laugh again, you laugh.

CAROLINE: I can't just laugh, there's nothing funny . . . *But she does laugh, ringingly, and he hugs her again.*

ANTON: Beautiful, beautiful laugh—now you sit, here, my chair and I make tea, you sit, sit. *She sits.* Something to eat, long trip from Edmonton, you tired. Come to visit your grandpa.

CAROLINE: *Laughing, trying to get up.* Grandpa, don't rush around, I don't need—I just thought I'd come, to see you.

ANTON: *Pauses.* What about school, that university?

CAROLINE: A bit of a break—nothing. How are you doing?

ANTON: *Still looking at her.* Fine, fine.

104

CAROLINE: All alone, with grandma gone.

ANTON: People get old, they die. You look like a woman now, but the pants . . . even the zipper in the front.

CAROLINE: *Laughs.* Oh, women wear pants in today's world. I don't even own a skirt.

ANTON: Your grandma never wear pants. Four, five skirts, but never . . . *Quick shift.* You have it, baby?

CAROLINE: *Astonished.* What?

ANTON: Baby?

CAROLINE: *Laughs, relieved.* That's not a problem any more. No. Still the same old grandpa!

ANTON: You have it baby, I kick your ass. Now go, make tea.

CAROLINE: *Hugely relieved, rises.* Sure. Your tea still in the cooky jar?

ANTON: Good place.

CAROLINE: *Off-stage.* Mom called, she's gone to Iran.

ANTON: You have good mother—bossy, but she helps your father, Wadu. You should be proud of your father.

CAROLINE: *Coming back, standing in doorway with empty teacups.* What?

ANTON: You should be proud of your father! Wadu smart man.

CAROLINE: *Unconvinced.* Oh. Yeah.

ANTON: When Wadu little, he sing, he always sing, 'Juz ty spiewasz, Skowroneczku' . . . come, you sing now in Polish, like little Wadu.

CAROLINE: I can't sing Polish.

Loud. You forget everything I teach you, every summer?

CAROLINE: *Sits.* Grandpa, it's twelve years, I . . .

ANTON: March, why you not in university? Heh?

CAROLINE: It's spring break—no. I wanted . . . I just had to leave.

ANTON: *Pause.* What your father say?

CAROLINE: We don't talk . . . much . . .

ANTON: *Busy.* All right, you sing in English, 'Welcome, Skylark'. Stand up, sing, sing!

CAROLINE: *Rises.* Okay, but not Polish. *She sings the 19th century folksong.*

How small are your wants, my warbler high and lonely,
A field of corn you need and bright, blue heaven only.
God bless you, skylark mine, I envy you your gladness;
For a man's life's not easy, with its toil and its sadness.

*She is in the spirit of the song, and when Anton breaks into Polish,
she sings that also with him, the memory coming easily, happily.*

ANTON and CAROLINE:

Bog pomoz, skowroneczku, dodawaj nadzieje,
I dla ciebie ja zarazem i dla siebie sieje.

*Anton's singing breaks down into coughing. Caroline's voice peters
out; the cough begins to frighten her. He coughs on and on. Finally
he takes out a white handkerchief and coughs into it. Caroline helps
him to the chair.*

CAROLINE: Grandpa—Grandpa—what. . . . *ad lib.*

ANTON: *Gesturing through coughing.* Smoke—cigarette—give—
cigarette!

CAROLINE: That's no good—it can't . . .

ANTON: *Roars.* Cigarette!

*Caroline hastily gives him one. He lights it, and gradually stops
coughing.*

ANTON: You see—always . . . it goes away.

CAROLINE: You still have it, so bad . . .

ANTON: It's the mines, coal mines in Crow's Nest Pass. See. *Holds
up the handkerchief.* See, still black, forty-three years, goddam
Hillcrest Mines! I carry in my lungs to my grave, somonabitch!

CAROLINE: Grandpa, is there something about a mine here, a
coal mine? Betty Mitchell was saying—

ANTON: No. No! This is Canada, no Poland; here stand on your
own land and you king. My land, my fence. *Gestures.* Here, here,
everybody out. Out! You stay here till you feel better.

CAROLINE: I want to stay—go see the river valley again.

ANTON: *On his feet.* Go fix goddam Ruby now—come on, come
one, sit on your ass all day? This is farm, no university.

Caroline's laughter is heard as she gets up. Lights out.

Scene v

The valley of the Battle River, near Anton Kalicz's farm. Prairie river music. Caroline enters, runs up the ramp, breathing in the vista.

CAROLINE: *Happy.* Still the same, oh—still the same. *She stretches out on the ground, totally at peace.*

Regal Dead music; they enter; Crowfoot and Aberhart still carrying the Princess Louise. They are all very weary. Crowfoot senses something and drops the Princess's feet; he comes forward, staring into distance.

CROWFOOT: I know this place. The wide low valley, the little river that curls back on itself. On the high bluffs the light gleams, and is gone . . .

PRINCESS LOUISE: Oh, that sounds so beautiful, so Matthew Arnold . . .

ABERHART: Yeah, Dover Beach. *Drops the Princess too.* Hey chief, chief, where are we?

CROWFOOT: This is the Battle River. The border between Blackfoot and Cree.

ABERHART: Battle River . . . in Alberta, why, where's the long wooden bridge, the—

PRINCESS LOUISE: *Popping up, alert.* Alberta you say. *Stands up.* This is Alberta? *She runs about, ecstatic.*

ABERHART: Of course, I saw that long ago. But where's the wooden train trestle, the longest in the world that used to curve across the vally like a fine woman's— *He has been shaping the Princess and he stops, confused.* Sorry, Princess, I—

PRINCESS LOUISE: *Concerned with herself.* This is my province!

CROWFOOT: Yeah.

ABERHART: But your name's Louise, what—

PRINCESS LOUISE: I was the sixth child, fourth daughter of Her Imperial Majesty Queen Victoria, the Princess Louise Caroline *Alberta.* Lorne named this province for me.

CROWFOOT: *Sarcastically.* Oh yeah.

PRINCESS LOUISE: *Staring about like the proud owner.* What a *wonderful, beautiful* place. *Her hands are undulating like hills.*

CROWFOOT: You see where the river turns back on itself, by that black shadow on the bank? This is the place.

PRINCESS LOUISE: At last!

ABERHART: *Puzzled.* You sure, chief? There's nothing here, they even tore down the longest wooden bridge in the world.

PRINCESS LOUISE: Chief Crowfoot could not be wrong, certainly it will be here in my— *They discover Caroline as she sits up, stretches. Ecstatic.* O look, an Albertan!

CROWFOOT: Yeah, in its native habitat.

Caroline comes down the ramp towards them and the river.

PRINCESS LOUISE: *Circling her.* Is it—male, or female?

ABERHART: It's hard to tell. By their works ye shall know them.

CROWFOOT: *Sniffing.* Female.

Caroline comes forward with a happy, mused expression on her face. She opens her arms as if she would embrace the whole circle of river, valley, banks and sky. Princess Louise moves as if to touch her.

CAROLINE: Remember me? Remember me?

CROWFOOT: *To Aberhart and Princess Louise.* Remember, we are allowed to interfere only once. Only once.

PRINCESS LOUISE: *Draws back, disappointed.* Yes, yes, I know. *But she is nevertheless fascinated by Caroline.*

ABERHART: Each of us has only one arrow to shoot, so to speak, eh chief?

CROWFOOT: *Heavy stage Indian.* Shootum only one arrow, from bow.

CAROLINE: *Calling softly.* Hello. Hello.

PRINCESS LOUISE: *Echoes, enjoying this.* Hello, hello.

CAROLINE: Remember me? I've come back. Hello-o-o-o.

PRINCESS LOUISE: Hello-o-o-o. *She trips across, laughing.*

CAROLINE: Ah-h-h-h-h, you smell so good, old friendly hills: George, Josephine, Esmerelda peeking over your shoulder. Every summer I'd be here, Grandpa's cows grazing among the willows, and the sky blue like the inside of an egg. Still so peaceful . . . *Crowfoot begins to move slightly towards her, intent.* What are you doing, lovely old river? Yeah I've changed. I'm not twelve, I'm not even a virgin. Changed a lot. I don't sit in the grass anymore and make up stories. Who'd listen? *Laughs suddenly.* Hey river, want to marry me? It'd be a trip. Sure. Come on, marry me? I'm yours. *Hesitates.* I'm too cluttered up? Okay, I'll sacrifice, I'll. . . . *She begins unhooking buttons from her jacket.*—here's my 'Abortion on Demand' button, my Morgenthaler button, my 'Save Chile' button, my 'fly the friendly skies with Otto Lang' postcard, oh . . . *Crowfoot is in his own space, very close to her.* Why are you always the same, so quiet, so filled with everlasting peace! Save me, river, I'll clear out your sludge, I'll bathe all your little puddles, I'll be faithful forever; just let me be part of you, floating with you, forever . . .

Crowfoot has been moving gradully into a rhythm beside her. At a strong movement he begins a slow chant that rises, rises, and he sways into dance. Aberhart and Princess Louise are in the background, watching intently.

CAROLINE: I'll even give up my tinted glasses. That's my last defence.

She takes them off; Crowfoot is growing beside her in his chant, dance, and suddenly she is aware of him as Regal Dead music sounds. She is not frightened, merely startled, and stands up; draws away a little as his dance reaches a crescendo, ends in a great, long cry.

CAROLINE: Oh—I—hi—hi . . .

She moves closer to him, but he is looking into distance.

CROWFOOT: How far can you see the river?

CAROLINE: Uhh, it's the Battle River, you see, long ago there was this big Indian battle here and they— *She comprehends the big Indian beside her; embarrassed.* Oh—sorry . . .

CROWFOOT: Look farther. *He points.* We hunted here, here I became a warrior, and here we died. Look there, at the bend the Cree attacked us, Siksikas and Sarcees, drove us back, and here we died in the great battle, twenty-three Blackfoot warriors, every one my friend, lying there and there . . .

He points, leading Caroline across the battlefield wtih his count.

PRINCESS LOUISE: *Puzzled.* The *great* battle, and only twenty-three dead? Why, when the English fight the Germans a grcat battle would be twenty-three thousand killed.

ABERHART: Twenty-three was a lot for them, Princess. They're not civilized, you know.

CROWFOOT: . . . and there and there. Eiynah! They died like warriors!

CAROLINE: *Very uncomfortable.* Yes . . . yes . . . well my grand-father's land goes up to that fence, it—

CROWFOOT: Look close, close . . . *He is bending her down.* Here we die the year of the Rotting Death, a woman and her child died here. *He picks up a tiny bone, offers it, but she cannot take it.* The legbone of the child.

CAROLINE: *Aghast.* I made mud-pies here, when I was eight.

CROWFOOT: Over six thousand Blackfoot—nearly two-thirds of all my people, men and women and children, died that year.

CAROLINE: *Softly.* I don't know anything like that . . . but I have a small history here too. One tree fort, collapsed, one . . .

He curls his arm about her shoulder; she is forced to turn though he does not touch her; warning music rises.

CROWFOOT: There, on the bank, where the black earth glistens—there, a girl with long hair like the sun twists in agony. She will suffer . . . leave now . . . now. The black earth that burns. Go now, go!

But she walks to the river. Crowfoot hesitates, then moves slowly back to the Regal Dead as warning music fades.

CAROLINE: . . . one broken arm under the willows. I belong here too . . . *She gestures herself into resolution.* Give me the bone of the child . . . just let me stay here.

She turns towards him, but he is gone from her sight. She stares about. The Regal Dead above are watching her.

CAROLINE: Hey, where are . . . I didn't even ask his—hey, hey! *She scoops up her belongings, exits searching.*

CROWFOOT: Women. They never listen.

ABERHART: *Puzzled.* Shot your arrow pretty quick there, chief. And a pretty strange target too, I'd say, eh Princess? Young girl like that.

CROWFOOT: The white man destroys everything. His whole history is a story of destruction, of killing and being killed.

ABERHART: No, no, chief, history is prophecy fulfilled, what you just did. All the prophecies of all the coming ages must be fulfilled before—

PRINCESS LOUISE: Now, William, really, I refuse to endure another one of your interminable sermons. Nothing will destroy my beautiful province where the sun shines so endlessly. Lake Louise . . . I want to go and see it, Lake Louise, isn't that mellifluous, Lake Lo—

John Siemens and his assistant Don Ritz run on stage, John rattling into a radio while Don sets up a detonator box.

JOHN: Okay, okay, we're fine now, watch your gauges, all set? Three, two, one, zero, go!

Don plunges the lever. A tremendous explosion at the Princess's very feet. She screams, flees back and the Regal Dead huddle together.

JOHN: Beautiful. Looks great. What's that reading . . . 976? . . . that's . . . 15%—whoopee! *He is laughing.* Don, it's 15% higher than number 63!

DON: This ain't a coal mine, it's a *gold* mine.

John ad-libs numbers into the phone.

CROWFOOT: *As they slowly separate.* See! Where are your pretty little trees now, your beautiful, *he gestures,* undulating hills.

PRINCESS LOUISE: What was that dreadful noise—and what is that dreadful hole? *Comes forward, pointing.*

ABERHART: That's progress! There's coal everywhere under Alberta and these fellows are just getting at the coal.

PRINCESS LOUISE: *Aghast.* This is a coal mine?

ABERHART: It's just a little hole. You can't make an omelet without breaking the egg you know.

Enter Caroline, staggered by the explosion.

CAROLINE: *To John and Don.* Hey, what're you doing—

DON: You stupid—what's the big idea!

Don moves in as if he would muscle her off; they yell inarticulately at each other.

JOHN: Quiet! I'll handle it—are you alright?

CAROLINE: Well, I'm in one piece, but—

JOHN: Didn't you see the orange markers, didn't you get the notice delivered to every farm family last week?

CAROLINE: Delivered! I'm walking on my grandfather's land and boom!—the landscape explodes!

JOHN: *Pulling out his notebook.* It's called a testing charge. What's your name?

CAROLINE: You've got no right to ask me anything.

JOHN: This is crown land, once a grazing lease held by Anton Kalicz but now crown land; you're trespassing on posted crown land.

CAROLINE: Crown land!

Don is standing back, trying to see her figure under her loose shirt and jeans.

JOHN: Now I've got a crew and half a million dollars worth of equipment waiting, so please move, well beyond that fence with the orange markers.

CAROLINE: Who are you guys? Imperial Oil?

DON: Calgary Power. Now just move—

CAROLINE: Don't you touch me, you capitalist pig!

JOHN: Don. Miss, Ms, whatever your name is, you're outa here—fifteen seconds or you're off with two boots in your rear end. Now move.

CAROLINE: Ah, who needs you, male dinosaurs. *Starts to leave.*

DON: *Laughing after her.* Hey, don't go away mad, we're not always like this.

CAROLINE: *Gives him the finger.* Screw you. *Exits.*

JOHN: Don, stow it. You go back to the truck, I'll handle this one myself.

DON: Oh, okay. *He exits.*

JOHN: *Into the radio.* Okay, we're ready here again . . . nothing . . . nothing. Give me a count when you're ready. Yeah, double charge on the last one.

PRINCESS LOUISE: *Not yet recovered.* I've seen the coal mines in the Midlands. The women and little children pulling coal cars in the black tunnels.

ABERHART: This isn't that kind of mine. The coal's just a few feet down. All they do is peel the top off, strip her back—

CROWFOOT: Scalp the earth, rip it off to the black burning rocks.

PRINCESS LOUISE: Worse and worse! My beautiful province one huge, muddy slag heap, like Wales, a slimy—

John plunges the detonator; a louder explosion than before. The Regal Dead huddle together more closely than ever, but they come out of it sooner; they are getting accustomed to the modern world.

JOHN: *Into the phone.* Got it! 16.5% higher? *Quietly jubilant.* Okay, that's very good for today, excellent. *Records.* Coal seams 34 to 37 feet thick. Man oh man, if we're careful the energy in this field will last longer than the Athabasca Tar Sands.

John exits. The Regal Dead come slowly forward.

ABERHART: You're right Crowfoot, and you're wrong. You're right, there's going to be an awful big hole here, but you're wrong if you think this will destroy the land or the farmers. This hole—coal mine—will transform the people and this province. Now you come with me and I'll show you the spawning ground of the politics of Alberta. *He is leading on.*

PRINCESS LOUISE: Spawning ground? Really, I don't much like lakes.

112

ABERHART: *Stopping and staring at her for an instant.* I meant a farm, Princess. That's where it happens in Alberta, on the farm.

PRINCESS LOUISE: Really? How interesting!

They exit to their music as lights fade.

Scene vi

Mitchell farm living room. Roger and Elton Preschuk are watching the hockey game on TV.

ELTON: *To Betty, off stage.* Joe Nussbaumer says they've invested so much money in the project already that you'd have a snowball's chance in—

ROGER: Hey, look at that Lafleur hey? Hup, hup, hup, son of a gun that Shutt, huh! *Laughing.* You see that shot, Elton, you see that?

Betty enters with the coffee pot.

ELTON: Maybe the replay'll—

ROGER: If they gonna re-play everything that Lafleur and Shutt do—ssseeessh, they go into that Washington goal like . . . *Looks up; Betty is standing there.* I wouldn't want to say.

BETTY: You want re-fills?

ELTON: Who were those guys, Betty, sitting up there at the meeting?

BETTY: I've been looking at the stuff again, that they gave out.

ROGER: Oh ask the wife, she knows, she knows.

BETTY: Well, somebody around here has to. It was the government up there.

ROGER: What?

BETTY: A cabinet minister. She is searching her papers. The Minister of the Environment, Yurko.

ELTON: Yeah, Nussbaumer's always yelling about him, Yurko Jerko he calls him.

ROGER: Ahh Betty, Environment, he just goes around looking in rivers and streams . . .

BETTY: No, he was there, I—

ROGER: . . . picking out beer cans and paper. What'd he be doing talking about expropriating farms, coal?

BETTY: He said the coal was here, I heard him, didn't you, Elton? Just ten feet down in some places, and they'll get it out so they—

Music; enter the Regal Dead, led by Aberhart.

ROGER: Hey, look, look!

The farmers freeze as if watching the TV.

ABERHART: Now here you have it. That one, *points to Betty,* knows the score, this one, *to Roger,* thinks he knows it, and this one, *to Elton,* is waiting for the re-play. And now we'll see some rigorous political debate.

The farmers unfreeze.

ELTON: Yep. Seven nothing for the Canadiens.

ROGER: *Disappointed.* Just a mucky scramble.

ELTON: Washington. There's still eight minutes left in the first period!

BETTY: And Canadian Pacific Minerals, they own nearly all the mineral rights here. He was the white-haired man, Elton, he never said a word.

ELTON: Why should he, if he owns it all?

ROGER: You think if they hadn't expanded so much there'd be better competition? I mean, the Canadiens are running all over these guys.

BETTY: For years there's been all these men coming around, 'Just run a test, madam, Alberta Soils Survey'.

ELTON: Yeah, but I never seen a single one of those, not for six months.

ROGER: There wasn't nothing at all going on, just before the election.

BETTY: So you do notice! What are you sitting here for watching that—

ROGER: I see who walks around my farm, and I see when. I got eyes in my head. But I don't figure there's anything to your—Yurko Jerko whatever sitting at a head table, yakking. When the time comes for the shit to fly they'll be at my door, asking me, I don't need to run after—

Betty stares at him; momentary freeze.

ABERHART: You see? The people aren't stupid. They know what's going on.

BETTY: That was what this meeting was about! That young—John Siemens—from Calgary Power said they were building the power station on Teske's east quarter and Canad—

ROGER: Calgary Power?

BETTY: Yeah!

ROGER: We've got Calgary Power right there. I'm watching the TV on Calgary Power! You're talking like I should be out watching the bulldozers come rolling over the hill right now.

ELTON: Fifty-five square miles are gonna have to go, they said, and Joe Nussbaumer was jumping up fit to be tied—

ROGER: Joe Nussbaumer is a hot-headed fool, Elton, don't let the wife spook you. She's being a bit—

BETTY: Joe Nussbaumer was holding up his part of the roof at that meeting while you were lying here, that whole auditorium was full of Joe Nussbaumers!

ROGER: You're starting to sound just like your mother.

BETTY: You leave my mother out of this.

ELTON: *Uncomfortable, getting up.* Well, eight nothing and the first period ain't even—I'll just—

ROGER: Elton, sit down, you gotta see if they'll score twenty, just sit down. *He notices Betty, standing rigid, staring at him.* Well, what are you staring at?

BETTY: Oh, I'm just watching the TV! Sit down, Elton. *He sits; Betty moves in on Roger.* How often do you think Canadian Pacific has been stopped from doing anything?

ROGER: This isn't the CPR, it's—

BETTY: You don't know what it is! You weren't there, you won't read anything, or listen, you sit here and watch that—that silly game—'because they'll always need the farmer, the farmer's the foundation of the world'—what's 80 farmers compared to Canadian Pacific Minerals and Calgary Power and—

ELTON: They'll finish us before breakfast, they won't even burp.

BETTY: Sure, and the cabinet was there, and you know our MLA Gordon Stromberg was sitting in the audience, and he didn't know anything about it either? The coal is down there, it has to come out, they say. Well, this is my farm too. Two quarters of it were cleared by my parents and if you want to sit till they come in and roll the land out from under you like a carpet cleaner well you can just sit here and you can cook and wash the dishes and the clothes too and—and— watch your hockey till your teeth fall out because I'm calling Joe Nussbaumer and we're going to have a meeting. Aren't we, Elton?

ELTON: *Jerks erect.* Uh-h—what?

BETTY: We're going to call every farm couple in Dodds-Round Hill district. And you'll help me.

ELTON: Well, I—sure, I guess, sure.

BETTY: You get the phone-book, start checking the names. And Roger . . .

ROGER: *Leaping to his feet.* Yes sergeant!

BETTY: You— *She laughs a little, self-consciously.* You make another pot of coffee.

ROGER: *Saluting.* Yes, sir!

He marches out, Betty snaps off the TV and follows him.

Crowfoot is laughing to himself, but the other two do not notice it.

PRINCESS LOUISE: *Clapping.* Bravo! Bravo!

ABERHART: Now there's a woman of grit.

PRINCESS LOUISE: And why not? After all, my mother ran the British Empire for 63 years.

They become aware of Crowfoot's rising, unbelieving laughter.

CROWFOOT: She wants to stop the CPR! Stop the CP bloody R! Ha-ha—

Lights out on his thunderous laugh.

Scene vii

Anton Kalicz enters his barn carrying a straw bale. He picks up a thick tangled rope; he is smoking as usual.

ANTON: Just twelve years old, no goddam good. *Throws the rope down, picks it up again.*

WADU (WALTER): *Calling off stage.* Dad, you in the barn, Dad?

ANTON: Hoh!

Wadu appears in trim business suit, picking his way.

WADU: Dad, hello Dad.

ANTON: *Happy.* Wadu, long time . . . *Comes forward, hesitates to embrace him, but they do; Anton carefully not touching him with his hands. Anton shakes Wadu, laughs.*

WADU: You're looking good.

ANTON: And you, all dressed up, tie, shiny shoes.

WADU: *Wiping his shoes.* The barn's not quite as clean as it used to be.

ANTON: You want to eat off the floor!

WADU: *Defensively.* No, no.

ANTON: *Working on the rope.* How's the wife? Having good time.

WADU: *Relieved.* Oh sure, sure, she phoned last night, from Tehran. She'll be coming back in a week or so I guess.

ANTON: *As rope frazzles out.* Somonabitch, no goddam good. *He picks up the ends; looks at them.*

WADU: I may as well say it to you right away, what I came about. I know you'll get upset as soon—

ANTON: Heh? Upset? I quiet, quiet, just like that.

WADU: *Apprehensively.* It's about this Calgary Power project, they're building—

ANTON: *Hands him rope.* Here, you get your hands dirty, eh. Hold it.

WADU: *The rope stretching out between them.* You heard of the Arabs, Dad? Oil?

ANTON: Sure, sure.

WADU: Well, we're the Arabs of North America. The coal under this land could buy the Shah of Iran.

ANTON: Nobody find coal under my land.

WADU: Ah dad there's so much—

ANTON: Shotgun, dogs, not one step over my fence, soil tests, nothing! This Canada, my land, off, off!

WADU: They don't have to test your land! They can test along the road, do contour map projections. Dad, there's a fortune under your feet, right here.

ANTON: How you know?

WADU: I know these things. Now look, you're getting older—

ANTON: *Quiet.* You getting older too. Just like me, every year one.

WADU: I worry about you here, alone. You've worked a lifetime, Dad, and I'll help you with this deal, they won't put anything over on you.

ANTON: Yeah, you always give me good advice, sure, you smart.

WADU: Look, this big company will pay you spot cash. No banks, mortgages, nothing.

ANTON: What I do, huh? Where I live?

WADU: You do anything you want, buy nice little apartment, travel, to B.C., Europe, Hawaii . . .

ANTON: *Half-interested.* Disneyland?

WADU: *Laughs.* Sure, the one in Florida *and* the one in California, anywhere you—

ANTON: No. No travel. No sell nothing.

WADU: What?

ANTON: You smart man, you give advice, but I sell nothing!

WADU: *Quiet.* Okay dad, okay. You sell nothing, but you know the east quarter, where you started. You own the mineral rights on that quarter.

ANTON: *A bit startled.* How you know that?

WADU: Because I have to keep your title duplicate in my office safe—you're too tight to rent a safety deposit box.

Old Anton begins to laugh; slowly, louder and louder, and Wadu joins him. They hold onto the partially spliced rope and laugh.

ANTON: I bought the land from CPR, work like hell chopping trees, your mother pile brush, and you, little Wadu, poke fire, here, there, burn, and three years I go in and lay the money on desk. 1938; big Depression, CPR bigshot there, say nothing, just look. Money in three years on ten year mortgage. 'Mr. Kalicz you do miracles.' 'No miracle,' I say, 'Work!' 'Okay,' he say, 'I give you bonus—mineral rights on the title.' 'What goddam mineral,' I say, 'Stone? All I find is stones, the bugger!' *Laughs.*

WADU: *Laughing too.* It's stones alright, but they're black and you can burn them! There's enough under that quarter alone to make you a millionaire. Don't sell anything, just give them the right to strip that quarter and put it back—

Caroline, preoccupied and swinging a milk pail, enters.

CAROLINE: Grandpa, Ruby doesn't look so good, she—

Wadu and Caroline see each other at the same instant. Momentary freeze.

ANTON: Somonabitch.

WADU: *Coldly.* What are you doing here? *Caroline stares at him, motionless.* Dad, how long has she been—

CAROLINE: It's none of your business. Grandpa, Ruby looks like she'll go down any minute.

WADU: Oh, you're playing the farmerette now—it's the beginning of April, why—

CAROLINE: How's mom? Has she toured the Shah's torture chambers yet, seen the picturesque rack?

WADU: *Enraged.* You leave your mother out of this. The end of your last year and— *He wheels on Anton.* How long has she been here?

CAROLINE: I'm old enough to talk to.

WADU: You're a quitter, you always were a quitter.

ANTON: *Drops rope, reaches behind bales.* Wadu, you want drink? Whiskey, good whiskey, always keep a little in the barn.

CAROLINE: Sure, it's afternoon, he'd be starting to drink by now.

WADU: Listen, I'll talk to you outside.

CAROLINE: You want to talk to me, you talk in the barn.

ANTON: *Comes to them.* Only one glass, the bugger ... *He rubs it on his overalls, pours.* You drink it, I use bottle.

WADU: No, no. What are you doing here?

CAROLINE: What about me, grandpa?

ANTON: Women don't drink. *He does.*

WADU: I've been trying to call you for three weeks.

CAROLINE: What are you doing here?

WADU: Everytime I call you, there's a new man answering the phone.

CAROLINE: So don't call so often. Hey, did you smell the Calgary Power money?

ANTON: *Arms around both.* Seven years, we haven't been together like this—

Wadu wheels away; Caroline stares after him.

CAROLINE: Well I'm fucked, it *is* the money.

ANTON: *Explodes.* Goddamnit, no swearing in this barn! *To Caroline.* This is my farm, I sell nothing, I proud of you, Wadu. When you little you say: I be farmer, like papa. But he grows up, study, study, his Mama so proud, always high marks, high, he never work on farm again, he—

WADU: Hey! *Coldly intense.* I worked on this farm, I worked, I'll never forget it, cold hand on my leg in the dark, cold floor, cold clothes, pull on the cold rubber boots, out into the suffering cold and milk some stupid cow, I worked here. Twenty years.

ANTON: I sell nothing!

WADU: You'll drop dead in this manure!

ANTON: Better I drop dead on Edmonton street?

They glare at each other.

CAROLINE: What should I do with this milk, grandpa?

WADU: You know, I ought to take you both outside and beat some sense into you.

ANTON: You want to fight?

WADU: Your mother is worried sick about you.

CAROLINE: It could be worse, I could have joined the Hari Krishnas.

ANTON: *Louder.* You want to fight?

WADU: Caroline, for god's sake, I'm your father, I love you.

They stare motionlessly at each other.

ANTON: *Loud.* You want to fight!

WADU: Yeah, you old bugger, I want to fight!

ANTON: Okay, okay, we fight right here, on the bales, we fight. Yeh!

WADU: What do you want, arms or legs?

CAROLINE: What are you two—

ANTON: Legs—uh no—arms . . . I get bale.

He hurls one down stage centre; they roll back sleeves, face-off across it.

WADU: You Pole bullshitter! Come on.

CAROLINE: Grandpa—dad—

WADU: But if I win, you sell the farm.

ANTON: And if I win, I kick your ass!

They kneel down, grip.

CAROLINE: Grandpa, don't he's tricked you! Dad, you—all right, I'm on his side, we're together.

She leaps down alongside Anton, her hand on his.

ANTON: *Roaring.* Woman, I fight my son!

Caroline draws back as Wadu laughs, settling into it.

WADU: Like this, so, like this. Ready, try it once, okay.

ANTON: Okay!

WADU: I've waited for this all my life. On three: one, two, three.

Their arms go rigid; hold. Caroline runs about whimpering, almost frantic.

WADU: *He is playing.* Is that the best you can do, dad, eh? Eh?

ANTON: *Strained.* No—no—more, lots.

WADU: Okay, do it then.

He exerts himself like an inevitability. Slowly the old man's arm begins to sink. With a sudden desperate inspiration Caroline seizes her pail, dumps the milk over Wadu's head.

ANTON: Ahhhh-ha! *Heaves the startled Wadu over.* I win!

Wadu roars. He leaps up, gestures futilely, and chases Caroline, seizes her, shakes her like a rag. She is laughing hysterically.

WADU: I should wring your stupid neck!

ANTON: *Exhausted on the bales, laughing.* Hey—

WADU: She won't last two weeks, you'll see.

He exits, dripping.

ANTON: *Laughing.* Wadu, you want it, second round?

CAROLINE: He's gone.

ANTON: *Winded.* What?

CAROLINE: He isn't very happy.

ANTON: Who?

CAROLINE: Dad. *She sounds on the verge of tears.* Mom's always going off somewhere.

ANTON: Wadu make himself happy, unhappy—he smart man. What you throw milk on floor like that for? Waste, feed calves—waste.

CAROLINE: Then lick it up. I'm gonna see Ruby. *She exits.*

Anton looks after her, laughs. Sits down with his rope. John Siemens appears in the door.

JOHN: Is it safe to come in?

ANTON: Huh?

JOHN: There was lots of noise. *Comes closer.* Hello, I'm John Siemens.

ANTON: What you want?

JOHN: You Anton Kalicz?

ANTON: You see my name on mailbox.

JOHN: Yes.

ANTON: Then why you ask?

JOHN: *Laughing.* Sure, sure, Mr. Kalicz. I want to talk to you, ten minutes is enough.

ANTON: *Working on the rope furiously.* Ten minutes, maybe— *Coughs deeply.* I die ten minutes.

JOHN: Your neighbours say you like to talk.

ANTON: I got no neighbours. *He is coughing more heavily and is fumbling for a cigarette.*

JOHN: And when you talk you have an old custom.

ANTON: Heh?

JOHN: *Louder.* An old custom: have a drink, and talk.

ANTON: I don't drink nothin.

JOHN: No vodka, no Polish whiskey?

ANOTN: When I was 21, my father take big bottle. He say, 'Drink,' so I take, one mouthful, he say 'Drink! Everything!' So I drink, till I—you know . . .

JOHN: Vomit.

ANTON: Somonabitch all over. Father say, 'So, enough for whole life' and smash bottle on ground. *He smokes speculatively.* I never drink again.

JOHN: *Pulls out a long bottle.* Well, I guess then I can just smash this. I don't drink either.

ANTON: Oh no . . . no . . . what is that?

JOHN: Polish whiskey.

ANTON: Let me see, *he peers* . . . yeh, yeh, that place, *he points,* the valley where I was born. We have one drink, celebrate my birthplace. *Takes a long pull.* Here—ahh, good.

JOHN: Here's to two men who don't drink.

He takes a sip; he is obviously not accustomed to it. Anton reaches for the bottle but John will not release it.

JOHN: And after the drink, your neighbour Williams says you sit down and talk.

ANTON: Neighbours know a lot, the buggers.

John surrenders the bottle to Anton, slowly. They move deliberately toward two bales, hesitate, sit down carefully together.

JOHN: Mr. Kalicz, I'm project engineer for Calgary Power; you've heard—

ANTON: Where is coal?

122

JOHN: Ten feet, there. *Points to Anton's boots.* Can you imagine a seam of coal 36 feet thick, twice as high as this—

ANTON: I hit it when I dig my well. Again and again. You smart man, you imagine a mile of rock, straight up, and you big as me working face of seam three and a half feet thick. On your knees with a pick, twelve, fourteen tons a day? That is coal.

JOHN: That is coal. You worked in the mines.

ANTON: I sell you nothing. Not one pound.

JOHN: I know you have the mineral rights on one quarter.

ANTON: How you know that?

JOHN: I have to know that. Mr. Kalicz, we need the coal, yours, everybody's, 300 million tons for our plant. You're right in the center.

ANTON: You need it, my coal?

JOHN: Yes.

ANTON: Then don't build nothing.

JOHN: Mr. Kalicz, look, it's going to happen, it's inevitable.

ANTON: What—inevi—

JOHN: *Slowly.* In-evit-able, it *will* happen. The plans are made, our data is—

ANTON: *Begins quietly, grows quickly to roar.* So the power, in-evit-able?

JOHN: Yes.

ANTON: The land ripped up, in-evit-able?

JOHN: I'm afraid so.

ANTON: Old Anton die, in-evit-able?

John is embarrassed, boxed in again by the old man. Anton rises.

Now you go. Get off my land.

JOHN: *Rising.* Mr. Kalicz, I—

ANTON: No, you say—

CAROLINE: *Off stage calling.* Grandpa, grandpa! *She rushes in.* It's Ruby, she's down and the calf's a breech, come on, oh!

ANTON: Goddam Ruby, always something wrong. Let her die.

CAROLINE: Grandpa, I can't do it alone, it's too hard— *She grabs the rope and sees John.* Come on!

She grabs his wrist, they are running off, around behind the back of the stage, invisible but audible. Anton follows them, still yelling, ad lib.

ANTON: No goddam good . . . it inevitable, let her die . . .

As they run around, shouting another part of the big barn appears in the circle of the ramp: Ruby stretched out. Caroline and John run in to her, Anton behind them.

ANTON: . . . let her die, good for nothing, to the knackers somonabitch!

He kicks at Ruby, John pushes him away.

JOHN: *Calm.* Easy, easy, it'll be okay, just get the rope. *Caroline does.* I'm going to have to turn it inside, so all four feet can come out. *He has rolled up his sleeves, works with the rope, up inside the cow.* When I say 'pull,' just do it, slow and steady—okay, pull . . . *She strains, he slowly turns something inside the cow.* . . . okay, good, now let go. *He gets on the rope with her.* Just steady, together now.

CAROLINE: We lost two already—oh . . .

JOHN: Steady . . .

They pull together; straining. Anton stands motionless at the edge of the barn. After a moment the calf emerges feet first, a small, wet red and white bundle. They ease up, John bends towards the calf, begins loosening the rope.

CAROLINE: Oh god—

JOHN: It's okay . . . the cow's all right, the calf's all right . . . okay.

CAROLINE: We did it! We did it! Oh! *She is laughing; a very vulnerable moment for them both.* Look, the perfect little ear.

They look at each other, smiling across the calf. John is wiping it with straw.

CAROLINE: You're a midwife! *Laughs.* I don't even know your name.

JOHN: We met, you know . . . the Battle River.

CAROLINE: *Laughs.* Oh yeah. I'm Caroline.

JOHN: I'm John.

CAROLINE: *As they shake hands.* Oooh, you're all slimy.

JOHN: So are you.

They laugh together, look at the calf.

CAROLINE: Hey little fella, how are you?

JOHN: It's a heifer.

CAROLINE: How can you tell?

JOHN: I've seen them before.

124

CAROLINE: I guess you have. Hi there! Well, we'll name you Johanna. You like that? *Pause.* I better get you some coffee, you want to come in?

JOHN: *Aware suddenly, checks his watch.* I have an appointment at three; I'm a bit late already. *He picks up his brief case with the tips of his fingers.*

CAROLINE: Oh . . . sure.

JOHN: How about coffee later. I'll pick you up.

CAROLINE: Oh sure, in your fancy car. Camaro?

JOHN: Porsche.

CAROLINE: Okay. *Pause.* I've never done anything like that before.

JOHN: *As he goes.* You were very good, really, real good. See you later then.

He goes; Caroline stands watching him.

ANTON: *Coming forward.* Goddamn Ruby.

Lights out.

Act II

Scene i

John's temporary office set up in an empty classroom in Round Hill School. Betty and Joe Nussbaumer, an older farmer in a perpetual state of suppressed fury, are standing, obviously waiting.

JOE: No, no, Betty, I'll let you do all the talking. But don't let this Siemens whitewash you, I know his type, he'll just snow you under—

BETTY: *Reasonably.* You'll be here; we were to come together and if you think—

Don Ritz enters.

DON: Mr. Siemens is sorry; he just radioed in. He's coming now.

JOE: Which side are you on, eh?

DON: *Startled.* What?

JOE: Farmers or bulldozers?

BETTY: Joe.

DON: I work for Calgary Power. Could I get you some coffee? *Looks off-stage.* Mr. Siemens, that's his car now.

BETTY: Coffee would be lovely, yes. *Don exits.* Joe, you agreed to keep . . .

JOE: I will, Betty, I will, but you've gotta take every advantage you can, we ain't playing for marbles. If his flunky is his weak link maybe we can get—

BETTY: We're talking to Siemens, straight.

John Siemens enters.

JOE: I know, I know, but we're gonna have to use everything we can. We'll need it with that slick—

JOHN: Hi . . . Mrs. Mitchell, *shakes her hand,* and you must be Mr. . . .

BETTY: *Quickly.* Joe Nussbaumer.

John reaches out; Joe hesitates, then quickly shakes his hand.

JOHN: Glad to see you both. Sorry I'm a bit late. Don getting you some coffee? Good. Please, sit down. *As they sit, he leans against his desk, but does not sit down behind it.*

BETTY: Mr. Siemens, we represent about eighty farmers who will be affected by your—ah—coal mine. We were all at that meeting at the auditorium and frankly, we were just . . . we are very unhappy with what we heard.

JOHN: Look, I'm John, can I call you Betty, Joe? We'll be seeing a lot of each other. Betty, I was unhappy with that meeting myself. Very unhappy; nothing seemed to go the way we thought it would. What was it that really disturbed you? The worst thing?

BETTY: The secrecy of it all.

JOHN: *Nodding unhappily.* Yes—go on, tell me.

BETTY: For three years all these . . . experts, ran around our farms, doing all kinds of testing and the wildest rumours went around. We never received one word of explanation, on anything. Then, suddenly, you're up at the front with Canadian Pacific Minerals and the Minister of the Environment nodding while you tell us you're building the biggest power plant in Canada and you'll have to tear up all our farms to get the coal to fire the plant. Just like that, finished. *Fait accompli.*

JOE: How'd you like it, mister, if for three years guys kept knocking on your door, coming in to test your plumbing, your foundation, the ceiling joists, and then all of a sudden the boss guy just walks in like he owns everything, tells you your house was too *valuable* for you to live in it any more. Out, get out, scram!

Don enters with coffee. John gestures; Betty takes a cup.

JOE: I don't want your coffee.

JOHN: Thanks, Don. *Don goes.* I'm sorry you got that kind of impression; but you have to see our side of the story too.

BETTY: That's what we're here for.

JOHN: The government tells the three power companies the province will need so many more kilowatt hours of electricity by 1981 to prevent a brownout and then—

BETTY: What's that, 'brown-out'?

JOHN: When your lights go dull because you use more electricity than we're producing. If our system is overtaxed too much, you're in the dark.

BETTY: You have a black-out.

JOHN: Right. So we do research on possible power sites; we have to do this ten years in advance, that's—

JOE: Ten years?

JOHN: It takes that long to get into production. We search the whole province: what's the best in long term, what's the best now so we can keep costs down? Now, there are thousands of square miles of plains coal under Alberta. One plan is—

BETTY: We know there's coal here. We used to heat our house with the coal we dug in our own ravine.

JOHN: Of course. So, we look at various sites. Three years of study, five million dollars, we recommend to the government that Dodds-Round Hill has the best possibilities for a thermal plant: most coal, most easily accessible, nearest to markets. We all need that electricity; it's right here, in the ground under your feet.

JOE: *Explodes.* So it is already decided, finished, it's happening—. scram!

BETTY: Joe, you agreed—

JOHN: It's okay, Betty, I don't blame anyone for getting angry. But it's *not* decided; the government hasn't said anything yet, and they have to say, 'Yes, go ahead'.

JOE: Oh, government, you had Yurko Jerko sitting up there thick as—

BETTY: *Very firm.* Joe! Either we listen or we're leaving.

JOE: Okay Betty, okay. *He sits, staring off.*

BETTY: You said there's so much coal in Alberta. Why haven't we heard anything about these other sites?

JOHN: There are four or five other sites being studied, but we can't talk about them. What would speculation do? Impossible.

BETTY: So you *are* keeping your information secret.

JOHN: No! Dodds-Round Hill is all in the open. That's why we had the meeting, that's why I've set up this office right here in town.

BETTY: But you didn't give us the reports on anything at the meeting. As far as we knew, you were making up figures to prove you were right.

JOHN: Because we didn't have the reports at the meeting. *Wheeling, opening files.* Here, I have no closed files on our physical studies, overburden data, ecological costs, employment charts, thermal plant, recreation usage of cooling lake, effluent fallout—you can study it all. *He is taking out thick files, giving them to Betty.* But I have to have your word, you won't show it to our competitors. *He picks up a blue book.* Here's Lougheed's 'A Coal Development Policy for Alberta'. Have you read it? *Hands it to Joe.*

Betty and Joe are rather staggered by this avalanche.

JOHN: The power needs of Alberta are enormous; we're the second richest province in the whole country and we can be the first. I tried to say these things—

BETTY: What *I'm* trying to say is, how concerned we are. My children are the fourth generation on our land . . . our whole community will be destroyed.

JOHN: I know, I know.

JOE: And Calgary Power'll just send us another community in the mail. Ha!

JOHN: But don't you see, a new community will arise out of this fact, not only agricultural, but industrial too.

JOE: Losing is like winning, eh? How stupid do you—

JOHN: No, Joe, everyone can win here. We all need this power to keep developing.

BETTY: Joe, we have to learn all this stuff, and figure out what's wrong with it.

JOHN: I'll explain anything you want.

BETTY: No, we'll get our own engineers to explain. Just give us the reports.

JOE: It'd take me three years to read all that stuff. I've got a farm to run!

BETTY: If we're going to fight this, we have to understand it. You can't expect people to listen if you don't know the facts.

JOHN: She's right Joe. I like that, very much.

BETTY: *To Joe.* You see?

JOHN: But just keep in mind, 80 farm families or 2 1/2 million Albertans.

JOE: *Rising.* Just get your cards on the table, mister, and fight fair and square.

JOHN: Not everyone wants to fight, you know.

JOE: Oh sure, the town lives off us, they—

JOHN: Not just the town. Three farmers already want to sell.

JOE: A hundred dollars an—who!

JOHN: *Not* a hundred dollars an acre. And if you want to know, ask your neighbours.

JOE: You said you'd be open and tell us . . .

JOHN: Not about confidential business deals. If you come to me, confidentially, I'll never—

JOE: *He wheels.* You slippery bastard! You'll wait for me! *He stomps out.*

BETTY: You're very . . . *she laughs,* persuasive.

JOHN: I'm afraid Joe Nussbaumer doesn't think so.

BETTY: What will it take to stop you.

JOHN: *Laughs.* An act of God.

BETTY: Oh, we've had those in Alberta too.

They laugh, easily. They find each other very likable people.

BETTY: *Suddenly very serious.* John, you're talking about my home. If you want to move me, you'll have to find the biggest shovel you can and heave me up, house and all.

JOHN: *Intense.* You think I like tearing up homes? I wouldn't touch this job if I wasn't confident the land could be reclaimed, as good or better than it is now. Betty, life is always change; we have to *work* to make that change progress!

BETTY: If you're standing on the edge of an abyss, the most progressive thing you can do is to take one step back.

JOHN: If you can show me any way we can build this enormous development of electricity without tearing up your farm, I'll get down on my knees and thank you.

BETTY: *Laughs, rising with her armload of files.* Well, I'll do my very best.

JOHN: Need some help with that?

BETTY: Oh, I'll take all the help I can get.

Laughter as they exit; lights out.

Scene ii

Out of the darkness at the top of the ramp come the voices of the Regal Dead, debating as usual. Light gradually up.

ABERHART: *Excited.* Did you hear that? Did you hear that?

CROWFOOT: A hundred years ago this year we gave this earth away and now the white man has at last decided he will chew it up and spit it out like a beast eating itself.

Light full upon them, lower stage in darkness.

ABERHART: No no no, chief. You never knew about all the food this land could grow, the grain, the cattle, the beautiful gardens, the potatoes and flowers.

CROWFOOT: We had flowers.

ABERHART: All right, flowers, but the power to grow all these other things was already there in the soil, waiting to be released. And we whites found it there, released it! Fed millions, all over the world. Now this other enormous power of coal, waiting to be released, placed there by God, is waiting to be released to lift man to his next stage of progress. These Albertans, in 1977, will develop the treasures *under* the earth, as my generation reaped them from the earth, as you people gathered them upon the earth. It is all there, the marvelous gifts of God, for us to use, for us—

ANTON: *Out of the darkness below.* Anna!

The Regal Dead are jarred out of their stasis; the light comes up on Anton in his kitchen. The Regal Dead peer down at him intently.

ANTON: Anna! You say nothing? Now? Do I sell the land?

Aberhart begins to move towards Anton.

All the time you talk. 'Anton, I die in that Canada. Anton, they don't speak Polish, we freeze there and nobody know what we say. Anton, you got such big stick, why you don't give me baby? Huh?' *He sits motionless a moment, begins to cough and fumbles for his cigarettes. Lights one finally into his coughing and it dies.* There is the farm now. Talk! *He smokes a moment, then jerks to his feet.* Goddam quiet here, the bugger.

He reaches for the radio; Aberhart is standing behind it and as Anton switches it on, his voice grows instantly out of it, as a battery radio would.

ABERHART: This is William Aberhart speaking to you from the auditorium of the Prophetic Bible Institute in downtown Calgary, Alberta. I once met a man who said to me, 'I treat my Bible as I would a beef steak: I eat the meat and throw away the bones.' That sounded good to me. For twenty years I read my Bible and in university I listened to the vapourings of modern theology. *Aberhart comes out from behind the radio, follows Anton down into the kitchen.* I read the first twelve chapters of Genesis, and it was nothing but the Bone of Allegory and I threw it away; the sun standing still for Joshua was simply the Bone of National Legend, and I threw it away; the Virgin Birth was neither more nor less than the Bone of Freudian Imagery and I threw it away. For twenty years! And then I read II Timothy 3:16: the light dawned upon me. There are no bones in the Bible! *All* scripture is profitable! And as long as I picked what I liked and threw

131

away the rest I could never receive any correction from it. *Seats himself across the table from Anton.* I never preached any better than that. Anton Kalicz you are a remarkable man.

ANTON: *Studying him.* Sure.

ABERHART: And I understand your problem.

ANTON: You always understand small man, Mr. Aberhart.

ABERHART: You are not a small man. You are a great man, a giant. Oh, I know, when they write the history of Alberta they will mention only the names of mayors, of premiers, of the sacrilegious writers, but you are the true sinew and muscle of this province.

ANTON: Sure.

ABERHART: You know, the name 'Anton' comes from the Greek.

ANTON: No, no Greek. Polish.

ABERHART: I know you're Polish, but the name comes from the Greek 'Anteus,' the giant wrestler, son of the Earth and the Sky. Whenever he was thrown down and touched the earth, he became all the stronger. You are such a man, whose strength is in the earth.

ANTON: Sure. I won't sell.

ABERHART: No, you won't sell. There's no company in this world could ever pay you enough for the land you have made fruitful, for the sound and smell of frost in the stubble in the morning. You'll never sell. You will give it away.

ANTON: Heh?

ABERHART: They will pay you some dollars, certainly. They must by law, but you love the land, we are but stewards of it. We vanish, the land remains.

ANTON: *Confused.* I sell my land!

ABERHART: Man was made to subdue the earth, and you've done it. Now you can give it away.

ANTON: But I have it, my land, I listen to you—I tell you, I work in the Crow's Nest Pass. Hillcrest Mine. *Aberhart stiffens; he knows.* Owned by Montreal millionaire, and I go down, dig coal. So, one day no orders, no work, two days, then shift boss come: go down, lay new track for coalcars. We pack bread, tea, I and my partner, go down. Singing Polish songs. Nice eh? Just as we come to turn in tunnel, bump. Bump! Rich bastard got nothing to test, mine full of gas. I'm behind roof timber; I'm blown out against the rock. My partner beside me . . . *He gestures futilely.* And deep down in the mine, they start bringing up the miners; bodies all twisted, not by rock: by the gas, explosion. So twisted. The doctors have to smash their legs, arms, so they can lay them in the coffins. 189 men. One poof.

132

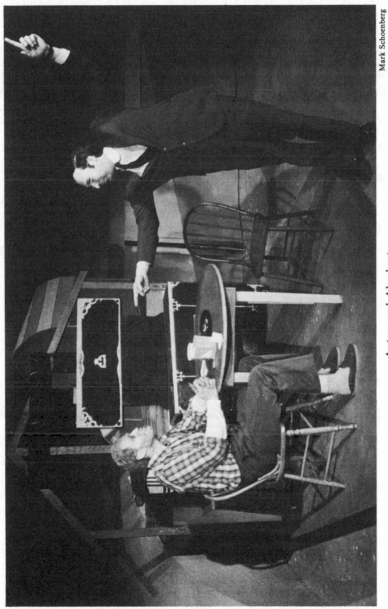

Anton and Aberhart

ABERHART: *Motionless.* The pain of man, endless like the waves of the sea.

ANTON: I work, but my soul is black. And then, one day—I sit in the kitchen, it is so black for me I cannot move, I cannot—and then comes the sign.

ABERHART: You were spared, Anton, spared.

ANTON: Out of the radio, right there.

ABERHART: Ahhh, ahhhh!

ANTON: It was you, Mr. Aberhart.

ABERHART: *As on the radio.* And I say to you, the people of Alberta, it is possible for you to own your own land, free from the mortgages and chattels and encumbrances of fifty bigshots that live in the east!

ANTON: Your voice is the sign. I move three hundred miles, to this farm. 43 years. And now you say . . .

ABERHART: Did you hear me, Anton? Did you hear me?

ANTON: I sell now? Give?

ABERHART: You have used the land in your way, now others are coming to use the land in theirs. The land gives coal.

ANTON: Goddam coal, follow me, everywhere.

ABERHART: Can you read the signs, Anton? Are you eating the meat and throwing away the bones? In the Crow's Nest you dug coal two thousand feet down; here God has brought it to within ten feet of the surface. Does He have to bring it out and put it in your stove before you will understand? *Rises.*

ANTON: *Thunderstruck.* What you say? The coal is the sign?

But Aberhart has vanished, is moving back to the Regal Dead. Anton remains transfixed, staring at the place where he sat.

PRINCESS LOUISE: *To Aberhart.* I never saw anything so despicable in all my life!

ABERHART: *Arriving, very satisfied.* Did you notice, I never told him directly what he should do? I just interpreted the signs.

PRINCESS LOUISE: You were beneath contempt. Using those biblical words, that phoney origin of his name . . . ugh . . .

ABERHART: Didn't like it, eh? I didn't think you would. How could you understand a man like that, a man who has worked every day of his life, who has laboured—what work have you ever done?

CROWFOOT: Work is for women, thought is for men.

PRINCESS LOUISE: Ugh—you are both—Crowfoot, you tried to warn that girl, you used your one chance!

CROWFOOT: *Enjoys scaring her.* It will be terrible when the digging machines come; when the earth screams—

ABERHART: *To Princess Louise.* All you are is a potted plant.

PRINCESS LOUISE: Potted plant!

ABERHART: An ornament of a feudal society. *The Princess is speechless with indignation, and fury.* A vestige of an outmoded world . . .

PRINCESS LOUISE: Ugh! *To Crowfoot.* Come, come, let's leave this dreadful, windy man, this *developer!* Come! *She hooks her arm in Crowfoot's and leads him away.*

ABERHART: *Slightly rhapsodic still, not noticing.* . . . a miscalculated ladder of being. What did you ever do for this province? You had your name pasted on it. Alberta indeed, a silly woman's name, *calls,* Alberta! A person who never even saw it. But Anton Kalicz: a poor immigrant who worked for over fifty years deep in the earth and on the earth, who worked and built and . . . this province should be named 'Anton'.

Anton at his kitchen table opens his eyes as at a revelation. Aberhart becomes aware that the other two are gone.

ABERHART: Princess? Crowfoot? Where are? . . . wait . . . wait . . . *He is running after them, calling.*

Slow lights out on Anton.

Scene iii

City lights of Edmonton; park bench below the Chateau Lacombe high on the bank of the North Saskatchewan River. Laughter; Caroline in jeans and shirt and John in suit come running towards the bench. John jumps in front of her.

JOHN: *Imitating a maitre'd.* Excuse me, madam, I'm afraid you can't sit on this bench, any lady that wears jeans—

CAROLINE: I'll have you know, fella, I ain't no lady.

JOHN: *Ushers her.* Then please, sit.

CAROLINE: Oh, why'd we go to the Chateau Lacombe anyway? Capitalist revolving pig-trough.

JOHN: Let me get this straight. We drove fifty miles because you said 'I want escargots,' so—

CAROLINE: *Gestures.* That's for you, Lacombe, sell-out to the CPR. That's to you, CP— *She turns, catches John in the same gesture.* —oh, you work for them too, you—

JOHN: The deal, remember, the deal. My magic carpet Porsche just whisked us away—that's all left, far away.

CAROLINE: Oh, that Porsche. *Sits down on bench again, legs sprawled out, head back.* What a sinful, lovely car to wheel around in.

JOHN: Porsches last a long time, they go 22 miles—

CAROLINE: The deal.

JOHN: *Laughs.* A good word, 'sinful'. When I first bought it and I drove home to my mother, I couldn't . . . I parked it in Lethbridge and took the bus home.

CAROLINE: That's where you're from?

JOHN: No, Coaldale.

CAROLINE: Coaldale! Hungarians and Mennonites!

JOHN: No—Ukrainians, Mennonites, Mormons, and Hungarians, in that order.

CAROLINE: The Poles don't have a chance.

JOHN: We just won't have 'em!

They laugh together.

CAROLINE: *Glances up.* You know my one real weakness? Food.

JOHN: Okay, let's go then and buy you a dress.

CAROLINE: Dress!

JOHN: You like the car, you want escargots, you need a dress. Let's see, something long, what do they call them, sheaths—

CAROLINE: Of course, *she gestures,* something long, black, clinging . . . *She collapses.* The parties my parents used to give, the women all laying it out for their husbands' deals.

JOHN: And you were so repulsed by it you hid under your bed.

CAROLINE: No, I was the decoration behind the bar. Skirt up to here, black nylons, and the drunken lords of Edmonton commerce leaning over me. *She makes a sound of disgust.* Once my dad got his hands on me. He was completely sloshed, 'Hey girl, you've got the nicest—' and then he recognized me. That was my last party.

JOHN: You wouldn't go?

CAROLINE: No—he wouldn't let me. *Leans back.* Oh, why don't we just drive . . . drive . . .

136

JOHN: Okay.

He moves into position as if the bench were a car; he switches it on, burbles as small boys do when they pretend to drive. Caroline bursts out laughing.

JOHN: Hang on!

Abruptly he throws decorum away, shifts gears, roars off. They seem to careen wildly forward, swaying in rhythm together as the car corners bends. Their motion becomes almost a dance.

CAROLINE: *Shouts above his noise.* Where are we going?

JOHN: Nowhere!

CAROLINE: What'll we do when we get there?

JOHN: Turn around and come back!

CAROLINE: No, go past, beyond nowhere, go! *As John roars on, mightily.* No, no, stop! Stop!

JOHN: *Screeching to a halt.* I was almost there—nowhere. What's the matter?

CAROLINE: I feel silly in this expensive car.

JOHN: Get off! You like it.

CAROLINE: I do. *Pause.* How's your love life?

JOHN: Not too hot. Got any ideas?

CAROLINE: No, the line is . . . *Claps her hand around John's shoulder, her fingers twitching on his breast.* Got any ideas?

JOHN: *Imitating her.* Got any ideas?

CAROLINE: I warn you, I wear three girdles, and I've buried a hat-pin this long in the one next to my skin.

JOHN: Oooch, what a terrible armoured tank you are.

CAROLINE: The better to destroy you, my friend.

JOHN: But what lovely—if I could only see them under all this greasy denim—long legs you have.

CAROLINE: The better to run away from you, my friend.

JOHN: And what radiant—it needs combing, but nevertheless— radiant golden hair you have.

CAROLINE: The better to dazzle you, my friend.

JOHN: And what kissable lips . . .

CAROLINE: Then why don't you, my friend.

And suddenly, he does. A long motionless kiss, only their lips touching. After a moment she is about to put her arm around him, then jerks it away. Finally both pull back. They sit side by side, staring before them, down into the valley.

CAROLINE: *Making conversation.* If you're a Mennonite, how come you went to university?

JOHN: Russian Mennonite, *very* progressive. Only one son could stay on the farm, so others had to get an education. But I was radical: I took engineering, not medicine or teacher training.

CAROLINE: Engineering is radical?

JOHN: It's the science—dangerous. Evolution and reasoning things out, everything rational. There was one man earlier in Coaldale became a scientist, and one day he couldn't handle it. He killed himself, in his lab. The church had a long debate about where they should bury him, and finally they dug the grave in the farthest northwest corner of the churchyard, just inside the fence. When I was going to university an old man took me aside, 'Be careful,' he said. 'Remember, remember,' and pointed to that farthest corner of the churchyard. *He laughs.* You know, that cemetery has gotten so big, all the 'believers' surround the grave, now.

CAROLINE: Some churches would've never even put it inside the fence.

JOHN: Huh? *Surprised, understanding.* Yeah, I guess that's true. But science never tempted me away from anything: it showed me the immutable laws of God that cause the universe to turn within itself more precisely, delicately than the most intricate computer. To build that bridge across the river, to send that jet through the sky, to—

CAROLINE: To belch that smoke out of that power house . . .

JOHN: No—that's just bad engineering, it—

CAROLINE: Of course, it's owned by *Edmonton* Power.

JOHN: No! That's mostly water vapour; it's bad because it makes electrical power from natural gas: one clean fuel from another clean fuel, a terrible waste of resources.

CAROLINE: Oh, they should be burning coal from Can Pac fields, dumping sulphur on—

JOHN: *Claps his hand over her eyes.* You won't see! Listen: I want to show you something.

CAROLINE: *Amused.* I've heard that line before.

JOHN: Quiet! I'm not one of your horny pamphleteers.

CAROLINE: Oh no, you're John Siemens, God's Engineer.

JOHN: Shush! *He turns her head, still holding her eyes shut, to one side, slants it up.* Look what do you see?

CAROLINE: The 99th floor—

JOHN: The 34th floor!

CAROLINE: Of the AGT Tower.

JOHN: Okay, that south-west corner, that's my office.

CAROLINE: Oooh my, glass all around, my, my, my!

JOHN: *Insists.* Will you indulge me—will you? From up there I can see where the river comes from the mountains, where it bends around the powerhouse where the fur companies built their forts two hundred years ago in the wilderness, where it curves off, east, over a thousand miles to Hudson Bay. and here are the factories, the hundreds of thousands of people living, working in peace and comfort, the lights of their houses playing with each other in a rhythm that imitates the stars on a winter night . . . the northern lights that the Innuit say are the souls of unborn children playing with their umbilical cords.

CAROLINE: Oh com'mon, if you're—

JOHN: This is my dream, you tell me yours later. Anything is possible for man, if we but dare. I want to take that coal out of the ground, light this province for thirty years and put the soil back and have it growing more grain than it ever did before. It can be done.

Caroline is motionless, looking at him. Slowly her glance follows his to the vista before them.

JOHN: I'd like to stretch out the ideas exploding in my head, stretch them out there wide for you to see: there are more than the lights of this city, from one end to the other.

Momentary silence; then into their freeze.

ABERHART: *Off stage calling.* Princess. Hey, chief. Chief!

Princess Louise and Crowfoot appear in a spot; she still holding his hand, pulling him.

CROWFOOT: *Heavy stage Indian.* Rules say: one arrow; and everybody got to stickum together.

PRINCESS LOUISE: I know, we can't lose him, but just make him wonder a little longer.

They vanish from the spot.

CAROLINE: I'm scared silly of you.

JOHN: I'm scared silly of you.

They look at each other; slowly they move together into an embrace. Aberhart appears in the spot; flustered but intent on his search. He is momentarily distracted by the park bench.

ABERHART: Hmmmm. Still the same old way of a man with a maid. *He turns, whispers.* Hey Princess, Chief.

John and Caroline still hold their embrace; Aberhart tiptoes off.

Lights out.

Scene iv

The Mitchells' living room: Betty and Roger Mitchell, Elton Preschuk, Henry Stutzman are sitting around the table with a slide projector on it: Joe Nussbaumer stands, the control in his hand.

JOE: As president of the Action Committee I've called this meeting for a special reason. It seems to me we've been moving too slow and I want to show you some—just wait, Elton, wait—Roger get the lights, I want to show you something and then we can talk it over. If you'll just hang on till you see what I've got here.

Roger flicks the light off: all that is visible is the projector light shining straight at the audience; it clicks.

Okay, there you have it, the Saskatchewan tractors of 1968, miles and miles, tied up all the roads, highways *click* —look at that face there: you see that? Determination. *Click.* There's Trudeau, shivering, *click,* and there's the wheat pouring out on the streets of Saskatoon. One big spout of wheat. *Click.* And there's our cow-calf people, camped in Edmonton on the steps of the legislature. See that: talking to Horner. *Click.* —that's Horner, right there, looking like he's got a real pain up him somewhere. *Click.* And there's the Quebec dairy farmers, last year, and you don't need to know French to understand them signs. *Click.* Here's the prize: Eugene Whelan, right there under the Peace Tower, Ottawa, yup. Milk and egg dripping all over him. Okay that's it. Roger, get the lights. *The lights flick on.* That was everyday Canadian farmers going about their everyday Canadian business, which is *action.*

ELTON: Yeah, that's good. How'd you get this all?

JOE: I put it together in five days. Now, here's my plan. Step one, we focus on Edmonton. Later we hit Calgary, but first Edmonton. Step two, we contact all the newspapers, the radio—

ROGER: They just got that one *Edmonton Journal.*

JOE: No, no, all the town papers, Canadian Press, every daily in Alberta, even *The Globe and Mail,* and all the TV stations, CBC, CTV, ITV, cable, everything.

ELTON: When are we gonna get that cable anyway?

JOE: Step three, we all of us hook up our tractors to our manure spreaders, loaded, and we head into town—

BETTY: Joe . . .

JOE: Betty, can you wait till I get to step five? All of us, eighty, ninety with loaded manure spreaders, down to Camrose, up number 21 past Sherwood Park and into Edmonton—

ELTON: Down 82nd Avenue, we're spreading the strong deep smell of the land—

JOE: Now you're getting the idea, Elton! But we ain't turned nothing on yet—right across the High Level Bridge and we don't stop for no lights either, city slickers look out for yourselves, right to the Legislative Buildings and—

BETTY: This is the silliest thing I ever—

JOE: Betty, I'm not through!

ROGER: *Laughing.* Get her, Joe, get her! You got the High Level Bridge blocked already!

He and Elton roar.

JOE: . . . circling the legislature, around under Horner's office, Lougheed's, till we're all wound up around them, five deep. And step four, we stop and yell: 'We will keep our land! We will keep our land!'

Roger and Elton cheer; Betty sits, stares; Henry Stutzman has been looking at his hands throughout, not moving.

BETTY: And step five?

JOE: Step five. we give them one hour while we talk to reporters and then, if they don't say the project is cancelled, you can keep your land, we start up the tractors, turn on the spreaders. If they take our land, we'll grow our crops on theirs!

ELTON: Whoopee! All them pretty little secretaries having lunch out on the lawns!

ROGER: Close your baggy lunches, girls, and get your asses off the grasses, we're a'coming through!

Elton rumbles like a tractor; they laugh uproariously.

BETTY: *Cold.* What do you think of it, Henry?

HENRY: *A hesitant, quiet man.* I don't want to lose my land, but I'm not spreading manure on any government lawn.

JOE: Oh, the government's dumping on you every day, Henry!

HENRY: Not on me.

ELTON: *Sobering.* What'll you do after you've dropped your load there, eh Joe?

BETTY: He'll go to jail.

JOE: Yeah! Maybe we'll go to jail! And everybody'll know we mean business, we can't be pushed—

ROGER: If we want to show 'em we mean business, why don't we just douse ourselves in gasoline and fry ourselves?

JOE: Were you listening to what I said?

HENRY: *Still looking down.* I don't want no TV taking pictures of me. I can't talk to them.

JOE: Did you listen!

BETTY: *Conciliatory.* Joe, pickets, confrontation . . . we decided a month ago we would—

JOE: A month ago! And every day more farmers are running to Siemens. We don't know who's sold, who hasn't, but all of a sudden some key person will go and our whole Protective Society goes pffft! We need action, now.

BETTY: But tractor demonstrations aren't the way.

ELTON: Yeah, that cow-calf camp-out didn't help, really. Those guys froze their butts for $4 a calf, and they'da got that anyway.

BETTY: Sure. And we've been doing things. We've talked to the Agriculture Minister Moore, we've talked to our MLA, we're working on a brief—

JOE: Our MLA Gordon Stromberg! He can't even farm, he's ruining his dad's good farm and he's—

BETTY: Maybe he's too busy being a good MLA to be a good farmer!

JOE: Betty, where've you been living all your life?

BETTY: I may be naive, but I think our politicans will listen to us if we can make a reasonable case.

JOE: God, reason! They listen if they think they won't get elected!

BETTY: *To the attack.* All right. And what kind of impression will you make on two and a half million Albertans? Eighty to ninety farmers driving their great big tractors down the streets and throwing manure on people and yelling, 'We want out land'? They'll out-vote us 3000 to one.

JOE: *To the men.* Are you just gonna sit there, do nothing?

ROGER: I always figure, hire a coupla lawyers and let them argue. They got all the time in the world.

JOE: Canadian Pacific'll drown you in lawyers!

HENRY: You never run for election, did you Joe?

ELTON: Oh no, Joe just runs for brick walls.

JOE: *Hurt.* Well, Elton, if that's how you feel about it—

BETTY: Joe, please, you went to a lot of work, and some of that may be of some use, but this is our land; our living. If we can't convince the government that Calgary Power and Canadian Pacific Minerals are wrong to develop here, now, then we better just keep quiet. We have to *know* more so we can prove them wrong. Do you have any idea what holes that big would do to the water table for hundreds of miles around? Well? Neither do I! We have to represent every single person affected so when we speak to the cabinet we know what we're talking about. We have to think bigger than the—

JOE: *Roars.* I'm thinking bigger than anybody here!

BETTY: You have to think bigger than your mouth.

JOE: Well, if that's the way you feel—

BETTY: Yes.

He stares at them a moment. The men are studying the floor. Joe grabs his projector, slams out.

ELTON: I don't feel so good about this.

BETTY: *Facing the facts like a true leader.* We'll feel a lot worse before this is over. But that's not our way. Now let's get busy.

Lights out.

Scene v

Anton Kalicz's kitchen. John Siemens is just entering. Anton stands behind his chair, waiting for him.

ANTON: I call you. Come in. You don't look so happy.

JOHN: Oh, I'm okay. It's hard work, getting this together.

ANTON: Everybody stubborn bugger, eh?

JOHN: That protective society is *working.*

ANTON: Okay, we drink and then I make you— *he coughs heavily—* happy. *He pours whiskey into the water tumbler on the table.* Here.

JOHN: Hold on, I don't drink—

ANTON: You drink. *He sits down, lifts his glass.* Nostrovia! *He knocks back a huge swallow; John drinks a little.* Alright now. I make you happy. I sell you my land.

JOHN: *He may have drunk too much.* Huh? Oh sure. *He laughs, drinks substantially.* Sure, Mr. Kalicz.

ANTON: You laugh at old man in his own house?

JOHN: You caught me a bit, *coughs,* by surprise.

ANTON: I say, I sell you my land, I sell my land! North quarter, west quarter where I have mineral rights, this quarter, on one condition.

JOHN: What's the condition?

ANTON: I keep this house and 120 acres around it, pasture, till I die.

JOHN: Till you die!

ANTON: Till I die. Old man not so dumb, eh?

JOHN: The house, sure, ten, fifteen acres, but 120 acres pasture—

ANTON: One hundred twenty acres!

JOHN: *Has his book out.* You're in the first four years—it's possible we could re-organize the excavation order a little . . . *He is studying his maps, book; unhooks his radio, buzzes.* Don: run this through the computer on the excavation listing: 8793/ 639427/8796686/ check that against the reading yesterday, 63-80-97.2. Yeah . . . Yeah. Okay, thanks, Don. *He switches it off, stows it away.* I can make you an offer, Mr. Kalicz. I buy everything and you live in your house, with 120 acres, for five years.

ANTON: You think I die in five years? Only 78!

JOHN: No, no, but you might not want to farm after that.

ANTON: I call Wadu; I ask him.

JOHN: *Very busy, calculating.* Sure, you call Wadu; we'll agree on a price and get the papers . . .

Anton goes; we hear his voice shouting in the manner of old people on phones. John hums a little, chuckling to himself as he works. Caroline enters in work clothes.

CAROLINE: Hi, I saw your car outside but you—

JOHN: *Not at all happy.* Oh hi, Caroline . . .

CAROLINE: *Coming close.* We agreed, you'd leave him alone and I wouldn't leave you alone.

JOHN: I have, I haven't said a—

CAROLINE: Then what are you doing here? Didn't he tell you I was in the barn? What— *She looks at the whiskey, his books, pencil.* John, that was our deal . . .

JOHN: He called *me.* He wants to sell.

CAROLINE: *Putting her arms around him.* Oh sure! I'll believe that when—

JOHN: *Hands on her shoulder.* Caroline! He's calling your father, he wants to sell!

Anton comes in, pleased with himself; Caroline steps back hastily.

ANTON: Wadu say eight years. *He sees Caroline, hesitates....* and we negotiate price next week.

JOHN: *Painfully.* Six years, and we negotiate price this Friday.

ANTON: You say six, just like that?

JOHN: Yes, six. Absolute maximum.

Caroline is moving towards Anton.

ANTON: Okay, six. *To Caroline.* He powerful man, eh? Just like that he says—

CAROLINE: Grandpa, what are you doing?

JOHN: Caroline—I—

ANTON: I selling my land. *Takes her aside.* But you got smart grandpa, all money now but I keep house, 120 acres for six years, live here, peace and—

CAROLINE: You can't sell the land, it's ours!

ANTON: *Close to her, whispers.* I sell now, get good price, I old and all the worry, people push this way, that way. *He thrusts her hands away.* But the others don't sell, nothing happen, you see.

JOHN: Caroline, please, he—

CAROLINE: Shut up, you snake. Grandpa, if you sell, everybody'll have to sell. You'll live here on your island and all around will be a *hole*, the bulldozers clanking all around night and day— *She wheels on John.* What did you say to him? What!

JOHN: He called me, he—

CAROLINE: *Enraged.* You goddamn liar! I drive and laugh with you, I—oh— *She beats at him in furious frustration.*

ANTON: *Pushing her roughly aside.* He is guest in my house! You don't swear at my—

CAROLINE: *Whirls on him.* You give in to the Germans so fast, you old man? You're no Pole, you're a scared, wishy-washy—

Anton roars a Polish curse, knocks her down. John leaps between them, wrestles Anton away.

JOHN: Mr. Kalicz please! . . . Caroline . . .

CAROLINE: You sell-out! You're nothing but a goddamn cheap sell-out!

145

ANTON: *Struggling in fury.* Get out, out of my house, get out—out!

JOHN: *Fighting to hold Anton.* Caroline go . . . go . . .

Sobbing, Caroline runs off; John and Anton separate, both their faces torn by dreadful emotions.

ANTON: Now you go. You go.

John stands a moment; they are both crushed. Then heavily he picks up his briefcase, paper, and goes. Lights do a slow fade on Anton sitting, head bowed, in his chair.

Act III

Scene i

Battle River music. The Regal Dead are united again, but not happily. They are picnicing on the river bluffs; Aberhart searches through the picnic basket for more food; the Princess has had quite enough to eat; Crowfoot eats on stolidly.

PRINCESS LOUISE: You Judas, you see now what you've done. Destroyed the old man's peace, and that young couple, their life together is ruined.

ABERHART: Nothing outward destroys a man and woman's life together, Princess. You know that.

PRINCESS LOUISE: Oh yes, it can. I loved Lorne when I married him, and yet—his melancholy, his travels, his—something came between us.

ABERHART: Something—or yourselves?

PRINCESS LOUISE: It was . . . Canada.

ABERHART: Canada!

PRINCESS LOUISE: A whole nation of colonials trying to get ahead. Do you have any idea what it's like standing in a reception line hour after hour receiving fat, comfortable merchants and their laced-up-tight wives? Not a single artistic temperament in the whole colony!

ABERHART: Come now, not one?

PRINCESS LOUISE: It drove me to fury: I swore at Lorne, I chased my dog in the gardens at Rideau Hall, I flirted with that old philanderer Macdonald, I . . .

ABERHART: Really? Old long-nose?

PRINCESS LOUISE: He was charming.

CROWFOOT: I met him three times: he was drunk every time.

PRINCESS LOUISE: Oh, his drunkenness is much over-talked about. He suffered great personal tragedy, and I was so ruthless towards him . . . he was the only powerful man, of dignity, in the whole colony that I could use against Lorne and—and . . . I drove too fast, too fast.

ABERHART: What happened?

PRINCESS LOUISE: *Deep within herself.* It destroyed the last of what was left between Lorne and me.

ABERHART: *Puzzled.* Driving your horses too fast?

PRINCESS LOUISE: The horrible tempting snows of Canada, so blazing white, tempting. I had the driver whip the sleigh horses over the trails along the Rideau River, whip, whip them! I wouldn't let him stop, I was screaming at him, whip them! Until the sleigh flew— over—I was thrown—dragged—my ear, my perfect ear . . .

ABERHART: Your what?

PRINCESS LOUISE: My ear was torn off. I almost died.

ABERHART: Oh, that's why you— *He understands her hair style at last.* And that destroyed . . . your marriage?

PRINCESS LOUISE: Oh how would you understand. For a delicate sensibility the dropping of a glove, a torn letter, can destroy—you go blundering about, preaching, selling . . . things . . . how could you understand. You sell out, to the first bidder.

ABERHART: *Angered.* We all have to deal with our world somehow, whether *you* call it selling out or not. Look at the chief, your big sensitive friend. Come on, tell her, tell the Princess Louise Caroline Alberta how you sold out. September 22, 1877. Tell her, O great chief!

PRINCESS LOUISE: Stop that! You have no consideration for the deeper feelings, none, none.

But Crowfoot raises his hand; rises slowly, with great dignity, to his feet.

CROWFOOT: I will show you, how it was. You, *he gestures to the Princess,* are the Governor Laird, who speaks for your Great White Mother—you sit, there.

She rises, sits with the dignity of a pompous man.

Behind you are your white councillors, all fat, happy and waiting to grab the first bit of land. You, *he gestures to Aberhart, who rises to his hand,* are Colonel Macleod of the North-West Mounted Police— you sit there.

Aberhart breaks into a march as he moves, sits.

Behind you stand the red police, guarding the high stacks of food. Laird, you have made your long speech.

PRINCESS LOUISE: *High, carrying tone of rhetorical male.* In a few years, the buffalo will all be destroyed, and for this reason the Queen wishes you to live in the future in some other way. She wishes that her white children come and live on your land . . . raise cattle and grain . . . she will also pay . . . *The voice is stuttering out.* . . . every year . . . a reserve . . . land set aside . . .

CROWFOOT: And you, Macleod, have spoken many times. You have never gone back on your word: your word is too hard for that. It sits like a stone and the whiskey traders break the wheels of their carts against it.

ABERHART: *High official tone.* There is only one law, the Queen's law. I will destroy the whiskey traders and you will obey the Queen's law. I am your friend . . . as my past promises . . . kept so the treaty . . . never broken . . . as long as the sun . . .

CROWFOOT: And my painted young men rode circles about the great camp, crying their cries, and Red Crow came at last and spoke, and Old Sun and Peigan Chief, and Sitting on an Eagle and Red Crow again. And that night I went to Pemmican, the ancient medicine man of my people. Three times I went to him, but he said nothing. Then, the fourth time, he spoke: *Crowfoot sits down like an old man; his voice goes high, breathing, ancient.*

'Your life will all be changed, all changed. Buffalo make you strong, but the food from this money will bury our people all over the hills. The whites will take your land, they will lead you by a halter . . . I say don't sign, don't sign . . . but my life is old . . . over . . . ' *He rises; his voice is normal again, sad.* And I looked at my people, fewer than there had ever been, and I looked at Laird. And then I looked at Macleod: the man with words like one stone. Behind you was piled all that food, and behind me stood my hungry people. And the words came to me:

'If the police had not come, where would we be now? Bad men and whiskey, and sickness, were killing us so fast, even fewer of us would be left today. I am satisfied. I will sign.'

He moves slowly to the Princess; one brief, strong handshake.

CROWFOOT: *Moving away.* I never did touch the pen, but my X is on the treaty. The police stood, guarding the food.

ABERHART: People have to eat, yes. Yes.

CROWFOOT: I never should have done it!

ABERHART: *Comforting.* You had to, chief, you had to.

PRINCESS LOUISE: Oh William, you have no comprehension of anguish of soul!

Crowfoot moves away from them; slowly he outlines a tiny square

149

reserve the size of a blanket around himself while they continue to argue.

ABERHART: Anguish yourself all you want, but that was done for all of us, in the name of your Imperial Mother. To give us land, to keep you in jewelry. Oh, don't look so shocked, you know very well what I mean.

PRINCESS LOUISE: Just because I understand suffering, am I expected to run about in blanket and loin-cloth?

ABERHART: Yes! If you want filet mignon, you kill steers.

CROWFOOT: We agreed to live in one small place, and you took the land and agreed to feed my people.

PRINCESS LOUISE: Oh, in every way we English are always the villains. Well, I don't believe that.

ABERHART: Nobody's a villain, Princess. We're trying to understand how the world is—was. Old Anton Kalicz is—selling out.

In its usual curve of the ramp, Anton's kitchen appears in shadow with the old man sitting motionless at the table; it has a whiskey bottle on it.

He is going to live in a small place . . . and he's sorry already. But a man has to decide, and live with his decisions.

PRINCESS LOUISE: Oh, men. Always the big, heavy decisions.

CROWFOOT: You haven't shot your arrow yet.

PRINCESS LOUISE: You're right. *Savouring it.* And you both have. Well! I shall see, I shall see. Come. *She beckons to them.*

There is a thunderous knock on Anton's door; but Anton doesn't move.

ABERHART: A decisive woman!

PRINCESS LOUISE: *Smiling.* Come. Come.

They follow her up the ramp where they vanish. The lights come up full on next scene.

Scene ii

Anton Kalicz in his kitchen, drinking. The knock is repeated, but he does not react. Finally Betty strides in, stares at him; he does not look up.

BETTY: You know where Caroline is?

ANTON: I will build a fence, heavy mesh wire . . .

BETTY: At our place, since you kicked her out.

ANTON: . . . pig wire, ten feet high, with three strands barbed wire sticking out the top . . .

BETTY: And she's still crying.

ANTON: . . . to keep out busy-bodies that tell me what to do. Everybody tell Anton what to do, the whole goddam world!

BETTY: *As loud as he.* And you can electrify it too, with all that power and fry every— *She abruptly tears herself out of it; pauses.* Well, it's not her first world that's collapsed.

ANTON: *Quietly.* I sit here laugh, cry, drink myself to death. Good life, old man, eh?

BETTY: I've tried to think of one good reason why you shouldn't sell. And I can't think of one.

ANTON: You understand it, old man?

BETTY: You should sell this farm for every penny you can get.

ANTON: Yeah! Every penny!

BETTY: It's exactly what I would have done. I mean, you're bound to be dead in five years.

ANTON: Six years.

BETTY: Six years. You've only known me—what . . . 40 years— *She gestures.* I can just drink myself to death, all alone, easy. Easy.

ANTON: Good. So. Everybody happy, eh?

BETTY: My granddaughter—ha!—runs around in pants, swears, cries too much—

ANTON: So everybody happy, eh!

BETTY: *Loud.* Oh, happy, happy.

ANTON: *Loud.* You mad because I get good deal, this goddam place!

BETTY: Why are you mad?

ANTON: *Shouting.* I not mad, I happy!

BETTY: I'm happy too. *Almost breaking down.* We're both happy, so let's dance. Come one, let's dance together, come on, come on.

She pulls him into it and they whirl, stagger about a circle and finally she thrusts him away; she is wiping her eyes, but does not make a sound.

ANTON: *Imploring her.* In Poland, Russians come and take our land, Germans come, take our land, then both come together, kill us, each other . . . who will take the land? In Canada, nobody take. I sell or I don't sell. Old, I have no one to give my land, so I make good deal. No one else sells, nothing happens.

BETTY: Jack Williams is selling.

ANTON: But . . . he has good son, strong . . .

BETTY: And Eric wants the farm, but Jack . . . well you know how it goes sometimes, between father and son.

ANTON: *Groaning, sits down heavily.* Oooi, oooi, oooi . . .

BETTY: *Softly.* You got a very good deal. Really. Because in Canada they take land too. It's not war here, it's expropriation. But it works more or less the same way.

She touches him, goes quickly. Anton stares at his hands, motionless. Lights out.

Scene iii

The scene-changing music now takes on the distant beat of machinery, of earth-moving vehicles clattering. It is still distant, but ominous.

The Regal Dead deep in discussion. The Princess Louise leads them and she is more interested in purposeful progress than conversation.

ABERHART: Oh, decisions are always painful, but they have to be made, eh chief?

PRINCESS LOUISE: Are you two coming?

ABERHART: I mean what did I know about politics, about government and high finance? I was just a funny looking fat man, that radio preacher, from Ontario, glasses, losing his hair. But I saw hunger in Alberta, and I did something for the spirit of the people: I gave them hope. I just rode forward with the people and God gave us the power . . .

PRINCESS LOUISE: William! I've got my arrow to shoot!

Crowfoot laughs.

ABERHART: *Exasperated.* Well why don't you then, for mercy's sake. We shot ours without everybody standing at attention.

PRINCESS LOUISE: *Smiling.* I want you particularly to notice. This is for persons of artistic temperament.

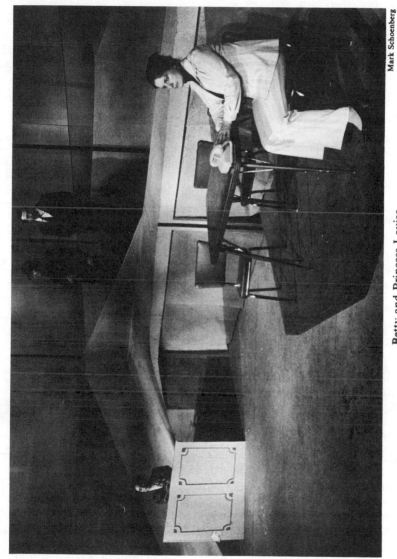

Betty and Princess Louise

ABERHART: *Interested.* I think you waited a bit too long.

PRINCESS LOUISE: We'll see, we'll see.

Below them Betty is sitting in her living room, deep in a brown study. The Regal Dead stand, watch her; Betty reaches for the telephone. Dials 1, then long number.

BETTY: Hello, hello; oh, is that you, Sheri? You sound so grown up, you're answering the phone, how are you . . . *ad lib.*

ABERHART: *To Crowfoot.* That's where progress gets you—no more smoke signals!

PRINCESS LOUISE: Sssssh!

BETTY: . . . Is your Mommy in . . . Sheri . . . oh, Marilyn . . . *She laughs.* No, no, long distance doesn't matter, it was so nice to hear her voice, she's so grown up . . . How's Fred . . . real estate in Red Deer is . . . oh good, that's good. And you? . . . no, no, just a bit tired, I haven't talked to you for so long. No . . .

Princess Louise begins to move towards Betty.

Princess Louise is moving around her, to the piano. Betty's voice is beginning to break a little.

Oh your dad's fine, fine, he's hammering some feed for the cows . . . Yeah, just wanted to call, hear your voice. Do come if you can, soon. Love you sweetheart, bye . . . okay, bye. Bye.

Betty hangs up, on the edge of tears. She sits thinking, wiping her eyes, Aberhart gently begins to read her thoughts.

ABERHART: Have to finish those minutes, get the steaks out, three calls to make, it's nearly eleven o'clock . . .

Into this come the quiet opening ripples of Princess Louise's music; she plays the opening bars of the Prelude in D flat, Opus 43, no. 1, by R. Gliere: delicate like fresh water folding itself over rocks. Slowly Betty becomes aware, turns, watches the Princess. The music rises, urgently surging; fades.

PRINCESS LOUISE: *Looking at Betty; smiling.* Beautiful, isn't it. *She stands up.* I first heard a master pianist play that at a command performance in— *She laughs, dismissing that.* I knew it was something I had to learn, and know, so I could fly with it when I needed wings. So I had the music brought and I sat down, *she does.* and I began. *Begins, hesitantly, better, then abruptly stumbles on a sour chord, two; she stops.* That wasn't right . . . something . . . again . . . *She begins again, gets a little farther, and discord.* No— *She tries again; disaster.* Three times! I seized the music, crushed it, threw it on the floor. *Suits action to words.* If you cannot play it right you just leave it, throw it . . . No. You don't just walk away. The right and beautiful is always so difficult, so achingly difficult to achieve, you do not just walk away. You bend down, *suits actions again.* Pick it up, smooth it out, and you try again, and again . . . *She is starting very slowly, gradually gaining the rhythm.* Until you . . . *She has captured the ecstasy and is flying to the end. She stops, rises, looks at Betty motionlessly facing her.* The beautiful things of this world deserve everything we have. Myself and Lorne were not able to have any children. This magnificent land is the only thing left with my name. It must not become one open, running sore of a strip mine! It must not!

She catches herself; she has become too categorical. She begins to sing, unaccompanied, to the tune of 'Lead Kindly Light':

> Although I cannot change the world
> To what it ought to be,
> I know that what I do is right:
> One step's enough for me.

She stands motionless.

BETTY: *Echoes her, hesitantly.* One step's enough . . . for me.

Lights out on her resolute face.

Scene iv

The machinery sound grows, closer now. Caroline enters Anton's barn, knapsack hung on one shoulder, wearing her tinted glasses. Anton comes from the opposite direction; they stare at each other for a moment.

CAROLINE: *Hard.* I just came to pick up my stuff; is my jacket anywhere here, the denim one?

ANTON: *As if nothing has happened.* You always leave things. I tell you, tell you. *He heaves on a bale.* On a farm you leave things lie, you never see them again. Cows eat everything.

CAROLINE: I guess I never learned. Have you seen it?

ANTON: You like that Betty? Good woman—talk too much, but good woman. You know, I dance with her once.

CAROLINE: Oh.

ANTON: High school dance, her graduation, *gestures lightly,* she nice big woman, young like fresh corn, sweet . . . I dance around the school. *He dances, humming.* And already young man, you know, *mimes tap on the shoulder,* so, I have to, she goes, and Anna standing there, black old woman, say in Polish, 'You dance once more, old man, and I kick your ass all the way home!' *He laughs uproariously.* She would, too.

CAROLINE: *Hard.* Have you seen my denim jacket?

ANTON: *A bit louder, but far from his usual roar.* I supposed to know every goddam jacket around here! *He heaves on a bale.* Maybe there, *gestures to loft,* hanging somewhere . . .

He works, Caroline drops her pack, clambers up the bales to the ramp. Anton calls after her.

This morning I come into barn, I hear voice. Strange, just cows and me, voice . . .

CAROLINE: *Returns with the jacket, cuts across his story.* It was there.

They look at each other a moment.

ANTON: *Pleading.* What else can I do? I have no son, take the farm. *Pause.* Why it matter to you, I hardly see you, ten years.

CAROLINE: *Puzzled herself.* It's . . . this month has been . . .

ANTON: Six weeks.

CAROLINE: That long? I guess . . . I'm being stupid, but it's been so good, hard work, days getting longer, grass coming out on the hills . . .

ANTON: You move first, you always get the best deal. In Poland they never ask, just come, take. *Eager.* What you want? I buy it, I rich man, million—Caroline, you don't tell it, nobody, but that coal royalty, $900,000! He tell me, that Siemens. *She wheels, he follows her.* What you want? Commune? Big house on river in Edmonton, maybe . . .

CAROLINE: Oh grandpa—I don't want a house!

ANTON: *Pleading.* What you want, Caroline?

CAROLINE: *She is discovering.* I don't know . . . I want . . . this barn and Ruby and the kitchen . . . yes, I want this place. *Astonished, then quiet.* This place, this land, to be something useful, to live here and . . . grow . . . living things . . .

Anton is staring at her.

On the whim. I could pay you as much as Calgary Power . . . not coal royalties, but the land price . . . I'd get a mortgage and . . . *Laughs.* I got one for The Women's Center in Edmonton!

ANTON: You want to buy my land?

CAROLINE: Yes.

ANTON: Three hundred twenty thousand dollars?

CAROLINE: That much?

ANTON: Five quarters, four hundred dollars the acre.

156

CAROLINE: That's a terrible amount . . . *Laughs nervously.* I didn't know you were worth so . . . *Laughs; laughs it through.* But I could—sure, everything, but that includes buildings, equipment, cattle . . .

ANTON: Okay, we make a deal.

CAROLINE: Wait a minute . . . four hundred an acre?

ANTON: Okay, you buy everything, nice and even: quarter million.

CAROLINE: *Staggered.* Two hundred fifty—I haven't got a cent—that's what you call a mortgage! Okay. Sure!

Anton moves suddenly.

ANTON: No you don't need it, mortgage. No. I have papers right here. *He gets a yellow envelope from behind the barn wall.* Right here, titles. You don't need money to buy a farm in Alberta. *He pulls out a pen, his voice gradually rising.* I work 43 years but Caroline just say 'yes', and it happens! One, *he slashes across the paper with the pen,* and it yours! Play here in summer, so nice, big warm sky, play, papa send you to school, the money comes—but then, oh, I too smart for university! What do I care, university, run to the farm, work a little here, there, but if I don't want to work Grandpa do it, so nice cows, nice land, mortgage just like that!

He is battering her down; she stands motionless in front of him; her shoulders are beginning to shake.

Your big decision: wear glasses! Change patches on jeans from one leg to other: that's what you decide! You insult me—buy my land!

She stands, head bowed, crying.

And now you cry. Grandpa stop, give little Caroline what she want, stop. No, Grandpa not stop! He get you, like you say it, right in the fucking nose!

CAROLINE: *Through sobs.* All right . . . all right . . . maybe my record is terrible, maybe I can't do it . . . I don't stick with things, I cry. I'm sorry I cry, I . . . *She tugs off her glasses, drops them on the bales, wiping her eyes.* But it means something to me, this place means more than anything I have ever . . . and what about you, your whole life's work just down a hole. You'll sit here and watch them rip up the land you plowed 43 years. Or move to Camrose, Leduc, Florida, and sit all day waiting for the mailman. So I'm young, impulsive, I—how old were you when you left Poland? How old? Eh?

ANTON: Twenty-five, but I a man with wife—

CAROLINE: And I'm a woman! Twenty-two. You go half way around the world, you make grandma come with you, how'd you dare, eh?

ANTON: Caroline, I'm sorry I—

CAROLINE: *Jerks away from him.* Oh, Caroline's just a woman, give her a dress, a big empty house where she won't have one damn thing to do but get drunk and fucked out of her skull! Just—

Anton, furious, jerks away from her and she grabs him, pulls him around.

No, no, no! This farm isn't just something you own! I am the last of your blood, and you owe me something. Not much maybe, but something. A chance at least. I helped you fight Dad for it.

They stand, staring at each other.

CAROLINE: *Hard.* My name is Kalicz too, and my grandfather is a big, powerful man. He was a coal-miner and a farmer and a story-teller and he was never drunk off his feet and he is a stubborn son of a bitch. *He jerks, but she stops him with a hand.* And he loves his son and he loves his granddaughter. Whether you like it or not, I am your granddaughter and I'm stubborn too. I won't let you sign away your land for some pieces of paper. I am taking over this farm.

Her left hand goes out, takes the papers from his right hand; her right hand rises to his. After a moment, his hand comes up to it; they grip. Both stand tall, erect like equals; they shake hands. Then Anton laughs a little; goes back to his bales.

ANTON: *Voice very reduced.* I tell you, don't leave things lying around . . . cows eat everything.

Caroline stands holding the papers. Lights out.

Scene v

The machinery sound is coming very close now; a steady hammering throb.

Office of the Protective Association in the Round Hill Fire Hall. Elton Preschuk is reading a letter to Betty, who is busy with papers.

ELTON: 'We view this Camrose City Council endorsement of the project as a *complete betrayal*'.

BETTY: *Busy.* Good, Elton. Are you finished?

ELTON: *Getting up.* Yep. In my perfect scrawl.

BETTY: I'll drop a copy at the *Camrose Canadian* this evening.

ELTON: Yeah, and you better send Gordon Stromberg one too; he's getting so lonesome yelling 'Dodds-Round Hill' in the Legislature, he tabled a lump of coal up there yesterday!

BETTY: He's crazy, God bless him. Now, you're away—

Caroline enters with papers; she is dressed in a skirt, shirt.

ELTON: *Moving.* Okay, gotta get Dr. Currie to his plane. *To Caroline.* You know, he was saying last night that soil is a *living thing.* You can't scrape off the top and pile it somewhere for awhile and then just put it back. You'll break the soil's—what was that— cycle?

BETTY: Nutrient.

ELTON: Yeah—'nutrient' cycle, you'll bust it. It'd be like taking your grandmother apart with a bulldozer, putting the pieces in a closet for a year and then opening it up and expecting her to cook you supper! *Pause.* You can't do that.

Caroline laughs; Betty waves at him.

I'm off, boss, I'm off! *Exit.*

CAROLINE: I finished summarizing the reports, here. I have to pick up some calf meal before the elevators close.

BETTY: Canadian Pacific have brought in their own expert.

CAROLINE: What?

BETTY: We just heard last night. Head of the biggest coal mine in West Germany. They've been stripping and reclaiming land, whole villages, for forty years.

CAROLIN:E Those bastards, CPR bastards!

BETTY: *More hopefully.* Well, if Dr. Currie's so sure, how could another scientist figure it out any different? We were at Forestburg and reclamation there looks terrible.

CAROLINE: Oh Betty, you buy scientists like you buy shares in Calgary Power.

BETTY: We did pay Currie expenses and $100 a day. That seemed real high.

CAROLINE: For that amount, he *has* to be honest! This German probably owes CPR a favor. They're all together.

BETTY: We've always had to face it: we'll probably lose.

CAROLINE: *Surprised.* If you think that, how can you keep going, every day . . .

BETTY: *Grins.* It's been exciting, working at something this important. You know, the Agriculture Minister received us the other day. And he listened to us very carefully.

CAROLINE: But he never agreed to anything, did he.

BETTY: They're important people, Caroline, they have to listen to everybody.

CAROLINE: Oh Betty, you're so . . . so . . . *She has to laugh.*

BETTY: What were you going to say? Simple?

CAROLINE: No, no, you're very complex . . . but . . .

BETTY: I'm naive.

CAROLINE: Yes . . . I guess . . . you're so direct and you're just taking on the Peter Lougheeds and Calgary Powers and Can Pac Minerals and you're . . .

BETTY: I'm just a farm housewife, and I've looked after my kids and I've raised my husband—well, more or less. And I drove tractor, milked when I had to and I got into this . . . and I like it. I haven't felt so good since—never. They're important people and they deal in billions of dollars but they're human. They need to talk to people like us to find out what's going on in the world.

CAROLINE: And did you see the big man, Football Peter? Did you?

BETTY: No, not yet.

CAROLINE: And you won't see him. *He'll* decide this and the closest you'll get to the human being Peter Lougheed is the TV set.

BETTY: Well, you're experienced, what's the best way for us to deal with this 'TV Peter'? Heh?

CAROLINE: Lougheed's got to make the *responsible* decision, you've got to make him think it's his own idea, and it's got to look like that to the voters.

Roger bursts into the room.

ROGER: *Heavy.* Shut her down, I'm the man with the news.

BETTY: We don't want to hear it, we know all about that German expert and we're planning new tactics—

ROGER: Are you interested, I mean, are you interested in what I have to report?

CAROLINE: Yes! Come on, Roger!

ROGER: The German, big double lined suit— *Looks far-sightedly at his hand.* aha, soil! Wind blown silt, very high in production, one of the best in the world, but only six inches? Six inches. In Germany we dig the coal under top soil forty feet deep. You have six inches.

BETTY: Roger, what, what are you saying?

ROGER: *Slowly.* Oh, you are interested?

CAROLINE: Roger!

ROGER: Forty feet thick in Germany, and there they spend $7000 per acre on reclamation.

BETTY: Seven thousand?

CAROLINE: *Beside herself.* What's he saying!

ROGER: He says, with six delicate inches, reclamation is impossible. No way Jose!

Betty and Caroline scream, grab each other, dance in a circle.

BETTY: *Great flurry.* We've got to get to the *Camrose Canadian* before they get him away from here!

ROGER: My gallant charger is off, com'mon.

CAROLINE: I'll get the media in Edmonton— *She grabs the phone. Dials.*

BETTY: We've got to get him on the TV . . .

Betty and Roger rush out.

CAROLINE: Hello. CBC? Evening news please . . . yes . . . yes . . . *ad lib.*

Enter the Regal Dead on the ramp. Aberhart is at their head; he is both indignant and angry. The Princess is walking with her hand regally on Crowfoot's arm.

ABERHART: Your artistic meddling has just given that poor woman false hopes. False, false.

PRINCESS LOUISE: *Sweetly.* I was just shooting my arrow, William.

ABERHART: *He is leaving them.* False encouragement is the worst possible . . . it simply prepares the way for going down, deeper, and deeper . . . *He is gone.*

CAROLINE: *Dialing.* CFRN . . . news desk please . . . yes. *Ad lib.*

PRINCESS LOUISE: *Detaining Crowfoot.* Oh, let him go, tramp it off. Three is such a crowd. Especially with him.

CROWFOOT: *Moving slightly away from her.* He'll miss his favorite engineer.

John Siemens enters, watches Caroline. He is not quite as nattily dressed as usual.

CAROLINE: Yes, at the Chateau Lacombe . . . if they haven't kicked him out yet. *She laughs.* Anytime. Bye-bye.

She hangs up, humming; is startled by John standing there. Crowfoot and Princess Louise observe them.

CAROLINE: Lo, the vanquished hero. Old Can Pac Min really laid a clunker this time, eh? Whooo-who!

John looks at her steadily, says nothing.

CAROLINE: Their own expert, they've got us all running, but their own expert . . . poof!

JOHN: Caroline . . .

CAROLINE: You need a job? I need somebody to work my summer fallow.

JOHN: It doesn't matter, Caroline.

CAROLINE: Oh, nothing matters with you. You're so progressive you don't feel triumph, you don't feel defeat, you—

JOHN: I told them all along, we have to develop our own, particular, reclamation system. And we will.

CAROLINE: What about Currie's grandmother, eh? What about that?

JOHN: Soil isn't *quite* as sensitive to bulldozers as grandmothers. Look Caroline, you're hurting yourself, you'll just get clobbered if you put—

CAROLINE: You have to win, don't you. You can't be beat.

JOHN: What do I have to do to convince you? You want some real information? The cabinet is meeting on this day after tomorrow.

CAROLINE: The cabinet, day after—how do you know?

JOHN: I have to know it.

Caroline grabs the phone, but John claps his hand over hers, stops her dialing. Princess Louise is very interested in these developments and pulls Crowfoot forward to see better.

JOHN: Stop it, Caroline. It's all in process now.

CAROLINE: So. What's in this for you, now?

JOHN: What we had going before, that's what's in it.

CAROLINE: That's nothing, it's . . . nothing.

JOHN: You were just playing around?

CROWFOOT: *Egging John on.* Get her, white man, get her!

CAROLINE: Okay, I wasn't playing . . . then. But I've taken over Grandpa's farm and every—

JOHN: I know. What do you know about running a big mixed farm?

PRINCESS LOUISE: *To Crowfoot.* Now really, what are you doing?

CROWFOOT: No damn good, a woman always have her own way.

The Princess laughs, looks at Crowfoot very appreciatively.

CAROLINE: What did you know about building thermal plants at 22?

JOHN: *Shifting ground.* You still don't believe me. You want to make a *real* phone call.

CAROLINE: Sure.

JOHN: Okay. Let's call Peter Lougheed. Ask him anything you want.

CAROLINE: Oh sure, hi Pete.

John dials.

CROWFOOT: He fix her now, you watch.

PRINCESS LOUISE: *Moving in fast.* You are such a splendid man, so intense.

JOHN: Hello Ian, John Siemens here. Look, could you get me through to Peter ... yes ... *To Caroline, hand over receiver.* What do you want to ask him? Quick!

Crowfoot is excited; Princess Louise too, but for a very different reason.

CAROLINE: Ask him if he still wears Stanfield shorts.

JOHN: Hello, Peter, just one question, I'm at Round Hill and a young . . .

Caroline signals frantically, 'No! No!'

Excuse me. *John glares at her, then, quite in control.* One question. Can I let it be known down here you are having a cabinet meeting Thursday? . . . I know the agenda is confidential . . . no? Of course, of course. Goodbye, Peter. *He hangs up.*

CAROLINE: You would have done it, too.

CROWFOOT: *Jubilant.* He fixed her, he fixed her!

JOHN: I always play for keeps. One more call. *Picks up, dials one digit.* It's for you. *Hands her the phone; she takes it, hesitantly; he bends to the mouthpiece, her ear.* I love you.

CAROLINE: *On reflex.* Say that again.

JOHN: *Staggered.* I—I love . . . you.

CROWFOOT: Somonabitch!

He roars in fury, hurling down his hat. The Princess begins to laugh.

CAROLINE: I'm sorry . . .

JOHN: I'm sorry too.

CAROLINE: I'm sorry I love you too.

Slowly she drops the phone; they move into an embrace.

PRINCESS LOUISE: You are such a magnificent man, in your rage.

CROWFOOT: *Becomes truly aware of her.* You want to go on watching that?

PRINCESS LOUISE: *Very close.* No. Love is not a spectator sport. It's action . . .

Crowfoot hastily goes for his hat.

CAROLINE: *Tearful, pushes away.* I am not doing this. I am in the office of the Dodds-Round Hill Protective Association, you are giving me some information, you will leave, I will . . .

JOHN: Look, it's not true, it's . . .

CAROLINE: I don't want to look! *She flees back into his arms.*

CROWFOOT: You really want me?

PRINCESS LOUISE: Yes. Yes.

CROWFOOT: You, sure, white princess?

PRINCESS LOUISE: Yes. Come. *She takes his hand, moves against him.*

CAROLINE: *Pulls away.* That's enough. Just go.

She wheels away, but John catches her wrist.

JOHN: I'll go, but you're coming with me.

He pulls her around; they run off together.

CROWFOOT: *Looking about, frantically.* Aberhart, where are you? *He attempts to run.*

PRINCESS LOUISE: *Cutting off his escape.* Princesses are just women. You know, Crowfoot, I always wanted to know more about Indian affairs. How many wives did you have?

CROWFOOT: *Cornered, grinning.* I can't remember . . . 16, maybe 20. But not all at once. *He touches her waist.* And none of them come wrapped in . . . steel.

PRINCESS LOUISE: That's nothing but whalebone, silly man, and easily removable.

She twirls his long braid over her shoulder and begins to lead him across by it. Suddenly he bursts out laughing, picks her up and carries her off over his shoulder; both laughing.

Lights out.

Scene vi

The rising mechanical throb of machinery will now ram the various places and people of the play together into a timeless, placeless confusion. The throb is excessively loud, almost thundering as out of the darkness first appears, in its usual curve of the ramp circle, Anton's kitchen with a very angry Wadu pacing before the seated Anton like a caged tiger.

ANTON: You proud of me now, eh Wadu? Caroline work the farm, I retire, get money . . . everything fine . . .

WADU: When will you stop hiding behind your Polish bullshit! You bitched and whined 43 years, farming's so awful! Nails you down! And now you let Caroline—my god Dad, that girl, what are you thinking!

ANTON: She make good farmer, work so hard, she—

WADU: She can't take it! Year after year, day after day! Dad, you've split this family into little pieces, my wife won't come home, she's in North Africa—Italy for all I know—

ANTON: What I do to your wife, huh?

WADU: She knows Caroline is out here, her only daughter shoveling manure! We had a chance to beat—

ANTON: Shovel manure! You listen, she farmer, she stubborn like you, she seeding all day, drive the tractor like—

WADU: Yeah, all of three months!

ANTON: When she ever do anything before, three months? Heh?

WADU: Oh, what's the use! Talking to you is—where's Caroline? *He wheels, furious.* I'll drag her back by the bloody hair, I'll— Caroline!

He strides away, up the curve of the ramp. There is a heavy beat of machinery noise.

ANTON: *Recovering in an instant.* Wadu? *Gets up.* Wadu! Come back!

Machinery beating. Anton moves unsteadily, like the very old man he is, in the circle Wadu has made towards the ramp, but the machinery keeps beating and both he and Wadu freeze into the position of their motion as in the opposite curve of the ramp Orest Kushnik's cafe appears; Betty with her friend Agnes enter. They are dressed in summer clothes, laughing about something that has just transpired. Orest follows them, silent and grim.

BETTY: *In high spirits, calling over her shoulder.* Orest, two fresh strawberry shortcakes, please.

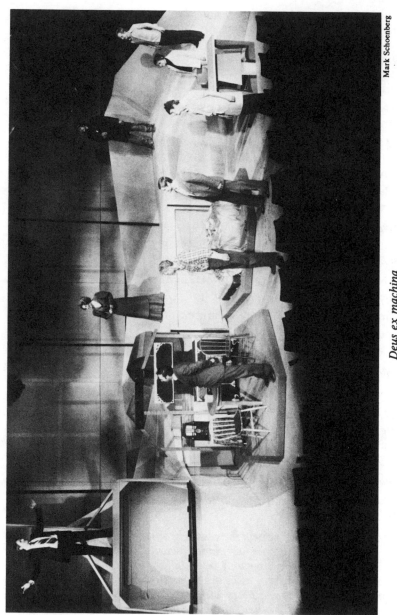

Deus ex machina

Orest grunts, goes.

BETTY: He's sure become a grouch. Well! I haven't relaxed like this since—we haven't had coffee in months, you know Agnes, that's terrible!

AGNES: You just don't have any time at all, for town people.

BETTY: *Not noticing.* Oh heavens, Agnes, I haven't had any time for anything. Everybody's on pins and needles now, the cabinet is deciding in Edmonton and—did you hear that German expert, they played his comments again last night on CFCW?

Orest brings the shortcakes; he places them down with a thump.

AGNES: No, I . . . I didn't . . .

The women look at Orest in some surprise. He has several pieces of paper in his hand.

OREST: Betty, can I have your attention. Raymond White left these bills this morning. *He slides them on the counter.* . . . and he wanted me to read you this letter: 'To the wonderful Betty Mitchell, ha ha ha ha!'

AGNES: Orest, for goodness sake!

OREST: *Continuing.* 'Thank you very much. I'm a citizen of Dodds-Round Hill too and I want to say, Betty Mitchell, that to save our lovely fields and hills we need more do-gooder fat-assed bitches like you.'

BETTY: *Starts up.* Orest, what—

OREST: You just sit and listen, for once: 'What do you know about raising a family in this town? I was laid off seven months ago. I got three kids and I'm slinging seed bags and that's finished in a week. I need the job, building that plant! I'm not asking for a house like yours, tractors, equipment . . . I was born here too, I just want to feed my family. Is that so wrong? You goddam meddling—' *He catches himself.* Raymond says maybe you can look after his bills too.

Orest turns, walks away to the foot of the ramp and freezes. The two women sit for a moment; Betty stunned.

AGNES: That was terrible, to read that that way, but there's a lot of hard feeling in town. We've been friends all our lives, Betty, I never had the courage to say it, but . . . well, how many farmers really care about us in town?

BETTY: We buy all our groceries here.

AGNES: I know, you do, but Bert . . . well, if you see a chance to maybe get really big . . . You've got all that land, you're really rich anyway, no matter what.

BETTY: Money? Agnes, we can't let Calgary Power break up our friendship!

167

AGNES: *Distraught, getting up.* That's why I said, let's meet here. Bert . . . doesn't want to see you around our place . . . anymore.

She runs past Orest, off.

BETTY: *Starting up.* Agnes, wait . . . Agnes! *She runs after her.*

The heavy machinery hammers immediately after her call; it is much closer, louder than before. Betty runs past Orest, who also moves forward on the beat, as do Anton and Wadu.

ANTON: *Calling.* Wadu!

Thunder of heavy machinery.

WADU: *Calling.* Caroline!

Heavy machinery. Abruptly all freeze again in the position of their running as, in the center between kitchen and cafe, Caroline's city pad appears. Caroline and John are seated back against back on the mattress. They wear nothing but loose, unbuttoned shirts; blankets are tumbled about them; a sense of omne animal.

JOHN: *Sad.* 'O, for a draught of vintage . . . Lethe-wards to sink . . . for Joy, her hand is ever at her lips, bidding adieu.'

CAROLINE: 'At *his* lips.'

JOHN: 'Her.'

CAROLINE: Keats wrote *his.* Keats?

JOHN: First year English. If you want to impress a prof, memorize lines.

CAROLINE: God, you are achievement oriented.

JOHN: Sometimes it comes in handy . . . 'For Joy, her shoulder.' *He is kissing it.*

CAROLINE: How often have you used that line?

He pulls away; she teases.

I could give you a useful course. Night course—'Sex for Profit'.

JOHN: Don't . . . *They link arms, rock.* . . . be such a smart-ass.

CAROLINE: *Lethargic.* Oh, I'm smart all over.

JOHN: We have a few minutes at most.

CAROLINE: And then . . .

JOHN: My radio buzzes.

CAROLINE: Are you *always* wired for business?

JOHN: It's wireless!

He scrabbles for the radio in his pants, indicates 'no wires'. Caroline gestures 'throw it away'; he does, with a clatter.

CAROLINE: *Collapsing, in laughter.* It was so funny . . . so . . .

JOHN: What?

CAROLINE: You wheeling the Porsche down those back roads . . .

JOHN: *Imitating her.* 'Betty mustn't see me in the car with you!'

CAROLINE: *Laughing.* And Joe Nussbaumer, pounding in posts with his front end loader . . .

JOHN: Like he had my head on every one!

They are swaying together in laughter; they collapse into kissing. Abruptly the radio begins to bleep.

CAROLINE: Ohh. Didn't you break it?

JOHN: *Not moving.* They're supposed to be indestructable. *The radio continues to bleep.*

CAROLINE: Take it.

JOHN: No. *He has moved down to kissing her thigh.*

CAROLINE: It'll never stop!

JOHN: *Gets up, grabbing the radio.* Yes. Just a minute. *He reaches for his pants, begins to put them on quickly.*

CAROLINE: *Laughing, leans over.* Hey Don! Yoohoo, Don.

JOHN: *Into the radio.* Yes. Yes.

He becomes totally business-like; Caroline reaches for her skirt.

Enter the Regal Dead above. The Princess looks satisfied. Crowfoot a bit grumpy; Aberhart has only found them after the fact.

PRINCESS LOUISE: *Looking down at the lovers.* I suppose, William, you think this is the pit of sin.

ABERHART: Oh no, young people in Ontario do that all the time. *Looks severely towards Caroline.* Now they'll just have to get married.

The Princess looks at him in astonishment; then at Crowfoot. They both laugh uproariously.

JOHN: No, the coordinates read 79, 183, 67.8 on the west side . . . *Angry.* Well if it's their fault, get after them! Okay, Don. Tomorrow morning.

He clicks off, puts the radio in his trouser pocket as he comes back to the bed. All is hazy-lazy for a moment.

CAROLINE: Which do you prefer, Tahiti or Bermuda?

JOHN: Bermuda's too close.

CAROLINE: Pitcairn's Island . . . did they ever find it?

JOHN: Yeah. Actually, I prefer your farm.

CAROLINE: Yeah. *She gets up, buttoning her skirt.* Tomorrow the cabinet meets.

JOHN: You know why reclamation won't stop the stripping?

CAROLINE: *Putting on her shoes.* Why?

JOHN: If reclamation costs too much, Canadian Pacific won't reclaim it.

CAROLINE: Oh. Just pay the fines . . .

JOHN: And forget it.

The impossibility of their lives is in their relative postures.

CAROLINE: *Softly.* You've done your work too well, my lovely lover-enemy. And I, I have to go take off my hay, so that when your bulldozers come they won't destroy everything— *Warning music from the Battle River rises as she remembers.* 'There, on the bank, where the black earth glistens, a girl with long hair like the sun twists in agony' . . . No, don't get up, no don't move, please . . . I have to fly somewhere . . . nowhere . . .

She runs; he scrambles to his feet, gets tangled in blankets.

JOHN: Caroline. *Heavy machinery.* Caroline!

He runs after her, calling. All the characters on stage except Crowfoot move with him. The noise of the machinery comes in thunderous jerks now and between each of their calls it grows louder and louder, its tempo quickening. Only Crowfoot is motionless, high on the left corner of the ramp.

ANTON: Wadu!

BETTY: Agnes!

WADU: Caroline!

OREST: Betty!

In the rush of searching, calling, the ominous roar of machinery, the Princess Louise becomes confused.

PRINCESS LOUISE: *Searching.* Crowfoot!

ABERHART: *Moving too.* Princess? Princess!

All the characters swirl about the stage, calling their loved ones in confusion as the machinery jerks become deafening; at the highest points of confusion and noise Crowfoot stands above them all, laughing tremendously, inaudibly. Then the machinery noise changes to that of a crane lowering; a gigantic orange apparatus begins to descend at stage right. All freeze, stare; every sound dies except that of the machine creaking down. It is an immense coal

170

scoop; obviously it is too shiny and new ever to have been used; yet. Inside the bucket is Peter Lougheed, the perfect deus ex machina. The bucket descends to a full and complete stop on the ramp.

LOUGHEED: *Riding the bucket in characteristic pose.* My dear people of Alberta, voters all. My government has with great care considered Calgary Power's application for a thermal electric plant at Dodds-Round Hill. My government is committed to provide every citizen with adequate electricity. However, this project would disturb too much prime agricultural land. Therefore, at this time my government will *not* give approval to Dodds-Round Hill development.

Screams, laughter, tears. Responses are similar to the characters' general attitude throughout the play. On second thought, however, their response changes and as they speak individually, their tone underlines the ambiguity of what has, and has not, happened. Nothing human has been resolved by this mechanical statement.

JOHN: *To Caroline.* I lost.

CAROLINE: *To John.* I guess I lost too; you'll have to move. *She goes towards him.*

BETTY: *To Orest.* There still won't be any more jobs around here, the young people will all keep leaving.

OREST: *To Betty as they sit down at the cafe counter.* We always had to get along on just the farmers.

Morosely they eat the untouched strawberry shortcakes.

WADU: Well Dad, the farm's safe.

ANTON: *Sitting down in his kitchen chair.* Couldn't sell it now even if we wanted to, somonabitch.

ABERHART: *To the audience, in total admiration.* What a politician! What a politician! If I'd been his age, had such a start . . . he's a chip off the old block!

PRINCESS LOUISE: *To the audience.* It's strange: I feel now as if I had a history here too. For I do care about this place.

LOUGHEED: *Still making his speech.* Alberta's demand for electrical energy doubled between 1967 and 1975 and will double again by 1983 . . .

CAROLINE: *To John.* Where will you have to go now?

JOHN: Hanna maybe, or Fox Creek.

CAROLINE: Want to help me run my farm?

JOHN: *Gestures.* Can't you see? He's given you three years, at most.

CROWFOOT: *Comes across, seats himself opposite Anton in the vacant kitchen chair.* A hundred years ago the white man took this country, and now they know the black burning stone is under the earth; and they will not be able to leave it alone. White men can never leave, anything, the way it was.

LOUGHEED: We have listened to you, and we have understood you. Thank you.

Lights out.

Medicare!

Rex Deverell

Medicare! was premiered by the Globe Theatre Company in Yorkton, Sask., March 12, 1980, opening in Regina, March 18.

The Company: Douglas Brown
Lee J. Campbell
Rita Deverell
Linda Huffman
David McCulley
Elizabeth Moulton
Pierre Tetrault

Director: Kim McCaw

Designer: Kathrine Christensen

Technical Director: Peter Urbanek

Medicare!
As a one man collective

Rex Deverell

My first experience working with collective theatre came with the Studio Lab Theatre in Toronto in 1970. Those were the heady days of experimental theatre. Living Theatre and the Performing Garage were in their prime in New York. The Studio Lab under Ernie Schwartz had created its own version of Dionysus in '69—an updated Bacchii with audience participation.

My wife, Rita Deverell, joined the Lab in 1970 as an actress. I also became involved in the development of new material as a writer and sometimes even as a performer.

This collective was director controlled rather than democratic. The work consisted of actor improvisation based on written text. The text might consist of classical pieces or children's literature, fairy tales or even a collection of songs brought in by one of the troupe. While I was there I worked on a new version of a Roman comedy, a children's play based on the Sambo story and a revue based on songs by Tom Sankey.

While textually oriented and collectively experimental, this was not documentary material. Nor do I think many of the members of the theatre were very politically sophisticated. Their concerns focussed on style and form and were revolutionary only in the sense of being somewhat anti-traditional. Nevertheless the experimentation in the area of audience participation was genuinely innovative.

At that time little documentary drama was being done in other theatres. Toronto Workshop Productions following in the Joan Littlewood mold was creating plays through improvisation and some of these were documentary in nature. Curiously enough Regina's Globe Theatre put together a play about Saskatchewan history called *Next Year Country*. The playwright was Carol Bolt. She rewrote it later and it was produced at an up and coming Toronto theatre under the title *Buffalo Jump*. The theatre was Theatre Passe Muraille.

As the seventies progressed Paul Thompson's Theatre Passe Muraille developed the improvised collective documentary to a state of brilliance. Such was the Toronto troupe's influence that the term 'collective documentary' now seems synonymous with Theatre Passe Muraille. A whole decade of actors has grown up who have adopted Passe Muraille techniques of reportage and character representation.

Meanwhile I went in a different direction. In 1971 Rita joined Saskatchewan's Globe School Touring Company and I began my evolution into a "prairie" writer. I wrote first for the school company and then for the main stage of the Globe. My work began to take on a kind of social/political thrust in both areas.

In 1975 the theatre, thinking I was sufficiently Saskatchewanized, put me on salary as a resident playwright. Writing in the traditional isolation was pushing me into a growing responsibility for my own artistic and thematic decisions. Nevertheless sometimes I felt a certain nostalgia for the old days when I worked with a collective to develop material. So when the Globe began to consider a new documentary I began to look forward to a collective creation. Ken and Sue Kramer, the Globe's co-directors, had long had the idea to create a play about the grain industry. They suggested we use not the Passe Muraille model but an earlier Stoke-on-Trent style.* What attracted them about the English method is that it insisted on a very literal adherence to original documents as the source for the dialogue.

We assembled a company and set to work. Our first task was to understand the issues, the story and, it soon became obvious, the rhetoric of the grain trade. It was a period of consultation and gathering. As the company divided itself into research groups we agreed we would seek any written material touching on issue or story. We set up boxes with files devoted to the specifics. If a file remained empty we would spend extra time figuring out what kind of documents might exist to fill it and then dispatch members of the troupe to find those documents. Then, of course, an alert researcher would bring in something unanticipated and a whole new category would have to be opened.

A curious phenomenon occurred. The troupe became politicized. It formed a strong opinion about the current state of the grain industry and federal/provincial policy. The actors began to feel that they had a responsibility to use the play to make a statement and that the play could enter the debate raging in the industry.

The next step was for the researchers to revert to players. We examined the documents in small groups and then

---

*Developed by director Peter Cheeseman at the Victoria Theatre, Stoke-on-Trent, in such documentary plays as *The Knotty, Six Into One* and *Fight for Shelton Bar.*

cooked up sketches based on them and using their words. For example, the text of the Foreign Investments Review Act was combined with the advertising of an American multinational in order to comment on Ottawa's relationship to multinationals. The actors invented a Cargill Grain Company playboy bunny who succeeds in seducing the Review Board. This without departing from the documentary texts.

As writer I stood back from the process and made suggestions as to what documents could be used, where they could be placed, how to structure the entire show.

We presented the show for a week, the actors reading their lines from hand held five by eight cards. The third act was a discussion with the audience. The cards allowed us to change the play based on audience contribution. We called the play *No. 1 Hard* which is both a grade of wheat and was a brand of rye whiskey. A few months later we took a revised version on the road for the Saskatchewan Farmers Union.

At the same time Saskatoon's 25th Street Theatre produced *Paper Wheat* which was a Passe Muraille style documentary covering some of the same material as *No. 1 Hard*. *Paper Wheat* was very successful and a national tour proved it accessible to a broad audience. *No. 1 Hard* played mainly for grain farmers and I think was seen to be a direct statement on current issues. The two types of documentary are worthy of comparison. *Paper Wheat* is character and vignette oriented. *No. 1 Hard* is closer to the living newspaper productions of the 1930's. The acting is inventive commentary on the text.

The next documentary we did at the Globe was *Medicare!* I wrote *Medicare!* based on what I had learned through the *No. 1 Hard* process. I wanted to preserve the authority of using literal documents as dialogue and add the flexibility and texture that comes in the creation of new characters and scenes from the imagination. On the other hand I did not want to move so far from the primary material that I would be creating a new imaginative piece. *Medicare!* was an extraordinary event in Regina but only insofar as it interacted with the original medicare crisis.

I regard my responsibility in this play (and the one that followed, *Black Powder*) to the event and its people, rather than to my own imagination. I'm not going to argue that one ought not to allow one's fantasy to fool with historical events. In fact I am intrigued by that possibility and I may do it next time. But with these important regional stories I think one owed it to the audience to expose the story and to celebrate the story's own language and its characters.

Now why do I call *Medicare!* a one man collective. I suppose because it employs methods and techniques which have been developed by collective docu-dramas over the last twenty years . . . and because it involved my own improvising upon what we started collectively with *No. 1 Hard*. Writing it by myself gave me the advantage of the deciding vote and that is faster than days of debate in the company. I could structure things more intuitively and not have to worry about explaining it to anybody. When it came to playing with the various kinds of rhetoric I was in a state of pure excitement, and I know that it would have been difficult to get a group of actors as interested in bureaucratic wrangling and the peculiar forms it took.

But I have to admit I missed the group process of the collective troupe. Especially, I missed the kind of wrestling with issues and facts which leads to a group political consciousness.

My problem was first to isolate my prejudices. I could appreciate the desire for socialized medicine far more than the attitude of the medical profession. I was bothered by my failure to understand and I hoped through writing that I would gain understanding. My concern took the form of a question: under what circumstances would I take similar action?

Whereas *No. 1 Hard* had been a commentary on issues, this play became an exploration of issues. It asks what happened, why and how.

To find out what happened I had to arrange the events in such a way as to expose a sequential story line. This involves some artistic (or at least crafty) decisions. Where are the builds and denouements, the contrasts, the ironic possibilities in juxtaposing scenes or events or speeches? Most of these decisions were made while assembling the script. During rehearsals, of course, I found I'd made parts of the play too fat and other parts too thin and, as is the case with any new play, more molding had to take place.

Now, in this process—which is common enough in the creation of any story—I was discovering what happened in a way other than reading a chronological list of events associated with the medicare crisis in Saskatchewan. I was learning the story's aesthetic, its shape. I was learning where it is beautiful, painful, grotesque and funny and how these things weave together. I gained a level of understanding.

Then I moved on to the question of why it happened. Already I have found out how the events are causally related. But now I have to worm my way into the characters of the drama. My entry is primarily through their speech. At this point the process departs from the writing of fictional drama and even traditional historical drama where speech is invented to fit the history. In the case of *Medicare!* I had a plethora of rhetoric available, not only in manuscript but also on audio tape.

Speech is for something. Words are not uttered without goal or motive. They always seek. Usually they seek power. Sometimes they defend and hide. Sometimes they probe. Sometimes they dazzle. Arranging the rhetoric of *Medicare!* was a kind of dramatic version of "found poetry". I had to show it, show its effect within the drama and allow it to have an effect on the present day audience. This was the second artistic (craft) task.

I could reconstruct the public story in the very words of the participants. But to go behind closed doors and into the back rooms I needed their memories (which could sometimes be obtained through interviews) and I needed a sense of what would make me act in such a way: a perception of the imagination.

As I set about making the composite characters of Drs. Scott and Wilson their speech came from arguments I heard made by physicians on either side of the issue. But it also came from my own internal argument. Could I accept self interest as a valid argument for denying a society a palpable social benefit? Well, if I couldn't accept it as valid, could I discover under what conditions I would feel as strongly about my own self interest. Yes. If I thought my independence as a playwright was threatened, that my judgements might be subjected to the opinion of petty bureaucrats, I might become fairly hysterical myself. And so between the found dialogue and the speculative dialogue I reached another level of understanding.

In the course of assembling plot and dialogue I was also arriving at an understanding of how the medicare crisis took place. By this I mean I began to hear the tone of people's voices and see the expression on their faces. The story was a cyclic progression of hope, fear, frustration and victory. I also began to feel the fatigue of politician and physician alike, the fear of the pregnant patient as the deadline approached, the heat of the Saskatchewan July.

It remained for me to construct a pastiche of scenes, monologues, narrative and action. I had to find a style for each unit that corresponded to its meaning. The "how" of *Medicare!* had to be multifaceted like the original. As I worked at this I discovered it possible to keep the time perspective of the play at two levels: the event itself and the event as remembered. Thus I could first present Walter Erb reflecting negatively about the development of the medicare bill and then immediately have him step twenty years into the past to introduce that bill as the then Minister of Health.

Of course none of this was worked out as systematically as I have just described. Sometimes I was floundering in the dark. Some of it came all at once. Some was based on a general impression and might not have been actually factual. And I'm aware that I may have left out things in a process of editorial judgement.

However, all told I think the play is impersonal enough to be authoritative and personal enough to be insightful. It represents a struggle between my creative ego and the dramatic power of history.

Playwright's Preface

Medicare and the political context

This play begins April 25, 1959 when Saskatchewan's Premier, T. C. Douglas first declared his intention to proceed with a medical care insurance plan. The play ends July 23, 1962 with the signing of the Saskatoon Agreement which ended a withdrawal of services by the province's medical profession.

It should be understood that the history of medicare in Saskatchewan did not begin or end with these dates. From the early days when farmers began to pool their wheat, Saskatchewan people have looked to co-operation as a workable way to solve common problems. When as a result of the Depression folk could not pay medical bills, health plans were set up by many local municipalities. The doctors would bill the municipal secretary-treasurer and be paid by him at the beginning of each month. The medical profession apparently participated in these plans enthusiastically. In hard times it was advantageous to do so.

These local plans came about largely through the efforts of a rural municipality reeve, Matt Anderson. Norwegian by birth, Anderson had never been able to understand North American resistance to state medical insurance. In Europe such plans were common and Norway had begun hers as far back as 1890. As a local reeve he lobbied through the Depression for a provincial or national plan and failing that legislation to permit local ones.

In the best Saskatchewan tradition, therefore, the impetus for state medicine came from the grass roots.

After the CCF came to power in 1944, they established a plan for hospitalization (the first in Canada). Those municipalities with medical plans gave over that part of their responsibilities to the provincial government.

There was still the question of how to pay for medical care beyond hospital costs—i.e. visits to the doctor—specialized attention, in short, doctor bills. The government had hoped to complete this part of their insurance program gradually, one region at a time. They began with the Swift Current Health Region.

Times were changing, however. The prosperity of the province was increasing. The medical profession no longer found the community controlled plans attractive. They campaigned against expansion of the regional plans and two regional plebiscites on medicare were defeated.

Meanwhile two doctor sponsored private medical insurance plans had been instituted: Medical Services Incorporated and Group Medical Services. Between them they were serving an ever increasing percentage of the population. Government medical insurance represented a direct threat to these companies and they would become a significant issue in the dispute.

Something needs to be said about the way in which the medical profession was organized in Saskatchewan. In 1959-1962 the College of Physicians and Surgeons, the licensing and regulating body of the profession, was also the Saskatchewan Medical Association, i.e. the lobbying quasi-union organization for doctors. This meant that the SMA had formidable disciplinary powers over its members, more so than the Medical Association of any other province. The medicare crisis was in effect a labor/management dispute between two governments, one provincial and the other professional. No small wonder that it often took on the tone of a war between sovereign nations.

It has been asserted with some justification that the community clinics which developed during the crisis were the most significant and progressive result of the time. As is indicated in Dr. Hjertaas' final speech these clinics declined numerically after the Saskatoon Agreement. Did the agreement and ensuing policy create an adverse climate for radical health care solutions?*

At the time of *Medicare!* the Globe Theatre was housed in temporary quarters. By some fortuitous accident, those quarters were The Trianon Ballroom. Eighteen years before the Trianon had been the sight of the nomination of Woodrow Lloyd to succeed Tommy Douglas as Premier. It was also where Premier Lloyd made a last ditch attempt at reasoning with a general meeting of the doctors. That same meeting voted for a withdrawal of services unless the government withdrew the medicare legislation. The Globe performs in the round and during more than one performance the audience could watch the real participants watching themselves portrayed on stage in the room where the same battle had been waged eighteen years before.

---

*Bill Harding, a long time Saskatchewan activist, has kindly sent me additional information about Community Clinics after the Saskatoon Agreement. I quote in part:

"The following week Woodrow called representatives of the Community Clinics to the Cabinet room and asked Lord Taylor to explain our role. He did so in the most arrogant speech I have ever heard. He described our role as caretaker only. There must not be any attempt to get involved in

Bibliography

Badgley, Robin F. and Wolfe, Samuel, *Doctors' Strike,* Toronto, Macmillan of Canada, 1967.

Lloyd, Diane, *Woodrow: A Biography of W.F. Lloyd,* The Woodrow Lloyd Memorial Fund, 1975.

MacTaggart, Kenneth W., *The First Decade,* Ottawa, Canadian Medical Association, 1973.

Mohamed, A. M., *Keep Our Doctors Committees in the Saskatchewan Medicare Controversy,* an unpublished M.A. Thesis, University of Saskatchewan, Saskatoon, 1963.

Taylor, Malcolm G., *Health Insurance and Candian Public Policy,* Montreal-Kingston, McGill-Queen's University Press, 1978.

Tollefson, Edwin A., *Bitter Medicine,* Saskatoon, Modern Press, 1964.

the policy side. We were to only provide services for the doctors—they would decide what was good for the community. And we mustn't get involved in methods of payment and all those sacred things. It was clearly the death knell of the clinics as we had envisioned them.

I responded angrily and told Lord Taylor that neither he nor the Saskatoon Agreement would determine the policy of community clinics—that the members of the clinics would make the decisions about their role in society. However most accepted this as 'political reality.'

. . . In my view we still have the task of completely restructuring our health services system." (W. M. Harding, letter to the author, Nov. 10, 1982.)

Act I

Scene i   The politicians

April 25, 1959. Birch Hills, Saskatchewan. The CCF (Co-Operative Commonwealth Federation) Party of Saskatchewan is holding a nominating convention for an upcoming by-election. The local movie theatre is filled to capacity. The stage is decorated with pictures of party leader, Premier T. C. (Tommy) Douglas. A large CCF flag hangs prominently. A large table serves as a lectern. The crowd is singing labour songs as the final ballots are being counted, growing silent as the Chairman begins:

CHAIRMAN: Ladies and Gentlemen . . . . Ladies and Gentleman, the ballots have been counted . . . the ballots have been counted, Ladies and Gentlemen . . . on the third ballot, with a hundred and eleven votes, the winner of the nomination and the next M.L.A. for the riding of Kinistino is Arthur Thibault!

Great applause—Thibault is a popular choice. He struggles to the platform amid backslapping and congratulations. The chairman shakes his hand and steps back to allow him to speak.

THIBAULT: Thank you, thanks—thank you . . . *The crowd finally quietens.* Mr. Premier, Mr. Chairman, Fellow CCF'ers, I—I don't know what to say. I didn't think I'd win. *More soberly.* Henry Begrand worked so darn hard for this riding—you know he was working for all of us and I guess we all feel kind of responsible for his death. *Stronger.* Well we owe it to Henry to carry on the good fight. I'm sure he does not want to be remembered by tears but by carrying on the work he has done. *Applause.* So let's roll up our sleeves and get at it. We've got a by-election June third—and we're going to win it!

Cheers.

I'd like to add my word of welcome to the Premier of our province, Mr. Tommy Douglas. We sure appreciate his coming all the way up here to Birch Hills to attend our Convention and I'll turn the meeting over to him now.

Tommy Douglas comes forward and congratulates Thibault on his nomination. When Douglas speaks he is spell binding. He is a combination of passionate idealism, charming elf-like wit, Baptist preacher and bantam weight boxer. He is greeted with thunderous applause.

DOUGLAS: Mr. Chairman, Delegates and Members, Friends. Let me tell you what you are doing by sending Mr. Thibault to Regina. You are advancing the day when a Co-operative Commonwealth is established not only in Saskatchewan but throughout Canada and the world! Our goal is to build a new society!

What's wrong with this one?

Fifty percent of the world's population hasn't got enough to eat and we are producing less food than we were twenty years ago. We see little wars cropping up. We are living in a boiling world! Is this the best society we can build?

Our society is owned and controlled by people not interested in the welfare of the community, only in making profits! We have political democracy but we do not have economic democracy.

We must beware that Capitalism does not creep in and take away our political democracy—because capitalists try to control governments to protect their vested interests.

VOICE: *From the audience.* You tell 'em, Tommy!

Laughter.

DOUGLAS: Elections are now being handled by big public relation firms to sell Ike, or Diefenbaker—just like any other product. Of course it should not be more difficult to sell soft soap than detergent.

Laughter.

They use slogans like "Use Brylcreem" or "Follow John!"

Laughter.

Get a slogan and you're in! And so bit by bit, economic power is reaching out to gain political power.

Our party is in favour of three kinds of enterprise: public enterprise, co-operative enterprise and private enterprise.

There is a little negative reaction from some in the audience but Douglas puts up his hand.

Oh, yes. We do not object to a man making a profit on his investment—but we do object to someone making huge profits at the expense of the people!

This draws applause.

Now let me tell you what the present CCF Government is

accomplishing for the people of Saskatchewan. The rural electrification program is within sight of completion. Electricity is established on fifty-five thousand of a possible sixty-five thousand farms!

Applause.

We are also studying the installation of sewer and water facilities in towns and villages by means of mass production and we hope to at least experiment with sewer and water on farms.

Applause.

Further we are in the act of planning a program of medical care for the province that will ensure that all residents can get the medical attention they need regardless of their ability to pay.

Louder applause as the lights fade on Douglas. Thibault steps out of the scene and addresses us.

THIBAULT: There wasn't much of a fuss when Mr. Douglas made the announcement—not that night, anyway. I'll tell you why I was for medicare. When I was eleven years old there were kids dying in my class at school of diphtheria . . . and that was years after the vaccine was available. People got the vaccine in the cities—but out in the boondocks children died. Of course that was a long time ago, but that sort of thing stays with you. I have stood at the foot of many a grave that would not have been there if there had been a medical care system.

There is a pause and then an ambulance siren shatters the silence. The stage is filled with an angry flashing red light. Thibault exits. The table becomes an operating table lit from overhead with glaring white light.

Scene ii   The doctors*

The siren stops as if the ambulance had drawn up to the emergency entrance of a hospital. The red light fades. Lights come up on the scrub area. Wilson, a middle aged doctor dressed in surgical greens, is scrubbing his hands furiously and mumbling to himself. Scott, the surgeon, enters, watches Wilson curiously and begins to scrub, as well.

SCOTT: You're going to take 'em right off one of these days.

WILSON: What?

---

*Scott and Wilson are composites of physicians who were involved in the medicare crisis. Their dialogue is semi-fictitious. Unless otherwise indicated the speeches of the historical characters are based on primary documents or reassembled from newspaper accounts.

SCOTT: The hands.

WILSON: *Looking at them.* Oh. *He shakes them dry, violently.* I'll charge it to Douglas.

SCOTT: Eh?

WILSON: The're going to ram it through, you know! They're going to ram it through!

SCOTT: Who?

They are putting gloves on.

WILSON: The government, the bastards!

A nurse leans in.

NURSE: All set, Doctor.

SCOTT: Let's go.

The patient has been placed on the operating table. All necessary instruments and apparatus are on hand. Besides Scott and Wilson there will be a nurse who hands Scott the instruments, another who hangs back a little to see to special needs and equipment, and an intern assistant to Scott. Wilson will be the anaesthetist.

SCOTT: *Gently to the patient.* Mrs. Engstrom . . .

PATIENT: *Dozy.* Dr. Scott?

SCOTT: That's right.

PATIENT: You showed up, eh?

SCOTT: *Laughing.* Least I could do.

PATIENT: Feeling pretty steady?

SCOTT: Like a rock. How about you?

PATIENT: I'm scared.

SCOTT: Don't be.

PATIENT: Easy for you to say.

SCOTT: Not a thing to worry about. Mrs. Engstrom, in a couple of seconds you're going to go fast asleep and the first thing you know you'll be waking up in the recovery room—I'll come by and visit with you.

PATIENT: Okay.

WILSON: Would you count to ten, please.

PATIENT: Pardon?

WILSON: Count to ten.

He administers a drug to the intravenous.

PATIENT: Oh. One ... two ..... three .... fo ... four ....
five.

She is out. Wilson places the mask on her face and monitors her blood pressure, pulse and respiration. The patient is swabbed and draped.

WILSON: She's under. All yours, Doctor.

SCOTT: Thank you, Doctor. *To the intern.* We'll make our incision here.

He begins to work with a scalpel. At first the operation is like a well-oiled machine. Instruments are handed automatically and few words are spoken.

SCOTT: Tissues.

He is handed tissue scissors.

Wet sponge, please.

Wet towels are packed into the incision.

Retractor. *The intern applies the retractors.* Retractor.

SCOTT: *As he works.* What's gotten into you, Joe?

WILSON: Politics.

SCOTT: *To one of the nurses.* If you'll give me a hand here a second. Just hold this back will you? *Tense for a second.* Hold it back! Alright—suction. *To Wilson.* Politics?

WILSON: They've been cooking this up all year. Douglas let it out in Birch Hills last night.

SCOTT: There's a bleeder.

INTERN: *To nurse.* Hemostat.

SCOTT: Let what out?

WILSON: State medicine. They're going to socialize us, Sid. BP good, 110 over 60.

SCOTT: I doubt it. *To intern.* See that?

INTERN: Yes.

WILSON: You're not worried?

SCOTT: Not much. I don't bother with politics much. No time.

WILSON: *Scornfully.* That's the attitude.

SCOTT: *To the other nurse.* We might have to transfuse her.

The nurse goes off and returns with plasma.

SCOTT: *To Wilson.* Government doesn't bother me, I don't

188

bother it. Who cares how a patient pays his bills: insurance, government—what's the difference?

WILSON: You want to be a civil servant?

SCOTT: Nope. Clamp.

A clamp is passed to him and he throws it on the floor.

Dammit, don't give me what I ask for—give me what I need! Scalpel.

A scalpel is passed.

She's losing a lot of blood.

WILSON: She started out with a hemoglobin of 10 point 9.

SCOTT: Better be safe than sorry.

WILSON: *Transfusing.* Blood's an expensive business.

SCOTT: What?

WILSON: Under medicare they might decide not to give you the choice.

Scott looks up sharply and there is a moment of suspended animation. The Douglas broadcast of December 16, 1959 is heard as if over a home radio.

ANNOUNCER'S VOICE: Ladies and Gentlemen, the Cross Saskatchewan Network, CKRM Radio, broadcasting over a provincial network of private stations presents, live from Biggar, the Premier of Saskatchewan, Mr. T. C. Douglas.

DOUGLAS' VOICE: All my adult life I have dreamed of the day when we would have in Canada a program by which health services would be available to all, irrespective of their individual ability to pay. Now the Government of Saskatchewan is convinced that the time has arrived when we can establish a prepaid medical care plan as the next logical step in our march toward a comprehensive health insurance program. . . .

Douglas enters in person and chats with the audience—the surgery continues in the background.

DOUGLAS: When I was a boy in Scotland before World War I, I fell and hurt my knee. A bone disease called osteomyelitis set in and for three or more years I was in and out of hospital.

My father was an iron moulder and we had no money for doctors let alone specialists. After we immigrated to Canada the pain in my knee came back. Mother took me to the out-door clinic of a Winnipeg hospital.

They put me in the public ward as a charity patient and I still remember the young house doctor saying that my leg must be cut off.

But I was lucky. A brilliant orthopaedic surgeon, whose name was Smith, came through the wards looking for patients he could use in teaching demonstrations. He examined my swollen knee and then went to see my parents. He told them, "If you'll let me use your boy to help teach medical students I think I can save his leg. His knee may never be strong again but it can be saved."

I shall always be grateful to the medical profession for the skill that kept me from becoming a cripple, but the experience of being a charity patient remains with me.

Had I been a rich man's son the services of the finest surgeons would have been available. As an iron moulder's boy, I almost had my leg amputated before chance intervened and a specialist cured me without thought of a fee.

All my adult life I have dreamed of the day when an experience like mine would be impossible and we would have in Canada a program of complete medical care without a price tag.

WILSON: *To Scott.* What's wrong with the way things are, eh? Tell me that.

DOUGLAS' VOICE: *On the radio.* That good medical care is available to the people of this province goes without saying . . .

WILSON: Right!

DOUGLAS' VOICE: But the fact remains that there are some people who are unwilling to seek medical care because of the high costs involved.

WILSON: They can get insurance! Why should the government get involved.

DOUGLAS: *To the doctors.* Unfortunately there are many people who cannot avail themselves of the voluntary plans, either because they can't afford the premiums or because they have congenital conditions which are not covered by them.

WILSON: I'll tell you why. Because they want to control everything, that's why. They want to get their grubby little socialist fingers into everybody's business and squeeze.

DOUGLAS' VOICE: In setting up the plan there are five basic principles which the government believes to be sound. The first is the prepayment principle.

DOUGLAS: *Explaining.* We feel that people respond better toward a program if they pay some portion of the cost directly on an insurance basis.

DOUGLAS' VOICE: The second principle is that a medical care program must have universal coverage.

DOUGLAS: The only way we can have a real insurance scheme is to cover the good risks as well as the bad, thus spreading the cost over the entire population.

DOUGLAS' VOICE: The third principle we have set is that there must be a high quality of service.

DOUGLAS: We believe that a medical care program must have as its major objective the improvement of the quality of care ... and it must not only be concerned with curing disease but also with the much more desirable objective of keeping people well.

DOUGLAS' VOICE: The fourth principle is that this must be a government sponsored program and administered by a public body.

DOUGLAS: In a government sponsored plan part of the cost can be borne out of general revenue, thereby keeping the per capita premiums at a figure which every family can afford to pay.

DOUGLAS' VOICE: The fifth principle upon which this plan will be established is that it must be acceptable both to those providing the service and those receiving it.

DOUGLAS: We have no intention of pushing some preconceived plan down the doctors' throats. We want their co-operation and from our experience with other health programs I am convinced we will get it. I would like to hazard the prophecy that before 1970 almost every other province in Canada will have followed the lead of Saskatchewan and we shall have a national health insurance program from the Atlantic to the Pacific. Once more Saskatchewan has an opportunity to lead the way. Let us therefore have the vision and the courage to take this forward step, believing that it is another advance toward a more just and humane society.

WILSON: Now, you see? The whole thing, right there. Not one bit of consultation. The whole thing—laid right out.

SCOTT: *Finishing the operation.* The election is in the spring, Joe. Joe. Alright, no more bleeding. We'll close her up. I think we've got it all. 2 - 0 chromic. *Begins suturing.*

There is a moment when the doctors and Douglas remain frozen, each satisfied in his own particular way. The lights fade.

DOUGLAS' VOICE: *Powerful in the darkness.* It is our intention to appoint an advisory committee on medicare. Three persons will be named by the medical profession, three by the government, three representatives from the general public and one appointee from the medical school. It is our expectation that the committee will submit their report by the end of 1960 and that we can get a province-wide medical care program started in 1961.

Scene iii   Not so fast!

Sound of typewriters. Civil servants rushing about with briefs and secretaries. The Minister of Public Health, J. Walter Erb enters. Erb was once an opera singer and brings a kind of operatic flair to his public pronouncements. He enjoys the limelight but is less enchanted by administrative responsibilities. A secretary, Miss Perkins, hovers nearby, taking dictation.

ERB: December 30, 1959 to Dr. G. W. Peacock, Registrar, College of Physicians and Surgeons of Saskatchewan—Saskatoon—whatever—you know the address. . . .

MISS PERKINS: Yes, Mr. Erb.

ERB: *Rolling.* I would request that the College name three physicians to sit on the proposed Advisory Planning Committee. It is our hope that this committee can be established as soon as possible thereafter. I am enclosing a draft of a letter which I propose to send to each member appointed. I am forwarding this draft at this time so that your Council may have an opportunity to discuss it. Sincerely yours, J. Walter Erb, Minister of Public Health. *To the secretary.* Do you have that letter yet, Miss Perkins?

MISS PERKINS: I think the Deputy Minister sent it up this morning. *Finding a letter and reading.* "Dear Blank. I am herewith submitting to each member of the Advisory Planning Committee on Medical Care certain comments and instructions . . ."?

ERB: That'll be it. You want to sum it up for me?

MISS PERKINS: Well, uh . . . *Reading fast.* It lays down the five principles that Mr. Douglas talked about . . .

ERB: Yes?

MISS PERKINS: And at the end it says they're supposed to prepare the final report not later than December 31, 1960.

ERB: That's enough time, do you think?

MISS PERKINS: Well, It's a year.

ERB: Alright, send it on.

Lights come up on Dr. Peacock, a plump roly-poly gentleman, and his secretary.

PEACOCK: Take a letter, Miss Hazelton, if you would.

MISS HAZELTON: Yes, Dr. Peacock.

PEACOCK: January 8, 1960. To J. Walter Erb, Minister of Public Health, Health and Welfare Building, Regina, Saskatchewan. Dear Mr. Erb: In the interest of better discussion and understanding, I am taking the liberty of asking if you would be kind enough to clarify the

192

following: "government has accepted the principle that a medical care insurance programme will be administered by a public body, responsible to the Legislature through the Minister of Health." Perhaps you can enlarge on the term "public body" and advise us what is meant. Yours sincerely, etc.* Fire that off, Miss Hazelton, would you.

From here on Erb will become increasingly anxious about the time that is passing. He is also desperately trying to stay on the Doctors' good side—perhaps too desperately. Peacock as spokesman for the doctors is playing a rather careful game.

ERB: Take this down, Miss Perkins. Dear Dr. Peacock . . . *To secretary.* Oh, what is the date today?

MISS PERKINS: January 12th.

ERB: January 12, 1960. Dear Dr. Peacock: One of the fundamental principles which the government considers important is that the administration of a program in which public funds are employed should be carried on in the democratic tradition of representative government. In other words it should be so designed that there is responsibility to the Legislature and through the Legislature to the people. The Advisory Planning Committee have the fullest freedom in making recommendations as to the exact form such an administration shall take. Sincerely yours, J. Walter Erb.

PEACOCK: *Dictating.* January 18, 1960. Dear Mr. Erb: The College of Physicians and Surgeons of Saskatchewan has studied the proposed terms of reference and is prepared to name three representatives—provided that the terms of reference are widened to investigate all aspects of health care and that there be no arbitrary time limit.

The telephone rings immediately.

MISS HAZELTON: *Answering.* Dr. Peacock's office.

MISS PERKINS: This is the office of the Minister of Public Health. Mr. Erb would like to speak to Dr. Peacock, please.

MISS HAZELTON: One moment please. *To her boss.* Dr. Peacock?

PEACOCK: Yes, Miss Hazelton?

MISS HAZELTON: Mr. Erb would like to speak to you.

PEACOCK: Put him on.

MISS HAZELTON: *Into telephone.* Dr. Peacock is on the line now.

MISS PERKINS: *To Erb.* Mr. Erb . . .

*See Tollefson, *Bitter Medicine*, for the full correspondence between the Government and the College of Physicians and Surgeons.

ERB: Yes, Miss Perkins?

MISS PERKINS: Your call to Dr. Peacock is through now.

ERB: Thank you. *Jovial.* Hello, Dr. Peacock!

PEACOCK: Hello.

ERB: Walter Erb here. How are you?

PEACOCK: Fine. What can I do for you, Mr. Erb?

ERB: We just got your letter here . . .

PEACOCK: Yes?

ERB: I think we'd better have a meeting.

Scene iv   Sabre rattling

The politicians and the doctors converge. Erb is accompanied by the Premier. Peacock is accompanied by E. W. Barootes—a Regina urologist. Barootes is tiny of stature but possessed of a vehement rhetorical skill.

BAROOTES: What I'm saying is that in this year, 1960, there are a great many things that are desperately wrong with our health care system in Saskatchewan and we need to look at all of it! Look at mental health with the Weyburn and North Battleford asylums—if you want to call them that. Prisons—that's all you can call them! What about places for geriatric and long term care? They are virtually absent in our province. What about rehabilitation centres? You know if there is one area of health care that is being cheated right now—if there is a group of sick and needy that are being cheated, it's the people who are under the purview and administration of the Department of Public Health! *Erb flinches.* Not the people who are paying premiums to Group Medical or M.S.I. or who are receiving care from their private physicians. We want to study the whole gambit!

DOUGLAS: *Responding calmly to this tirade.* Well, Dr. Barootes, I agree that these are vital facets—but the step we are undertaking right now is a prepaid medical insurance plan . . .

BAROOTES: That is best done by the citizen at large—and most easily funded!

DOUGLAS: I have no objection to widening the scope of the committee. We'll take your new terms of reference to the cabinet. We agree to recommend that the five principles—that is prepayment, universality, improved quality, government administration, and

Lee J. Campbell as Tommy Douglas

Sabre rattling
L. to R. Dr. E.W. Barootes, Alex Jupp, Tommy Douglas

mutual acceptability—these five principles will go in the preamble to the terms of reference rather than in the terms themselves . . . is that what you want?

BAROOTES: You can't dictate to the committee what decisions to make.

DOUGLAS: That was not our intention.

BAROOTES: Good. Now . . . *Consults notes.* we don't think there should be any government employees on the committee.

DOUGLAS: I think we've gone about as far as we can go.

ERB: Thank you, Gentlemen. This has been very constructive.

The meeting is over.

Scene v   Further delays

Everyone is back in his office. Douglas can be seen with his own secretary.

PEACOCK: February 8. Council is still of the opinion that the "five basic principles" outlined by the government should not be part of the body or of the preamble of the terms of reference. We feel a covering letter would be enough. However, we are prepared to concede this point. But the Council remains convinced that the composition of the committee which was recommended by us would assure a more unbiased study of the whole medical care program. Therefore the Council now recommends that a representative of labour and an appointee of the Chamber of Commerce should replace the government employees, thus adding two more lay members. G. W. Peacock.

ERB: February 10, Dear Dr. Peacock: With respect to the principles set forth in the preamble, I want to say that this does not imply that the members of the Committee must be in agreement with these principles. I would urge that your representatives be named as expeditiously as possible. J. Walter Erb.

PEACOCK: March 2. T. C. Douglas—copy to Mr. Erb. Dear Mr. Douglas: The district medical societies have informed the Council that they are unanimously opposed to the College appointing any representatives to the committee based on the terms of reference outlined in Mr. Erb's letter of February 8 and that the five basic principles should be removed from both the preamble and the committee's terms of reference.

DOUGLAS: *Struggling to remain civil.* Peacock, March 15. You *speak now of . . . Consulting a letter.* "terms of reference which are sufficiently broad to determine all the health needs of the public," which would entail a study of everything from dental services to the available supply of qualified nurses. The government is quite prepared to have the proposed committee conduct a broad investigation but this must be related to the provision of a medical care program!

With reference to the Chamber of Commerce and the trade unions, I have already indicated that the government would welcome this.

Insofar as the government's representation on the committee is concerned, I must insist that we reserve the right to name whatever persons we think are best qualified to interpret the government's views on this matter. We have not endeavoured to dictate to the College the nature of the personnel whom they will nominate and we feel the same privilege must be extended to the government.

The government has stated that no arbitrary time limit will be placed on the committee. It would seem fair to assume, however, that the people of the province will expect the committee to make reasonable progress.

May I remind you that the five basic principles have already been removed from the terms of reference and placed merely in the preamble. You confirmed this agreement and I must say it is extremely difficult to carry on negotiations if points upon which we have already reached agreement are to be renegotiated.

It will be necessary to make some announcement in the Legislature fairly soon and I hope it will be possible for the College to name its appointees at an early date. Yours sincerely, T. C. Douglas.

PEACOCK: March 29. Dear Mr. Douglas: The Council of the College of Physicians and Surgeons met in Regina on March 26 and reviewed all the correspondence between its officers and the government. Council has concluded that it had been agreed upon that the Advisory Committee could carry out a full, unobstructed study of all health needs as they relate to medical care of patients.

However the Council was disturbed to see and hear the statements made by the Premier and members of your government which refer only to the preconceived plan of your party to institute a compulsory, province wide and government controlled medical care plan.

The Council wished, therefore, to recall its resolution of October 25, 1959, as being opposed to such a plan and committed to a plan of support and extension of existing insurance plans. Having made this clear, the College therefore submits the names of its appointees to the committee, serving as individuals and at liberty to express their personal opinions: Doctors Jack F. C. Anderson of Saskatoon, Clarence J. Houston of Yorkton, and E. W. Barootes of Regina.

The lights fade slowly on the various offices. Barootes comes forward and addresses us.

BAROOTES: We had refused to join such an infamous group at first. It would have been like participating in a scheme of torture or some religious ceremony which you didn't agree with. But finally, when we thought the terms of reference had been broadened and that the Committee was not just a method of delivering up to Mr. Douglas the fatted calf he wanted, we agreed. And I must say that the late Mr. D. B. Rogers, at that time the editor of the Regina Leader Post and a neighbour of mine helped a great deal in our coming to that conclusion. He spoke to me many times about it and he finally suggested that we would get no more concessions from the government and that we needed to be on the committee, not just for our own sakes—but for the sake of the people of Saskatchewan, so that the opinions and advice of the medical profession could be at least heard, if not heeded.

With that, he exits and the lights fade out.

Scene vi   The election: Key man cells

Wilson is addressing a small group of doctors. The atmosphere is conspiratorial. Scott is the only one who doesn't seem to be taking this seriously. Wilson uses a chalk board for diagrams.

WILSON: I'm going to run through the organization as it's been laid out by the College and then you can ask questions, alright? Alright. First we've got five new committees: Community Relations, Medical Relations, Public Information, Medical Economics, Special Projects. Alright? Okay. Every doctor in the province is part of a cell group like this one and every cell group has a key man, who is responsible for passing information on up the tube or down it— whichever. That's me.

SCOTT: Sounds like Communism.

This was meant as a joke but isn't taken as one.

WILSON: It is based on the American Medical Association and it works very well there.

SCOTT: Sorry.

WILSON: Now, the Community Relations Committee will set up a speakers program on behalf of doctors for service clubs, labour organizations, churches, etc. Medical Relations is responsible for getting us information kits about the pros and cons of different kinds of insurance plans—you know, voluntary as opposed to compulsory plans. Public Information will deal with the media. Medical Economics refers to statistical information about potential costs. Finally, Special Projects: that's a kind of catch-all for special problems. All these committees are fully operational and have been since January. In addition we are requesting that each doctor in the province contribute to an emergency fund and the amount we are assessing is one hundred dollars.

DOCTOR A: In addition to our dues?

WILSON: In addition to our dues.

SCOTT: What's this for?

WILSON: A kind of war chest.

DOCTOR B: What are you going to do with it?

WILSON: Let me put it this way. This is an election campaign. Do you think the CCF is broke?

DOCTOR B: Oh.

WILSON: We're getting some professional public relations people in here. We're going to fight fire with fire.

SCOTT: *Mumbling.* Good God.

WILSON: Pardon, Dr. Scott?

SCOTT: This hundred dollar contribution . . .

WILSON: Yes?

SCOTT: . . . that you're charging us. Is it voluntary?

WILSON: Not exactly.

SCOTT: Is it compulsory?

WILSON: It's just an assessment.

SCOTT: And what if we don't want to pay?

WILSON: How many don't want to pay? *No response.* Don't be a shit disturber, Sid.

DOCTOR A: *Enthusiastically.* We're out to get rid of the CCF government, right?

WILSON: We're not saying that, okay? That's political. But if the Liberals get in, Thatcher and his boys say they'll hold a plebiscite. We'd stand a good chance of winning. We managed to defeat the plebiscites to set up more regional plans like Swift Current, didn't we? As for the other parties—the Conservatives say they are opposed to state medicine and I don't think we need to count Social Credit.

DOCTOR A: If we can keep the buggers from getting fifty percent of the vote we might win anyway. Did you see this in the Leader Post tonight? *Reading from a news clipping.* "Premier T. C. Douglas admitted Wednesday afternoon that his government will have a problem deciding whether or not the people want the CCF Medical Care Plan if the party is returned to office with less that half the popular vote. In 1956 they received only 45% of the popular vote. 'You know the solution,' Mr. Douglas told his supporters. 'Get out and work to gain a mandate for medical care!' "

WILSON: We'll remember that.

Blackout.

Scene vii   The campaign trail

In the darkness we hear a voice echoing over a public address system.

VOICE: The leader of the Liberal Party of Saskatchewan and the next premier of our province, Ross Thatcher!!!

Great applause. Thatcher appears in a spotlight. He is a belligerent scrapper of a politician who bounced from a hardware business in Moose Jaw left to the CFF and then right to the leadership of the Liberal Party. Now he is on the scent of blood.

THATCHER: *Roaring at a liberal rally.* The CCF is trying to ram their medical care plan down our throats! If the Douglas government is returned we will get a medical care plan. Alright. But suppose they are returned with only a 35% majority? Are the rest of us then going to have this forced on us by this minority?

Sweetly. The Liberal party if elected would, after the heat of the election has subsided, examine various plans, determine their costs and then the facts would be laid before the public and a plebiscite held. Although the CCF has had plebiscites on egg marketing, time, and liquor, they won't hold one on medical care. Why? *Rising to a climax.* I'll tell you why—because they are afraid to after the overwhelming defeat of such a proposal laid before residents of three rural health regions in recent years! That's why!

Applause.

VOICE: Ladies and Gentlemen, the Premier of Saskatchewan, Mr. Tommy Douglas!

Applause. The lights cross fade to Douglas.

DOUGLAS: *As if finishing a speech to a CCF rally.* Fifteen years ago when the people of Saskatchewan first elected a CCF government I promised that we would set up health services available to all without counting the ability of the individual to pay. I made a pledge with myself, long ago, in the years when I knew something about what it meant to get health services when you didn't have the money to pay for it—I made a pledge with myself that someday if I ever had anything to do with it, people would be able to get health services just as they are able to get educational services, as an inalienable right of being a citizen of a Christian country.

Applause.

CHAIRPERSON: Mr. Douglas has agreed to answer questions if there are any? Yes?

LADY: *From the audience.* Tommy, my question is not whether or not we should have medicare—but how come it has taken so long to bring it in?

AUDIENCE MEMBER: Yay!!!

Applause.

DOUGLAS: Well, the answer to that is simple. Money. You can't have a program like this unless you have a sound financial base for it. Mr. Diefenbaker—*There may be some hisses from the audience but Douglas stops them.* No—Mr. Diefenbaker has introduced a plan by which Ottawa now shares in the cost of a hospital insurance program with the provinces. We have had our own hospital care program for 13 years, so we can take this new federal money and use it to create a plan to pay doctors' bills.

A gentleman rises in the audience.

CHAIRPERSON: Dr. Hermitte.

HERMITTE: *British accent.* Mr. Douglas, in 1948 the British Labour Party promised a health plan to cost 80 million pounds a year. Now, in 1960, that plan costs 800 million pounds. Could Saskatchewan stand a similar rise in cost—say from 30 million to 300 million dollars?

DOUGLAS: Well, Doctor, 80 million pounds was about $7.50 a person—but even the present cost in Britain is only about $40.00 a person a year. It costs me much more in a private plan now.

If the British Health Plan had not been popular with the people why didn't the Conservatives toss it out when they returned to power in 1952? They knew then that if they had done that, the people would have tossed them out with it.

HERMITTE: That is an exhibition of the dishonesty of a political party in power. They wouldn't toss it out even though the plan is doing harm to the country. Good God, the taxes are crippling enough in Britain.

DOUGLAS: *To the audience.* I want you to get the logic of the doctor's position. He says this plan is so well liked that no party dare do away with it. If the people like it, why shouldn't they keep it? Doesn't the doctor believe in democracy? This smacks of a selfish attitude. The attitude is that those rich enough to pay their doctor bills easily must also pay heavy taxes to support a medical care plan.

There is a burst of applause and cheers and then all fades with the lights.

Scene viii   Elections: The doctors' panel

The lights rise on a group of doctors sitting motionless behind a table as if in a newspaper photograph. A reporter stands beside them.

REPORTER: Last night representatives from the College of Physicians and Surgeons held an information panel before a somewhat hostile audience in Regina.

The panel comes to life. There is a round of displeasure from the audience.

FIRST DOCTOR: The people in the Swift Current Health Region are happy with their Medical Care Plan because they don't know what it is costing them. When you add up personal taxes, deterrent fees and extra fees to specialists it is costing each person in the Swift Current Region $28.02. The voluntary plans—Group Medical and Medical Services Insurance, on the other hand provide the same services to their members for $20.00 per person!

Commotion from audience.

AUDIENCE MEMBER: That's because they don't insure anybody who can't pay the premiums!

SECOND DOCTOR: I am a general practicioner who worked for six years under the National Health Plan in Britain. It's compulsory. Once you sign up with a doctor you have to move out of his area or make a special application to the government to change . . .

AUDIENCE MEMBER: That's a lie!!!

SECOND DOCTOR: A doctor handles four times as many patients in spite of the fact that there is the same doctor-population ratio as here. Each year the money to be set aside for health is in direct competition with money for other government projects. The system is uneconomic and spoils the personal relationship between the physician and the patient.

AUDIENCE MEMBER: Why?

SECOND DOCTOR: Why? Because the doctor is an employee of the state rather than of the patient. Not only that, because the doctor is responsible to the government any kind of secrecy or confidentiality between the patient and the doctor is destroyed. The system over there is sickness conscious rather than health conscious. I even had a person visit my office who had no more wrong with him than a simple mosquito bite.

THIRD DOCTOR: Less than ten percent of the population of this province need help paying their doctors' bills. *Audience reacts scornfully.* Yes, any thoughtful examination of the statistics will show you that 90% are already covered through existing plans, government or voluntary, or that they can afford to pay bills. That leaves one man out of ten, one out of ten who needs help. Since one man needs crutches the government thinks that the other nine men ought to have them too. I question any claim that it is cheaper if all men wear crutches. No! Let the plans cover them and support the plans with grants where necessary. I suggest to you this is the most sensible alternative.

FOURTH DOCTOR: State medicine has always meant a loss of freedom for doctors because of interference by politicians and civil servants in the practice of medicine. A doctor has been trained to make scientific decisions on behalf of patients. Under the bureaucracy of state medicine, doctors would not be allowed to complete these scientific judgements. But there are much more insidious examples of political interference—cases where politicians would expect to get deferential treatment, perhaps. Government medical care means that the person is giving up responsibility for his own body. When you give that up you give up freedom of your body. The only question is when will the government assume responsibility for your mind.

AUDIENCE MEMBER: So what do you want from us?

AUDIENCE MEMBER: Who are you campaigning for?

AUDIENCE MEMBER: Ross Thatcher?

FIRST DOCTOR: We are not politicians. The CCF say that they will go ahead with this if they are elected. We regret becoming embroiled in a political matter.

Blackout.

Scene ix   The campaign heats up

ANNOUNCER: J. Stavely speaking in Pangman on behalf of the Liberal Party.

STAVELY: *Spotlight.* Socialism born in Saskatchewan must die

203

in its native province. We are witnessing its death throes now! *Spotlight out.*

ANNOUNCER: Mary Batten speaking in Estevan on behalf of the Liberal Party.

MARY BATTEN: *Spotlight.* In my home town of Humbolt every doctor has stated that he will leave if this plan goes into effect. CCF and Labour are moving together to form a new party and I dread what will happen to Saskatchewan when that happens. I tell you the farmer is going to be left out. The fact is that the CCF spends more on propaganda than people. This socialistic province has in the past 16 years become the poor relation of all the Canadian provinces. I say to you, throw off the shackles of socialism and bring industry, population and good government back to the province!

Blackout to whoops and applause.

Scene x   A few more words from your doctor

The old family physician hobbles in and sits in a large leather chair.

OLD G. P.:   *Extremely sincere.* Ladies, I appreciate your kind invitation to talk to you about health care. It is indicative to me of your real concern and interest in this vital topic. I am going to chat to you as if I were sitting with you in my office. Over the years, you and I have had many such chats. It is a relationship which I, as a Doctor, cherish. I am going to touch on some notions which I know are causing concern.

Today, your personal Doctor renders many services to you as women patients which do not really fall into the category of medical care in the strictest sense. Many times we have sat down in our office with a woman and discussed emotional situations which crop up during pregnancy or other critical periods in a woman's life.

We know that under Government administration we would be prevented from rendering these vital services. It could very easily be that this type of condition under state medicine must be referred to a psychiatric clinic or a mental hospital, a situation that I, as your personal physician would deplore.

Your Doctor is interested in you personally. He gives you personal services. He exhibits personal concern over you and your family and your problems. He is greatly disturbed about any possible change in this personal relationship. It could mean the end of your personal Doctor. *He relaxes and calls off stage.* How was that?

The high-powered imported P. R. man enters, furiously making notes on a clipboard.

P. R. MAN: Not bad, not bad. I wonder if you could just repeat the last line a little more sincerely, you know . . . *Laying it on with a trowel.* "He is greatly disturbed about any possible change in this personal relationship. It could mean the end of your personal Doctor."

OLD G. P.: *Trying to imitate the P. R. man.* He is greatly disturbed about any possible change in this personal relationship. It could mean the end of your personal Doctor.

P. R. MAN: *With a slight sob.* "It could mean the end of your personal Doctor."

OLD G. P.: *Following.* It could mean the end of your personal Doctor.

P. R. MAN: *Following.* Good. We have a few other things for you to try on for size . . . *He hands him a sheet of paper.* Read this for me, will you?

OLD G. P.: *Reading.* "A government controlled plan offers a latent but potential threat to certain dogmas of the Catholic Church relating to maternity, birth control and the state. The Pope has written a letter opposing state medicine." *He looks up.* That's a little strong, isn't it?

P. R. MAN: You gotta play all the angles. Trust me. I've been in this racket a long time. *Hands him another sheet.* How 'bout this one?

OLD G. P.: *Reading.* "The concept of universal medical coverage is not new and the approach by government to seek support is just the same as it was when first enunciated by Karl Marx in his Communistic Theories of the last century."

P. R. MAN: Good! And this one.

OLD G. P.: "Compulsion is an evil word. The government of Saskatchewan says that it is going to establish a compulsory program of prepaid medical care for the people of this province. Government claims that the universality of this plan is best for everyone. It is adopting the methods of an ancient tyrant by telling, not asking, the individual what he needs or wants. It should make us all cringe with fright to think of the dangerous future ahead under an elected body that has forgotten that government must be for the people, by the people and of the people."

P. R. MAN: *Delighted.* Fine! Fine! That'll get them!

The old g. p. is not convinced but he has to trust the expert. Blackout.

Scene xi   The wind up rally

Lights up on Douglas amid thunderous cheers and applause. Douglas is at his fiery best.

DOUGLAS: *Waving some of the same pamphlets that the old g. p. had been reading.* This is some of the most scurrilous trash that was ever printed in this province—hack writers hired by the College of Physicians and Surgeons have deliberately distorted the facts and figures.

THATCHER: *In another corner.* Douglas sounds like a broken gramophone record. Medicare, medicare, medicare. He hides behind this in order to avoid dealing with the real economic issues that face this province. Why doesn't he put it to a plebiscite?

DOUGLAS: I would rather lose fighting for a cause that will ultimately win than win fighting for a cause that will ultimately lose. We will not hide behind a plebiscite!

Tumultuous cheers.

GENESOVE: *Beside Thatcher.* Dr. Genesove, Member of Parliament, Liberal. A little honesty, a little integrity, a little consultation on the part of Mr. Douglas might have resulted in the development of some kind of plan on which both the legislature and the doctors could agree.

DOUGLAS: The doctors are saying that under a medical care plan you won't have a choice in what doctor you go to. How many of you have been in hospital under the government's hospital plan?

Many of the audience members put up their hands.

Were any of you told which hospital you must enter?

Massive "no". Douglas grins as our attention returns to Genesove.

GENESOVE: Can you blame the doctors? These men are not politicians. Living a life of personal identification with his patients' needs, the doctor was suddenly pitchforked into the middle of a political controversy. He didn't know what hit him!

DOUGLAS: If the doctors are intimidated into pledging not to co-operate with the CCF medical plan, the Saskatchewan College of Physicians and Surgeons could lose its licensing powers. No doctor need be intimidated. If one doctor's licence is cancelled because he gives service under the plan then I would remind the College that what the Legislature has given the Legislature can take away.

DOCTOR: *Standing with Genesove and Thatcher.* Mr. Douglas is now threatening the College against intimidating its members if the CCF is returned to power and implements its medical scheme. We believe the true action of intimidation is being performed by Mr. Douglas.

206

DOUGLAS: *Music swelling behind him.* The College's silly propaganda is being written by hack writers who got their training fighting again Truman's health plan in the United States, and against every progressive measure put forward on this continent in the last twenty years. They know that Saskatchewan is the beachhead. If they can't stop the plan here, they can't stop it sweeping across Canada.

One of the documents they have distributed tells us that the CCF plan threatens dogmas on birth control and maternity held by the Roman Catholic Church, and that the Pope had written a letter opposing the Truman plan.

Mr. Von Pilis who works for the Saskatchewan Farmers' Union read this in the paper and he telephoned the College to send him a copy of the Pope's letter. They told him they would have to call the American Medical Association in Chicago. When the letter arrived it was found to have been written not by Pope Pius but Msgr. Giovanni Montini. and it didn't relate to the Truman plan, it was written to a man in France. And it wasn't against state medicine, it was in favour of social medicine and vaccination of children.

Some people have questioned the wisdom of arousing the antagonism of doctors before an election. I'm not afraid of opposition if our cause is right. You and I have fought the battles of the common people with no other weapon than a good conscience and the support of the rank and file of the people and I ask no other support than that!

Great applause.

Election day will decide what kind of society the people want. There's one that I call the jungle society: this is the capitalist or free-enterise one that I call the jungle society: this is the capitalist or free-enterprise society, which believes in the principle of every man for himself. I don't believe in that kind of society and as long as there's a breath in my body I'm going to fight to change it.

I promise that if the CCF is re-elected, we will never stop working to build a society grounded upon the principle of co-operative living, social justice and human brotherhood.

The music swells and a thousand people rise to their feet.

Scene xii   Election night

The music has ended and Tommy Douglas appears in a spotlight alone, looking somewhat forlorn.

RADIO ANNOUNCER: *Heard over a speaker.* And now the final wrap up of today's election results. The Co-operative Commonwealth Federation Party under T. C. Douglas has been returned to office with an increased majority of two seats. The Liberal Party of Mr. Ross Thatcher has gained three more seats. In term of the popular vote, the CCF has received 40%. That is actually 4% less than it received in the last election. Mr. Douglas?

Douglas looks up.

Would you tell us what effect these election results will have on the CCF Medical Care Plan?

DOUGLAS: Yes.

He takes a moment. Then he straightens his shoulders and seems to grow larger.

The victory of my party is a clear mandate from the people of Saskatchewan to implement a medical care plan.

RADIO ANNOUNCER: Mr. Thatcher.

A light comes up on Ross Thatcher.

THATCHER: I serve notice that this is the beginning of a Liberal upsurge. I feel most emphatically that with such a minority vote the CCF party has no mandate whatsoever to proceed with state medicine.

RADIO ANNOUNCER: The College of Physicians and Surgeons.

PEACOCK: It must be clear to everyone that members of the College of Physicians and Surgeons remain united and unalterably opposed to compulsory government controlled medicine.

There is a moment with the parties frozen in their various stances as the lights slowly fade.

Act II

Scene i   The Thompson Commission

The lights rise on Barootes in a committee room.

BAROOTES: There was only one half afternoon of the Thompson Committee that I missed. The fact that we were being overruled, that nobody was listening to us, the bickering—finally it got to me in the stomach. I was so ill that I had to leave the meeting and I spent the rest of the afternoon and most of the night vomiting.

Erb enters, smiling grandly.

ERB: And so it gives me great pleasure to announce that the chairman of the Advisory Committee is Walter P. Thompson.

Doctor Thompson, a rather distinguished gentleman, takes his place at the head of the board table.

BAROOTES: Dr. Thompson is a brilliant geneticist, former president of the University of Saskatchewan, former teacher of mine in fact. However he was under the conviction that the best way for doctors to be paid was as he had always been paid as a member of a university faculty—by salary. On the Committee he would remind us of the Mayo Clinic where it is true that doctors are paid by salary— but I reminded him that the patients pay on a fee for service basis. It ought to be no concern to the patient how doctors divide up their money. The important thing is that the patients pay on a fee for service.

ERB: From the general public, Mrs. Beatrice Trew.

BAROOTES: She served on most of the CCF special committees.

ERB: J. H. Whiting.

BAROOTES: A farmer who admired W. P. Thompson and would always vote the same way.

ERB: From the government, T. J. Bentley.

BAROOTES: Former Minister of Health.

ERB: Dr. V. L. Matthews and Dr. F. B. Roth.

BAROOTES: Assistant Deputy and Deputy Minister of Health. Civil servants.

ERB: From the Medical School, Dr. I. Hilliard.

BAROOTES: Another university faculty member.

ERB: From the Saskatchewan Federation of Labour, Walter Shmishek.

BAROOTES: He was a radical back then—in favour of communes and things. He submitted a minority dissenting report in favour of salaried doctors and against an independent commission for the plan.

ERB: D. M. McPherson, representing the Chamber of Commerce.

BAROOTES: *Unqualified approval.* A brilliant business mind.

ERB: And of course from the College of Physicians and Surgeons, Doctors Anderson, Houston and Barootes.

BAROOTES: *Going to sit at the table with Thompson.* At any rate they gave us a lot of documents they wanted us to study. Whenever I or the other doctors on the Committee asked—nay demanded to circulate material that might provide a counter-balance to their arguments they would attach a note that said "This material is being forwarded at the request of Dr. Barootes." Condemned before it was even considered. They wanted us to study the systems of Britain and Norway and China—systems that had grown up in a society totally alien to our way of life or our way of thinking. It was a frustrating and unhappy experience.

Lights out.

Scene ii   Stalemate on the Thompson Committee*

Somewhere in the government offices. Thompson and Douglas enter. Erb is hurrying to catch up.

THOMPSON: *Distraught.* I tell you, Tommy, we're getting nowhere, absolutely nowhere! Houston, Barootes and Anderson are over there trying to filibuster every motion. We can't get one proposal off the ground. Those boys are digging in for the rest of their lives! If we keep on like this we won't see any kind of a medical care plan. How did I get on this damn committee?

DOUGLAS: You put yourself on it. You asked me.

*This dialogue while based on research obviously has to be speculative.

210

THOMPSON: Well, you didn't have to make me the chairman.

ERB: With respect, Dr. Thompson, you have to have patience.

THOMPSON: I've had a great deal of patience.

ERB: The doctors are fine people, under it all. They'll come round. You have to keep on talking.

THOMPSON: That is exactly what they want us to do, don't you see? Keep talking—talking—talking . . .

ERB: We can wait.

DOUGLAS: No.

ERB: *Startled.* We didn't put any limits on the time. We promised.

DOUGLAS: We can't wait. Next spring. That's the deadline. We're going to have the plan in operation before the end of April.

ERB: That's arbitrary.

DOUGLAS: No—necessary! Think, Walter. We want people to see it working for two full years before the next election.

THOMPSON: *Heated.* You could have had the report on your desk today, you know.

ERB: How?

THOMPSON: If you'd hand-picked a Royal Commission right from the start . . .

ERB: *Sarcastically.* Oh, the College would have loved that!

DOUGLAS: *Feeling some of the frustration.* The College! What's going wrong? We should be able to work hand in hand with the profession on this.

THOMPSON: I'm sorry, Tommy. But it's so damn frustrating!

DOUGLAS: *After a moment.* Well, then. How do we solve the problem.

ERB: Give it longer.

The other two look at him balefully.

ERB: What else can we do?

THOMPSON: In the terms of reference, you said you might ask for interim reports from time to time.

DOUGLAS: Yes?

THOMPSON: The committee might be able to produce an interim report within a reasonable period.

DOUGLAS: *Understanding.* Ah.

THOMPSON: Would that be enough to justify proceeding with the legislation?

DOUGLAS: How long would you need?

THOMPSON: Two or three months.

DOUGLAS: The Legislature will be called for October. Can you have the report in by early September?

THOMPSON: I think that is within reason.

DOUGLAS: Walter?

ERB: *To Thompson.* So you are going to ask the Committee to . . .

DOUGLAS: No, you as Minister of Health are going to make a written request for an interim report.

ERB: Yes, that's right.

Blackout.

Scene iii Moving fast

Lights rise on Erb and Douglas. Erb has a memo in his hand.

ERB: *Protesting.* But I can't do this!

DOUGLAS: *Exasperated.* Why not, for heaven's sake?

ERB: Well, the—the report isn't in yet.

DOUGLAS: We've got to move fast, Walter. We should have all the machinery geared up and ready to go the minute the legislation is passed.

ERB: *Reading the memo.* You want me to organize a Commission to run the medicare plan.

DOUGLAS: Precisely. Get names. Get people appointed.

ERB: But what if—what if the interim report comes in and they've found some way to work with the voluntary plans . . . it might change the whole administrative structure . . . .

DOUGLAS: Line up the Commission, Walter. If your people can't do it, I'll find somebody who can.

Blackout.

212

Scene iv   Douglas and the federal NDP

A reporter in a spotlight.

REPORTER: *Rapid reportage.* Negotiations between the Canadian Labour Congress and the CCF are now in the final stages and the birth of a new federal political party is imminent. The question of the future national leader of the New Democratic Party is a natural one. Of the names put forth, Saskatchewan's T. C. Douglas is the most prominent.

Spotlight up on Douglas.

DOUGLAS: I do not intend to leave Saskatchewan.

REPORTER: The wiry prairie spellbinder and former Baptist minister is under great pressure from those within the party to let his name stand for election.

DOUGLAS: I have no intention at this time of offering myself for the leadership of the new party.

REPORTER: In Saskatchewan, Mr. Douglas has led the CCF into five election campaigns and emerged victorious five times. The fact is that Douglas is a winner and the only logical choice as the first leader of a new political force on the Canadian scene.

DOUGLAS: If it is offered to me and if the Saskatchewan party is willing to let me go I will accept the leadership of the NDP.

REPORTER: David Lewis, National President of the party said yesterday he hoped Mr. Douglas will be given unanimous support at the founding convention to be held July 31 to August 3, 1961.

DOUGLAS: I am resigning my office as premier of Saskatchewan in order to seek the federal leadership of the New Democratic Party. However I shall remain in Saskatchewan until the CCF Medical Care Plan is established.

VOICE: *Heard over a P. A. system amid the sounds of a large crowd.* Ladies and Gentlemen, the votes have been counted. The results are: Hazen Argue, 380 votes. Tommy Douglas, 1,391 votes. The leader of the New Democratic Party of Canada is Tommy Douglas!

A thundering cheer. Blackout.

Scene v   A delegation

Lights up on Erb and Douglas.

213

DOUGLAS: Any word on the interim report?

ERB: Should be ready any day now.

DOUGLAS: It was supposed to be ready last week.

ERB: They tell me they've had a lot of trouble over there. I expect they'll come through by the end of the month.

DOUGLAS: *Gently.* Don't you think, then, you had better prepare a draft of the act?

ERB: Now?

DOUGLAS: So we can move as soon as the report comes in. If we have a rough draft we can incorporate additional material from the Thompson Committee.

ERB: But it might go in a totally other direction . . .

DOUGLAS: Walter, we're the government—we have to make the final decisions on this. Get your department working on it, alright?

ERB: We had better wait on Thompson.

DOUGLAS: We are waiting on Thompson . . . but we have to be ready.

ERB: My people aren't going to know what Thompson wants.

DOUGLAS: *Exploding.* To hell with the Thompson Committee! Your people know what we want!

At that moment a secretary's voice cuts in over the intercom.

SECRETARY: Dr. Dalgleish to see you, Sir.

Douglas looks inquiringly at Erb.

ERB: The new president of the College of Physicians and . . .

DOUGLAS: *Into the intercom.* Send him in.

Dalgleish enters. He represents a new phase of the dispute. He has a determined, gloves off approach.

DALGLEISH: We understand you have called the Legislature into special session next month.

DOUGLAS: That is true.

DALGLEISH: To pass medicare?

DOUGLAS: Yes.

DALGLEISH: And you haven't seen the recommendations of the Thompson Committee?

DOUGLAS: Not yet.

DALGLEISH: Then we have to assume that you have made up

your mind as to what kind of medical care program you want to propose to the Legislature. Do you want to tell us what it is?

DOUGLAS: Doctor, that will have to wait until we've considered the Thompson Committee's general recommendations.

DALGLEISH: Then there is no draft legislation.

DOUGLAS: *Looking at Erb.* No.

DALGLEISH: May I reiterate the College position on the scheme?

DOUGLAS: Please do.

DALGLEISH: Simply that we will not co-operate in fulfilling a compulsory, government administered scheme.

DOUGLAS: I'm afraid that is precisely what the government intends to proceed with . . . a universal, compulsory medical care plan administered by an agency responsible to the government.

Pause.

DALGLEISH: May we see the legislation before it is presented to the Legislature?

DOUGLAS: We usually discuss proposed legislation with any organization that might be affected by it.

DALGLEISH: Thank you, Mr. Douglas. *Exits.*

DOUGLAS: We shouldn't antagonize them.

Blackout.

Scene vi   The interim report—leaked?

Reporter in spotlight looking miserable.

REPORTER: September 29, 1961. In spite of a publication embargo which was to have been lifted later this week a summary of the report of the Thompson Committee on Medical Care, correct in virtually all details, appeared in the Toronto Star, Wednesday. Premier Douglas told the Leader Post that anyone who had been following the progress of the committee could supply details by guessing.

The committee majority report recommends a health plan with universal coverage, comprehensive benefits, a moderate premium and administration by a public medical care insurance commission. A minority report signed by the representatives of the doctors and by the representative from the Chamber of Commerce recommends a scheme utilizing the existing voluntary insurance plans.

Scene vii   The act

Walter Erb in the spotlight.

ERB: On October 5th I received a call in my office from Mr. Douglas' secretary requesting that I and my Deputy Minister come over immediately to the Executive Council Chambers to discuss certain urgent aspects of medicare. So we went over to the Executive Council Chambers and found Mr. Douglas together with the Federation of Labour and the vice-president of the Canadian Labour Congress and other gentlemen from the East—and Mr. Douglas had a copy of the draft Act. It was the first I or my Deputy had ever laid eyes on it.* And here these union people were getting some input into it. I thought this was most irregular. The doctors didn't get a chance to see it until it had become a bill and was tabled in the house.

I had mentioned to Mr. Douglas that the doctors had not seen it. Well, he said that it was up to me to call the doctors. Well, heh, heh, I didn't have the Act and of course he being the Premier—and he was carrying the ball to a great extent—that certainly it was he who should have invited the doctors because I don't know who invited the Canadian Federation of Labour. I thought it was quite irregular.

There is a transformation in Erb as he rises to introduce the legislation in the house. He is in his glory.

Mr. Speaker, I would like to say that I feel sure that all honourable members of this legislature share with me the pride that this historic responsibility and opportunity affords. For what we are in the course of doing here and will have done is that we shall have written a new magna carta for the health and well-being of the people of this province. Moreover I am sure that we shall set the pattern for other jurisdictions to follow in the years to come. It is in this spirit, then, Mr. Speaker, that I hope this bill will be debated and finally that future generations will acclaim the men and women of this legislature for their vision, their courage to pioneer and their sensitivity to human needs. I move second reading of Bill 1, an Act to provide for Payment for Services rendered to Certain Persons by Physicians and Certain other Persons.

There is loud parliamentary desk thumping. Walter Erb is glowing with pleasure. The lights fade.

---

*This speech was taken from an interview with Mr. Erb recorded in 1979. Perhaps he should not have spoken for his deputy minister. After the first production of this play the author received a letter from R. G. Ellis, Q.C., solicitor for the Department of Health: " . . . The Bill was initially drafted by me with the assistance of the Thompson Committee secretary, John Sparks, and under the general supervision of the Deputy Minister, Dr. Roth . . . There was no by-passing of the Deputy Minister . . . the reference to the labour officials being responsible for or influencing the contents of the Bill was the only part of the play that to my knowledge was inaccurate. Yours sincerely, R. G. Ellis."

Scene viii   Meanwhile back at the college

The assembly of the College of Physicians and Surgeons. There is a curious parallel between this body and the legislature. As the lights rise there is a great hubub of protest in progress.

CHAIRMAN: *Shouting over the noise.* Members of the College! Doctors! Gentlemen! Order! Order! There is a motion on the floor. Would you read the motion, please.

CLERK: "Therefore the College of Physicians and Surgeons of Saskatchewan reiterates its refusal to accept a government-controlled medical scheme as outlined in the legislative draft and declares that it cannot co-operate in such a plan."

CHAIRMAN: All those in favour? *Pause.* Any opposed? *He counts.* The motion is passed 441 to four. Would you read the second motion?

CLERK: "That the members of the Association continue to give service to their patients but agree that they will sign no individual contracts to service an overall health plan as presented in the draft Bill."

CHAIRMAN: Any discussion?

MEMBERS: Question, question!

CHAIRMAN: I will put the question. All those in favour of the motion? *Pause.* Opposed? *Pause.* The motion has been passed 443 to one.

Applause. Blackout.

Scene ix   New premier, new cabinet

We hear the sounds of yet another nominating convention.

VOICE: *Over a P. A. system.* Olaf Turnbull, 109 votes, Woodrow Lloyd, 425 votes. Mr. Turnbull?

TURNBULL'S VOICE: I would like to move that we make it unanimous and welcome the new Premier of Saskatchewan, Woodrow Lloyd!

A light rises on the reporter.

REPORTER: Last-night at the Trianon Ballroom in Regina the CCF-NDP elected a new leader to succeed Tommy Douglas: Woodrow Lloyd. A former Minister of Education and Provincial Treasurer, Mr. Lloyd has been described as a shy man who has

217

avoided the limelight and yet one of the most strongly principled men in the party.

A light rises on Woodrow Lloyd and his cabinet. Lloyd is a careful, quiet man—but implacable when convinced his course is the right one. The doctors may not know it yet but he will be their most formidable opponent.

LLOYD: I would like to announce a few changes in the cabinet. *He indicates the various members.* Allan Blakeney will become Provincial Treasurer, Olaf Turnbull will become Minister of Education in addition to his current responsibility for the Department of Co-operatives. Bill Davies will be taking over as Minister of Health and Walter Erb will be moving to Mr. Davies' former position as Minister of Public Works. *This is clearly a demotion for Erb and he knows it.* Yes?

REPORTER: Mr. Lloyd, has the fact that Mr. Davies has a background in organized labour anything to do with his appointment to the Health Portfolio?

LLOYD: *Smiling.* I don't think so.

REPORTER: Do you think you will have trouble negotiating an agreement with the medical profession?

LLOYD: I am not anticipating any difficulty.

Blackout.

Scene x   Standoff

Light rises on Davies, the new Minister of Health. He is on the phone.

DAVIES: Now that the legislation has been approved perhaps we could have an informal meeting. It could be useful.

Light rises on Dalgleish on the receiving end of the call.

DALGLEISH: I doubt that the Council will want to discuss the Act.

DAVIES: I was thinking we might discuss the make up of the Medical Care Insurance Commission.

DALGLEISH: We've already made our position clear.

DAVIES: But we could talk about it.

DALGLEISH: I'll take your request to Council and be in touch with you.

DAVIES: I'll look forward to hearing from you.

They hang up. Dalgleish picks up the phone again and it rings in Davies' office.

DALGLEISH: Mr. Davies, we do not wish to take part in a discussion on the organization of a Medical Care Commission.

DAVIES: Well, we were thinking of a more general exchange of views anyway—and maybe in the course of it we could talk about ways and means of implementing the Act and that would include the initial step of creating the Commission. We'd rather not proceed unilaterally on this. Do you have any dates free?

DALGLEISH: Not until the middle of December, anyway.

DAVIES: *Quickly.* How about the 12th or the 16th?

DALGLEISH: We'll get back to you.

He hangs up and the light goes down on him.

DAVIES: *Speaking into a dictaphone.* Dear Dr. Dalgleish, it is now the 28th of December and your reply has not yet been received. Yours sincerely, Bill Davies, Minister of Health. *He picks up a phone.* Hello, Doctor. I'm calling to ask if you would allow your name to be considered for appointment to the Medical Care Insurance Commission.

Lights up on Doctor A. at a phone.

DOCTOR A: I'd like to, Mr. Davies—but I think just under the present circumstances I had better not.

He remains motionless as lights rise on Doctor B.

DAVIES: *Phoning.* Excuse me, Doctor, but I'm calling to ask if you would allow your name to be considered for an appointment to the MCIC.

DOCTOR B: Given the attitude of my colleagues I have to say no—but thank you very much for asking me.

He remains motionless as the lights go up on Doctor C.

DOCTOR C: No, I couldn't. Thank you, but no.

Doctor C. freezes as the lights go up on Dr. Hjertaas, a Prince Albert surgeon.

HJERTAAS: You'd be better to get someone more central to the College.

DAVIES: We've tried.

HJERTAAS: Well, if I'm your last resort. . . .

Blackout.

Scene xi   The political front

Thatcher rises in the legislature.

THATCHER: Very respectfully, I ask the minister in view of his trade-union past, how many examples can he give of a union negotiator signing a contract in which he has no part in making the terms? How many? Having failed to persuade the college to enter into direct negotiations the new minister tried different tactics. He set up a commission and handed them the task of meeting with the doctors.

Mr. Speaker, how could the government reasonably expect that if the doctors would not sit down with the government they would sit down with a commission that after all was only a creature of the government?

The Thompson Committee in its report suggested that the chairman of the Commission should be a practising doctor. They suggested this in order to keep politics out of the appointment. Apparently the minister couldn't find a doctor who would act as a goon for the government—so it was a member of the civil service, a well known CCF party worker, Mr. D. D. Tansley who was persuaded, or maybe a better word, who was told to take the appointment. Now, Mr. Tansley may be a very able and capable civil servant; but I hope that the minister, before this session is through, will get up and tell the house just what he knows about medicine.

Scene xii   Getting the doctor's co-operation

Cross fade to Tansley.

TANSLEY: D. .D Tansley to Dr. Dalgleish. I and other members of the Commission will be happy to discuss any aspect of the plan with you or any group of your colleagues. We are willing to meet publicly or privately, formally or informally, at a location and time convenient to you.

Blackout.

VOICE OF REPORTER: Dr. Dalgleish?

Cross fade to reporter and Dalgleish.

DALGLEISH: Yes?

REPORTER: Will the profession refuse to meet with the government under any circumstances?

DALGLEISH: Let them repeal the Act.

REPORTER: *Amazed.* Do you think they'll do that?

Blackout.

Scene xiii The starting date

Lights rise on house.

DAVIES: Mr. Speaker, I would like to make an announcement on the orders of the day on a matter of some public importance. I am able to report this afternoon that the Medical Care Insurance Commission has recommended the starting date of the medical care plan. That date is July 1, 1962.

MEMBERS: Hear, hear!

THATCHER: *Scrambling to his feet.* Mr. Speaker, just a question! Could I just ask a question of the minister before he takes his seat? Could I ask the minister if he has any assurance that even on the July first date he can get the co-operation of the medical profession to make this plan work?

CCF FRONT BENCHER: Saboteur!

THATCHER: It is not sabotage at all. The July first date doesn't mean anything if you can't get some doctors to co-operate. I think it is a fair question.

DAVIES: I have confidence that some arrangements can be effective by July first. *Levelling at Thatcher.* Otherwise I should not bother making this announcement.

THATCHER: Mr. Speaker, may I now direct another question to the Minister of Health? Is the minister yet in a position to announce any progress which he has made in arranging for a meeting between his government and the medical profession in order to discuss the proposals for a medical plan?

DAVIES: Mr. Speaker, I have a letter from Dr. Dalgleish, the president of the College of Physicians and Surgeons, saying that a letter could be expected soon—but I have not received that letter.

The lights narrow on Davies dictating a letter.

DAVIES: March 22, 1962. Dear Dr. Dalgleish: I share to the full your concern over the present atmosphere which surrounds the relationship between organized medicine in the province and the Medical Care Plan. In my opinion it is only through a meeting that the air can be cleared.

The government has instructed me to invite representatives of the College to a meeting with members of the Cabinet at 10:00 a.m.,

221

Wednesday, March 28. It is proposed that the agenda be left open. Attendance at this meeting would be without prejudice to previously stated positions or conditions on either side. This date has been set as the latest possible time this year at which the government can consider amendments to the Saskatchewan Medical Care Insurance Act.

Lights broaden out to the house again.

THATCHER: Mr. Speaker, I should like to direct a question to the Minister of Health. Did the College of Physicians and Surgeons yesterday again decline to participate in the government medical plan? If so, how does the government intend to proceed in implementing their scheme without doctors?

DAVIES: Mr. Speaker, discussions took place yesterday between the College and the government. These talks were, as indicated, of an exploratory nature. We will continue this weekend. I believe that is all that is in the public interest that I should say at this time.

Cross fade to Scene 14.

Scene xiv   Negotiations

The weekend negotiating session. Davies walks into the scene from his place in the legislature. Lloyd, Erb and other cabinet ministers represent the government. There is a small delegation of doctors for whom Barootes is the chief spokesman. The scene opens with everyone talking at once. Finally Davies breaks through.

DAVIES: I'll tell you what—we'll take the Act and revamp it. We'll remove any suggestion that we're interfering in your professional business.

DOCTOR: Why don't you let the voluntary plans do it—just give them money for people who can't afford the premiums.

DAVIES: No, no. We can't give that many tax dollars to private companies. There has to be a public body responsible to the Legislature.

BAROOTES: *Bright idea.* Wait a minute. If that's the case, why don't you have a regulatory board—a kind of public body. It would, say, approve the private agencies—supervise their books—that sort of thing.

There is a moment while this sinks in.

DAVIES: *Slowly.* Maybe we're getting somewhere.

BAROOTES: *Picking up steam.* You know, this authority—let's call it a registration board—could make sure that the agencies have satisfactory reserves of funds, and that they cover your comprehensive range of benefits . . .

DAVIES: Could it be the MCIC itself?

BAROOTES: *Reacting.* I don't think so. It should maybe only have three members—one representing you, one us, and one agreeable to both sides.

DAVIES: Could it control the premium the agencies would charge?

BAROOTES: No.

DAVIES: The amount of extra billing done by the doctors?

BAROOTES: I wouldn't think so.

DAVIES: The essential services to be provided?

BAROOTES: The private agencies would compete to give the best possible range of services.

DAVIES: Well, let's think about it. You draw up the proposals and we'll look at them again.

The doctors leave the cabinet to discuss this new development.

ERB: I think we ought to go for it. I know it's only half the loaf— but it's better to take the half loaf when we can.

ANOTHER CABINET MINISTER: It would be universal, eh? Everybody would be in on it.

LLOYD: *Thinking hard.* No—"universally available." That's their distinction. People can opt in or out.

DAVIES: At least we're talking. I'm relieved we've gotten this far.

ERB: That's right. There's no use antagonizing them. They're providing a vital service. We can't have a plan without them . . .

LLOYD: *Suddenly.* The bastards are sucking us in!

Everyone turns to him.

They are. Medicare is nothing if it isn't the pooling of the resources of every individual in the province. No, we're not going to back down on this! We're going to control the costs of premiums, we're not going to continue designating indigents with special insurance cards. No! We won't back down!

A moment and then blackout.

Scene xv The amendments of April

Lights rise on the house. Davies is speaking and waving a newspaper.

DAVIES: Mr. Speaker, there was an editorial in yesterday's Leader Post entitled "Strait Jacket for the Doctors." *Reading from the newspaper.* "At the same time a well-authenticated report was in circulation that the government was on the verge of agreeing to work out an arrangement with the doctors until T. C. Douglas arrived in Regina." Mr. Douglas, so this report declares, brought pressure to bear on Premier Lloyd to scuttle negotiations. Quote: "One of the major plans in the NDP program is the compulsory, government-controlled, nation-wide medical care plan, and if the Saskatchewan government agreed to the proposed compromise with the doctors, this allegedly would have kicked the props out from under the NDP campaign." *Davies throws the paper down on his desk.* Mr. Speaker, I want to say that there is not a shred of substance to this so-called "well-authenticated report." I want to categorically deny that any such overt pressure has been applied by either Mr. Douglas or the New Democratic Party.

It is apparent indeed to me that the Leader Post continues to assist the cause of the Liberal party and their continued opposition to a provincial medical care plan in carrying out such an unworthy and unfounded report.

The amendments before us today establish the commission as agent of the beneficiary with respect to any matter relating to payment for an insured service. Provisions of this kind are common in insurance contracts and in fact there is one in the doctor sponsored MSI plan. These amendments do not seek to regiment or to confine or abuse any professional person in this province . . .

GOVERNMENT MLA'S: Hear, hear!

DAVIES: They actually seek a method whereby conflict can be reduced to a workable method. I want to say this too, in all sincerity, that while we wish to guard the right of some eight hundred physicians in the province, we must be mindful also of the needs and the right of some nine hundred thousand citizens that are also involved in this.

MLA'S: Hear, hear!

Meanwhile Thatcher has been outside the chamber conferring with Barootes and showing him the amendments which have been proposed. He now storms in.

DAVIES: Mr. Speaker, with these remarks I move that Bill No. 69 be now read a second time.

THATCHER: Mr. Speaker, Bill No. 69, an Act to amend the

Medical Care Insurance Act, is now before this Legislature. I think it is significant that it has been brought forward in the dying days of the session. I suggest it is also significant that this is the first real task the new Minister of Health has been given—to pilot it through. I rather doubt the former Minister of Health would have taken on this job. I think he had too much responsibility, too much integrity, probably that is why he is not the present Minister of Health.

The Minister of Health who spoke a moment ago was the former rough, tough, union boss . . . *Actually Davies is a notoriously gentle person.* He was a good one, opposing compulsory labour legislation, opposing compulsory arbitration. Yet today he has brought down a bill which imposes compulsory arbitration of a kind which is as vicious and authoritarian as any that I have ever seen. People say why should the Liberals worry about the doctors. They are wealthy, they are powerful, they can take care of themselves. I have had some people telephone me and ask me that question. Some of them won't even give their names. Mr. Speaker, if the government can take the rights of the doctors away today, they can take the rights of some other minority group away tomorrow. Who will be next?(!)

OPPOSITION MLA'S: Hear, hear!!

THATCHER: Is any minority group safe from these socialist planners? Liberalism believes in the rights and privileges of a minority and our party will defend those privileges at every opportunity, whether or not it is politically expedient.

Obviously the socialists will no doubt use their majority to ram this bill through the house. I think such a course should cause misgiving on the side of the house to your right, Mr. Speaker. Already there is a shortage of doctors in Saskatchewan . . .

CCFer: Here we go. . . .

THATCHER: It is steadily becoming more acute. Last night a gentleman telephoned me from Carlyle and he said, "Our doctor already said he is leaving town and going to North Dakota in a month." And they are pretty concerned about it. Our doctors don't have to remain in this province to be socialized!

CCFer: Nonsense!

THATCHER: Well, nonsense! Are you going to put them in jail to keep them here? Aren't you going to let them go if they don't want to be socialized? Mr. Speaker, the province of Ontario has stated they can take five hundred doctors. There is a place for five hundred doctors if some of ours want to go.

CCFer: Is that a threat?

THATCHER: No. No, it is no threat at all. In Manitoba when the federal Royal Commission was there, statements were made that Manitoba could take many of our doctors. Alberta has already taken some. They have said they can take more. The states of Minnesota and North Dakota can take more. Already this exodus has started. The time has come for this government to put the affairs of the people of Saskatchewan first and put the affairs of the NDP and Mr. Douglas second.

Cheers and desk thumping from the opposition.

Now what is the position of the Liberal party toward this whole political act?

CCFer: They have no position.

Guffaws from the government.

THATCHER: I repeat, the Liberal party does favour prepaid medical insurance, and there is a vast difference between that and state medicine. We opposed the third reading of the Act last fall; we feel obliged to vote against this bill today for the same reasons.

Thatcher sits down to Liberal desk thumping.

Scene xvi   Doctor's office

Wilson is finishing an examination. Liz is a rather nervous middle aged lady. She is coughing and her nose is congested.

WILSON: *Auscultation.* Deep breath. In, out. Again. Alright, Liz, if you want to get dressed. . . .

LIZ: Do I need to worry?

WILSON: Nope. I'll give you a few pills—should clear up in no time. You're not allergic to penicillin, are you?

LIZ: No.

WILSON: *Writing a prescription.* Good. Three times a day until they're gone.

LIZ: I wanted to ask you something else.

WILSON: Fire away.

LIZ: Are you thinking about leaving?

WILSON: *Stumped for the moment.* Leaving?

LIZ: Because of Medicare?

WILSON: *Switching gears.* Oh. *Pause.* Maybe.

LIZ: You can't. I mean it's not just me—I've got the kids—I mean it'd be alright for some families with healthy kids—what about Terry?

WILSON: I know. *Pause.* Listen, it's getting more and more—difficult—uncomfortable—to practise in Saskatchewan. I don't want to move away. This is my home, for heaven's sake. But there are some awfully tempting offers—and there's a point where staying here could be absolutely intolerable.

LIZ: I guess so.

WILSON: Maybe if the government feels enough pressure they'll get rid of the scheme—I don't know if the people—people like yourself, Liz—made some kind of move . . . the doctors have sure tried and we just come up against a stone wall.

LIZ: But what can we do?

Wilson shrugs hopelessly.

Organize a petition?

WILSON: Might help.

LIZ: Okay. I don't like getting into politics.

WILSON: Neither do I.

LIZ: But this really makes me mad. *Wilson does not want to say anything—he just hopes she will stay mad.* Okay.

WILSON: *As she starts to leave.* Hey, you forgot this.

He gives her the prescription and she rushes out, just barely avoiding a collision with Dr. Scott who is on his way in.

SCOTT: Is that woman alright?

WILSON: She's alright.

SCOTT: She looks like she's just heard she's terminal.

WILSON: A little hysterical, Liz is. But she's alright.

SCOTT: *Slumping into a chair.* It's been a long day. Are you finished?

WILSON: Yep—except I have to check in at Memorial on the way home. I've got a lovely duodenal coming along.

SCOTT: Yours or somebody elses?

WILSON: Nothing wrong with me that a change in government wouldn't cure.

SCOTT: *Getting up and stretching.* I'm on my way and praying that Kitty James doesn't decide to pop tonight.

WILSON: She due?

SCOTT: Overdue.

WILSON: Listen, I wanted to ask you something. What are we going to do about May 3rd?

SCOTT: What's happening May 3rd?

WILSON: Dammit, Sid! Don't you ever read your mail.

SCOTT: I'm behind.

WILSON: The general meeting of the College, Sid—Trianon Ballroom, Regina, May 3rd and 4th. It's going to be a good one. Everybody's up in arms.

SCOTT: *A little too sorry.* Gosh, Joe—I don't think I can get away.

WILSON: Would you be able to cover for us, then?

SCOTT: *Relieved to be off the hook.* Sure. *Second thought.* Who is "us"?

WILSON: Every doctor in town.

SCOTT: Every . . . even old Chess?

WILSON: Him, too.

SCOTT: Hope he survives the trip? What's up?

WILSON: It's these new amendments. They're going to be able to come after us—look at our books—decide if we're charging the patient too much—take us to court . . .

SCOTT: Aw, come on. . . .

WILSON: They are!

SCOTT: What are you afraid of, Joe?

WILSON: I'm not afraid. I'm mad—I'm mad at the CCF—I'm pissed off at guys like you who bury your head in the sand and just refuse to recognize what's coming . . .

SCOTT: No, you're scared. But what are you scared of? You know something? I've got an advanced carcinoma of the cervix in the morning. I know it has spread. I'm not sure if I can even save the woman. The family is out of work. They're not in any group plan. They can't afford major surgery. Thank God—thank God!—the cancer program will pay the shot! You tell me a family like that should go without medicare because you don't want anybody looking at your books and finding out you've been cheating on your income tax!

There is a long pause.

WILSON: You know me better than that.

SCOTT: I'm sorry. *Pause.* What's happening with us? I'm sorry.

WILSON: I guess I am scared. You're right. You know what I'm scared of, Sid—I mean if I get off the soap box?

SCOTT: What?

WILSON: I want to be my own boss—that's all. I don't want to work for anybody else. Just me and the patient. That's the way it's always been. I want it to stay that way.

SCOTT: *Mixed emotions.* Okay, Joe. Go to your meeting. I'll stay on call.

There is a moment and then blackout.

Scene xvii The Trianon Ball Room

The general meeting of the College. The room is in an uproar. Dalgleish is presiding while Barootes recounts the history of negotiations to date. He is in full rhetorical flight. As he is speaking, copies of the Leader Post will be passed among the delegates.

BAROOTES: And I say to you that never since the days of Charles the Second has there been such legislation reversing the civil rights and liberties of citizens!

The crowd explodes in agreement.

These amendments are deliberate, malicious and vicious. If this act is proceeded with it will be impossible for doctors to practise medicine in this province the way they have been accustomed to in the past. They leave us no recourse if we are sued by some crackpot.

The government wants us to try it for a year. Well, I want to know at the end of the year just who is going to decide whether or not the plan is satisfactory. Which of you knows any social security measure once enacted that has ever been rescinded? And that is where we stand today. Thank you.

There is a standing ovation.

DOCTOR: *Rising in the audience and holding up a newspaper.* Mr. Chairman! Mr. Chairman! I think the meeting should know that the morning edition of the Leader Post has just come out. Look at the headlines. "CCF Cabinet Minister to Sit as Independent, Erb Quits Government Over Medicare!"

The meeting goes wild. Through the commotion, Premier Lloyd makes his way to the platform. He shakes hands with those on the platform.

DALGLEISH: Order! Order! Order!

Silence is established.

DALGLEISH: Premier Lloyd has asked to speak to this meeting and it is proper that we should listen to what he has to say. Without further ado, may I introduce Premier Woodrow Lloyd.

The applause is sparse and deliberately unenthusiastic.

LLOYD: Mr. Chairman, Physicians and Surgeons of Saskatchewan. Basically the issue at stake is a very simple one: a common, overriding objection to promote and protect the health of our people. In this a great responsibility rests on the government and the medical profession. I must say that I find disconcerting some suggestions that governments do not have such a responsibility and moreover are not to be trusted when they attempt to discharge it.

The doctors show exaggerated boredom.

Emphatically. Attacks on the integrity of government as an institution can undermine the foundations of the very liberties we prize so much.

Some hissing.

The people of Saskatchewan for many years have clearly expressed their concern for the provision of adequate health services. They have done so because experience has indicated the inability of most of us to adequately provide such services for ourselves and our families. I express confidence that misgivings or fears regarding medical care insurance will be dissipated once you give the program a fair trial.

Laughter.

I am aware of, and greatly respect, your concern for a proper doctor-patient relationship. If this relationship is adequately protected under existing voluntary plans I am unable to see how its essential components can in any way be interfered with by the Medical Care Insurance Act . . .

VOICES: Wrong! Wrong!

DALGLEISH: Please don't interrupt the speaker.

LLOYD: May I say, Doctor, I'm used to it.

This wins a certain amount of respect.

Patients will be free to select the doctor in whom they place their trust and doctors in turn will be free to accept this trust.

Surely the depth and true meaning of this relationship cannot be altered by the manner in which the physician is remunerated.

There is another side. There has been a great deal of discussion recently over concepts of rights—the rights of individuals, the rights of groups, the rights of professions. I want to deal with the rights and proper expectations of the people of Saskatchewan. I repeat that, as patients, we are perfectly willing to place matters involving medical judgements entirely in the hands of a highly-skilled group such as you are. In enacting the Medical Care Insurance Act, however, we have said that we as consumers of medical services, and as taxpayers, *with emphasis,* have a right to a say in how we pay our medical bills.

My appeal is to what has been termed "the ancient wisdom of your profession." We seek not to change the ends of medicine. We do seek to find ways and means to adapt the financing of medicare to twentieth century society and the legitimate expectations of that society. In this the "ancient mission" need not be lost. Its achievement can be advanced. I invite you to join in a bold attempt to consolidate past gains and to move toward new horizons in the field of medical care.

There is silence. Dalgleish gets up.

DALGLEISH: Thank you, Mr. Lloyd. We appreciate your coming here, but I and many of my colleagues regret that nothing new has been brought forward for discussion at this meeting. Now, members of your cabinet and others have repeatedly stated that the views of the medical profession in this province have been represented hitherto only by the council or hierarchy of the College. Today you see over two thirds of the nine hundred or so doctors of Saskatchewan. And so, without prior consultation of this body, I propose to give the opportunity to individual doctors to indicate personally how they feel. All those opposed to the plan, the Act, the amendments, and who refuse to give services under it, please stand.

Most stand applauding.

DALGLEISH: *After letting the message sink in.* Those doctors who wished to state their approval of the plan and indicate they would like to participate, please stand.

There is general amusement. Finally one rises.

DOCTOR: Mr. Chairman, your question actually involves three different issues . . .

He is hissed and booed. Finally he gives up and sits down.

DALGLEISH: Order, order.

ANOTHER DOCTOR: *Rising.* Mr. President, I represent a delegation from the Swift Current Health Region where, as everybody knows, a form of medicare has been in effect for a number of years. You could say it has been given a "fair trial" in Swift Current. I and my delegation would like to move that we withdraw medical services in this province on July 1st, unless the Medical Care Act is repealed.

Another uproar breaks out. After speaking to the doctors on the platform, Lloyd leaves to be pounced on by reporters. The lights narrow slowly.

REPORTER A: Mr. Lloyd, were you surprised by the vote against the plan?

LLOYD: No, not really . . .

REPORTER B: Are you going to withdraw the plan?

LLOYD: No—as I said earlier, we intend to continue.

REPORTER C: Did you know about Mr. Erb's resignation?

LLOYD: I received it early this morning.

REPORTER A: Did you expect it?

LLOYD: It came as something of a surprise.

REPORTER C: Do you care to comment?

The lights now narrow on the premier.

LLOYD: It has always been the fate of reform parties to have some of the faint-hearted fall by the wayside. Each time the movement has emerged stronger than before.

Pause and blackout.

Scene xviii   The K.O.D.

A highway near Grenfell. A teenager in a militia uniform flags down a motorist.

MOTORIST: *Rolling down his window.* What's wrong?

SOLDIER A: Are you going into Grenfell, sir?

MOTORIST: Well, I was hoping to.

SOLDIER A: Are you going to the anti-medicare meeting?

MOTORIST: I don't think so.

SOLDIER A: Thank you, sir. Go right ahead.

He starts up again and another young soldier pops out and flags him down.

SOLDIER B: Excuse me, sir?

MOTORIST: Yes?

SOLDIER B: Are you going to the anti-medicare meeting?

MOTORIST: No, I'm not.

SOLDIER B: Go right ahead, sir.

The motorist is confronted by yet another soldier.

SOLDIER C: Would you roll down your window, sir?

MOTORIST: What is it?

SOLDIER C: Are you going to . . .

MOTORIST: The anti-medicare meeting?

SOLDIER C: That's right.

MOTORIST: Okay.

SOLDIER C: Pardon?

MOTORIST: Why not?

SOLDIER C: *Uncertain.* You're going there?

MOTORIST: Yep.

SOLDIER C: Would you give me your name and address, sir?

MOTORIST: Jim Blake, 1024 Railway, Melfort.

SOLDIER C: *Handing him a white envelope.* Here you are, sir.

MOTORIST: What's in this?

SOLDIER C: Oh, some pamphlets, some petitions and some "Freedom for our Doctors" windshield stickers. If you need parking, Lance Bombardier Parker will help you at the end of the street.

MOTORIST: Thanks—by the way, would you mind telling me something?

SOLDIER C: What's that?

MOTORIST: Why is the Canadian Militia handing out this anti-medicare stuff?

SOLDIER C: Oh, we're not.

MOTORIST: Say that again?

SOLDIER C: We're just directing traffic, sir.

Cross fade to the rally. Liz, Wilson's patient from Scene 16, is on the platform.

LIZ: There are 300 people here from 36 different communities. Surely we can act together to keep our doctors. *Reading a formal motion.* I move that we form an organization, designated as the Keep Our Doctors Committee, with the sole purpose of circulating petitions within the areas represented here.

MAN: *From the crowd.* I second that motion!

LIZ: All in favour? Carried!

Sound of the militia marching to a bugle band. Lights slowly fade to the end of the act.

Act III

Scene i   Signs and letters

Wilson enters and nails up several signs. They read as follows:

TO OUR PATIENTS

This Office Will be Closed After
July 1st, 1962
We Do Not Intend To Carry On Practice
Under
The Saskatchewan Medical Care Insurance Act

Not until now do the houselights go down. We hear voices from every side quoting letters sent to the various provincial newspapers.

VOICE A: *Man.* Dear Editor: These are truly dedicated men, the finest and the kindest that could be found anywhere. The plan is just a vote catcher . . . *Voice B begins and Voice A continues.* . . . a gimmick to appeal to the selfish, the niggardly, the money pinchers and a few deserving unfortunates just to help a few top socialists accelerate ushering in the welfare state-socialism.

           VOICE B: Dear Editor: Regardless of your own profession, would you honestly want it socialized? . . . *Voice C begins.* . . . So let us not wait until it is too late!

           VOICE C: Dear Editor: It is disgusting to say the least that the doctors are playing politics and therefore disregarding their duty . . . *Voice D begins.* . . . to serve the people to the best of their ability.

           VOICE D: Dear Editor: It is the same tactic announced by Joseph Goebbels in 1933 when he said . . . *Voice E begins.* . . . "The physician at the sick bed must realize the nation and its future are above everything." Signed Worried.

           VOICE E: Dear Editor: Some people will have a funny way of laughing . . . *Voice F begins.* . . . when they drive our good doctors out of the province. They need doctors too. Signed Freedom.

VOICE F: There is a tendency to brush aside the humanitarian side of life but this cannot destroy the need for helping each other. Signed Justice.

WOMAN: *Solo.* Dear Editor, I am married and expecting a baby. I am called an expectant mother.

I am going to have the baby on July 2, (July 1 being a holiday). What I would like to know is, is this here an emergency? To me, it sure is.

If the doctor will not deliver my baby, should I ask the mailman—he is a kind looking man and he delivers things. In this case should I send the bill to the Postmaster-General?

Signed: Pregnant and Puzzled.

Scott enters, sees Wilson's signs and pulls them down. Exit. Spot lights begin to rise on speakers around the playing area. First on Liz standing before a microphone.

LIZ: These are dark days for Saskatchewan residents but they are darker indeed for our doctors . . . and all because a promise was broken by one man and the breaking of that promise endorsed by his successor.

A light on Dr. Bachynski standing in the audience.

BACHYNSKI: The fifth of your principles required acceptability to those providing and those receiving services. If the majority of the medical profession does not consider your plan acceptable, will you then find it more convenient to forget your principles and force them into submission, or what is the plan?

A light on Douglas answering Bachynski's question.

DOUGLAS: I would think, Doctor, that's somewhat of a reflection on my integrity. I have been in the public life of this province for twenty-five years, Doctor, I don't know how long you've been here, but I have been in the public life of this province for twenty-five years and no one, not even my political opponents have suggested that I have forgotten my principles. You can no more take a doctor and make him practise medicine than you can take a horse to the water and make him drink. We recognize that.

LIZ: Yes, a pledge has been well and truly broken—and what degradation and bitterness it has left in its wake. Small wonder our doctors have become so disillusioned. I have personally talked with doctor after doctor and without exception they feel very badly about having to take the stand they have taken—to provide only emergency service at no cost to the patient—instead of normal practice. It goes against their basic principles as doctors. But they cannot, and will not surrender the freedom to which all men are entitled in a free country—I wouldn't, would you?

235

Lights fade on everyone except Douglas.

ANNOUNCER'S VOICE: And so the last of the polls are reporting and it looks like Mr. Diefenbaker will be leading a minority Conservative government in Ottawa. In Saskatchewan the Conservatives have been victorious in most ridings, including Regina where Tommy Douglas, campaigning once more on the medicare issue, went down to a resounding defeat.

DOUGLAS: Naturally I'm disappointed. But I have to say that the words of the poet come to mind—

> A little I'm hurt but yet not slain
> I'll but lie down and bleed awhile
> And then I'll rise and fight again.

Lights fade on Douglas. Scott arrives and puts up signs saying that his office will be open on July 1 and that he intends to practise under the Act. He leaves. Wilson returns with more of his signs and puts them over Scott's.

WILSON: *Addressing the audience.* I put it to you. You accept our advice in your homes on problems very vital to you concerning yourself and your family that an appendix or a gall bladder or a stomach ulcer must come out. You accept these decisions from us. Now we are advising you again. We cannot object to government collecting money to pay medical bills. We do object to government monopoly and we do object to the many unnecessary controls with the payment of medical bills. We object to conscription of doctors and the strangulation of our profession, and we fear what else will come in the future if this Act comes into force.

Wilson leaves and a reporter appears in a light to one side of the playing area.

REPORTER: The Attorney General of Saskatchewan, Robert A. Walker, speaking in Birch Hills Friday night. . . .

Walker appears in another spotlight.

WALKER: I would call the doctors' attention to the criminal code of Canada which states "Everyone who wilfully breaks a contract knowing that the probably consequence will be to endanger human life is liable to imprisonment for five years."

The two spotlights fade. Wilson and Scott confront one another over the signs.

WILSON: On July first, why don't you take your holidays?

SCOTT: Not on your life.

WILSON: You want to break up our partnership?

SCOTT: Is that the choice?

WILSON: You could look at it that way.

SCOTT: No holidays.

WILSON: That's it, then.

SCOTT: That's it.

The lights fade slowly out on Scott and Wilson as a chorus of Keep Our Doctors committee members keep the hysteria mounting.

K.O.D. meeting

Keep our doctors meeting, Legislative Building 1962

237

K.O.D. CHORUS: 46,000 Saskatchewan citizens petitioned against the cold, ruthless, naked power of dictatorial might. 46,000 people were denied fair consideration. Write, telephone, wire your MLA and insist that he speak for you as your elected representative. Stop implementation of medicare plan, July 1, unless agreement can be reached with doctors. Sponsored by your Keep our Doctors Committee.

MEMBER OF THE CHORUS: J. Walter Erb, former Minister of Health.

ERB: The situation is critical and the government must take the step that any responsible government would—and that is to back down!

K.O.D. CHORUS: Who will care for your children?
Who will care for your loved ones?
Who will be your family doctor
After July first.
Will illness wait for Premier Lloyd's Flying Doctor?

REPORTER: July first seems to hold a peculiar jinx in the history of Regina. On July first, 1912 the city was devastated by the Regina Cyclone. On July first, 1935 the Regina Riot took place. Tomorrow, July first, 1962 the doctors go on strike.

K.O.D. CHORUS: Your doctor is leaving!! It will be too late when the pain comes in the middle of the night, when the baby starts choking, when the good farm worker is mangled in the power take-off, when the car plunges off the road and scatters dusty bodies in the ditch, when the heart attack comes . . . if this sounds emotional, even hysterical, good.

REPORTER: Last minute attempts to bring the two sides together have failed and the fear in the air is almost tangible.

Scene ii   Reporters

A highway gas station east of Regina. A car drives up to the pumps and a bell rings inside the garage. The driver is "Reporter A", a camera equipped woman journalist from a large eastern daily. Eventually the garage attendant emerges wiping grease off his hands.

ATTENDANT: Mornin' ma'am.

REPORTER A: *Rolling down the window.* Good morning!

ATTENDANT: Fill 'er up?

REPORTER A: Yes, please. And check the oil, too, okay?

ATTENDANT: Sure thing.

He goes to work. The reporter gets out of the car and watches him.

REPORTER A: Nice day?

ATTENDANT: Couldn't be better. *Pause. Attendant notices licence plates.* All the way from Ontario?

REPORTER A: That's right.

ATTENDANT: Heading out to the coast?

REPORTER A: Oh no. I'm from the Telly.

ATTENDANT: The what?

REPORTER A: The Toronto Telegram. *Pause.* The newspaper.

ATTENDANT: *Vaguely.* Oh, yeah. She's down a quart. Want me to give her a squirt?

REPORTER A: I guess you'd better. Say . . .

ATTENDANT: 10/30?

REPORTER A: Why not? Say . . .

ATTENDANT: Yeah?

REPORTER A: What do you think of the doctors' strike?

ATTENDANT: Oh, I don't pay it much mind.

REPORTER A: Really?

ATTENDANT: I'm pretty healthy—I don't get sick much.

REPORTER A: So you don't feel it's very important.

She is scratching a few notes.

ATTENDANT: Fairly important to some folk, I guess—but I don't get too involved. *Closing hood.* That should do you.

REPORTER A: Do you mind if I take your picture?

ATTENDANT: *Wiping his hands.* I'm not 'zactly presentable. . . .

REPORTER A: *Snapping the shutter.* Don't worry, you look just fine. How much was that?

ATTENDANT: $4.20—with the oil. Thank you, ma'am.

Reporter A drives off and the attendant is about to return to the garage when Reporter B arrives.

REPORTER B: Fill it up, please.

ATTENDANT: Okee dokee.

REPORTER B: How're you doing?

ATTENDANT: Oh, not bad, not bad. Want the oil checked?

239

REPORTER B: Naw. Should be okay. I hear the doctors are on strike.

ATTENDANT: So they say.

REPORTER B: How do you feel about it?

ATTENDANT: Well, I hope they don't stay out too long.

REPORTER B: *After waiting a moment to see if he is going to add anything.* Do you think they have a right to strike?

ATTENDANT: I never thought of it. Maybe not. That'll be three bucks even.

REPORTER B: *Getting out of the car with a camera.* Do you mind if I take your picture?

ATTENDANT: *Posing.* Go right ahead.

REPORTER B: *Taking the picture.* Thanks. Keep the change.

ATTENDANT: Thank you. What paper are you from?

REPORTER B: Winnipeg Tribune.

He drives off and Reporter C arrives.

ATTENDANT: What can I do for you, ma'am?

REPORTER C: Hi.

ATTENDANT: Hi.

REPORTER C: Fill it up, okay?

ATTENDANT: Right.

REPORTER C: *Getting out of the car with a tape recorder.* I'm with the CBC.

ATTENDANT: No kidding?

REPORTER C: No, I'm serious.

ATTENDANT: I suppose you want to ask me about the doctors' strike.

REPORTER C: *Surprised.* Why, yes.

ATTENDANT: Fire away.

REPORTER C: *Into the machine.* Do you have any reactions to the current withdrawal of services by members of Saskatchewan's College of Physicians and Surgeons?

ATTENDANT: One or two.

REPORTER C: Yes?

ATTENDANT: Well, first of all it's sure bringing a lot of reporters into the province. Now, in regard to the doctors themselves: I'm not sure that a doctor should go on strike—granted that the government is trying to ram something down their throats but even so, you'd think they could talk the whole thing out and get it stright . . .

REPORTER C: Good—that's first rate. *She shuts off the tape recorder.*

ATTENDANT: *Not to be stopped now.* On the other hand you've got to ask yourself whether we need this health insurance at all. Now my wife she's a great believer in insurance. If you listened to her you'd be turning over your whole pay check to insurance companies--life insurance, death insurance, this insurance, that insurance . . .

REPORTER C: *In her car.* Thanks a lot. How much was that?

ATTENDANT: $3.72.

REPORTER C: Here you are.

ATTENDANT: But me, I couldn't care less—you know what I mean? Just live from day to day—take things as they come. You're from the CBC—it's like the Happy Gang, you see? I listen to the Happy Gang all the time. *Singing.* Keep happy with the Happy Gang—Keep happy with the Happy Gang—Keep happy with the Happy Gang . . .

REPORTER C: *Revving up.* I've gotta go. Thanks!

ATTENDANT: *Shouting behind her.* Because if you're happy and healthy, to heck with being wealthy, eh? *Waving.* Bye. . . .

Lights fast fade to black.

Scene iii   Tragedy

A spotlight rises on a grief sticken woman. She is Vicky Derhousoff. The following is taken from a newspaper interview and indicates a woman without many resources, operating at the limits of those resources.

VICKY: My baby died in my arms Sunday and I blame the government of Saskatchewan. If they had not forced the doctors to strike, my Carl would be alive today.

He took a slight fever about noon Saturday and I thought it was teething rash. I kept him clean and comfortable and fed him only liquids the rest of the day and just water through the night. Pete, my husband, and I took turns watching over him through the night. Sunday morning I noticed he was covered in red splotches and realized he was really sick.

Pete called the operator in Preeceville and asked her where any doctors might be located. There are two there. She told him both doctors had left messages that they would not accept any calls after midnight and had gone away for a vacation. My husband then called the hospital in Preeceville and asked the nurse if she would look at the baby if he was brought in. She told him she could not give any advice and said we should take the baby into the emergency centre at Yorkton.

Mr. Gregory at the general store said he would drive us—after Pete told him he was not sure if our old car would be able to go fast enough. I held my baby in my arms beside my husband in the back seat. Mr. Gregory and his wife Mary were in the front.

It was an awful feeling to go past the hospital in Preeceville and the other one in Canora and know that ordinary help was that close.

All during the ride Carl seemed to be sleeping but he was breathing kind of funny. Just as we got a few miles from Yorkton he suddenly stiffened in my arms and stopped breathing.

Screaming. "Pete! He's dead!"

He took him from me and started to breathe into the baby's mouth. He kept doing that the rest of the way to the hospital.

When the doctor told me Carl was dead I nearly fainted.

I don't blame the doctors, I know how they must feel. I wouldn't want anything crammed down my throat. In fact, I have been against the medical plan from the start. It's too darned expensive and Pete has been out of a job since last fall.

Light slowly fades on her. Meanwhile the reporter appears in another spot.

REPORTER: Mrs. Vicky Derhousoff of Usherville, Saskatchewan whose child died apparently of meningitis, en route to hospital in Yorkton, 90 miles away. We have Dr. Sam Landa on the line from Saskatoon. Dr. Landa is responsible for the doctors' emergency service. Dr. Landa, do you have any comments to make on this tragic situation?

Landa appears with a telephone. He looks and sounds fatigued.

LANDA: This is exactly what we were afraid of. We are trying to keep the emergency system working. It's all in place and we have the province fairly well covered. Doctors are working around the clock. But this little boy—this little boy may have had a very rapid form of meningitis—we won't know until after the coroner's report is in— and it might not have been possible to do anything for him—I don't know—but anyway nobody wanted anything like this to happen.

REPORTER: The doctors who are staffing the emergency centres—are they working under the medical health care plan?

LANDA: No, we won't work under that scheme.

REPORTER: You're working for free, then?

LANDA: Yes.

Lights fade to black.

Scene iv   Emergency

Scott's office. Scott bursts in shouting back over his shoulder.

SCOTT: No—take him down to the Memorial—I don't care! Right away! I'll try to get somebody.

He dials the phone. Lights come up on Wilson who has obviously been at home with his feet up. He picks up the receiver casually.

WILSON: Yes?

SCOTT: Joe, I need an anaesthetist.

WILSON: Sorry, Sid, no deal.

SCOTT: I've got a kid with acute appendicitis here. I have to go in.

WILSON: You know what to do.

Sound of a siren in the background.

SCOTT: I don't have time to worry about the emergency set up.

WILSON: Sorry, Sid.

SCOTT: Joe, this kid is going to die.   *No answer.* You son of a bitch! Listen, Joe, you've got ten minutes to get down to the Memorial Hospital. If I don't see you there and that kid dies, I'm going to the media, Joe. I'll tell them the whole story and by tomorrow everybody in this damn country is going to hear that a kid died tonight because Joe Wilson refused attendance!

WILSON: *After a moment.* You're bluffing.

SCOTT: Try me.

WILSON: Hell. *Pause.* Alright, I'm on my way—but you haven't heard the last of this. You're going to pay.

However Scott has hung up and is reaching for his car keys.

Blackout.

Scene v Airlift

Lobby of the Regina airport.

P.A. ANNOUNCEMENT: Trans Canada Vangard Service from Montreal, Toronto and Winnipeg is arriving. Passengers may be met at Gate 1.

REPORTER: *In the lobby.* Nine British doctors, including a woman are arriving here today after a twelve hour flight from London to begin short-term practice to fill vacancies created by the current doctor shortage in Saskatchewan.

The doctors begin to file through the lobby.

REPORTER: *Approaching one of them.* Excuse me, are you one of the doctors the government is bringing in?

DOCTOR A: *Not stopping.* I suppose—yes.

REPORTER: Would you mind answering a few questions?

DOCTOR A: I'd very much rather not. Thank you.

REPORTER: *Chasing another.* Excuse me . . .

DOCTOR B: Are you from the press?

REPORTER: Yes.

DOCTOR B: Sorry.

REPORTER: *To yet another.* Would you mind if I asked you a few questions? *No response. The reporter turns back to the audience.* The doctors remained tight-lipped when they stepped from the TCA Vanguard aircraft.

The reporter has missed the woman doctor.

DR. FISHER: I'm one, too.

REPORTER: Oh! I'm sorry.

DR. FISHER: Well, you see, I heard about it and I thought that— well, that it shouldn't happen, you understand. So I thought I'd come over and see if I could help. And here I am.

REPORTER: Did you sign a contract?

DR. FISHER: I don't think any of us signed contracts—but we have a guarantee from MCIC—is that what you call the agency?— that our air fare, accomodation, registry with the College of Physicians and Surgeons, all that sort of thing will be taken care of, you see—oh, yes—and that they will meet us and give us an allowance while we are getting settled—*Catching sight of someone off.* Oh, hello there. . . .

Exits.

REPORTER: *Speaking to glum gentleman who has been waiting.* Are you here to meet someone?

DR. LAIDLAW: No.

REPORTER: *To the audience.* As the group left the airport they passed by one of Regina's well known physicians, Dr. J. M. Laidlaw, who is leaving Saskatchewan to take up practice in Illinois. *To Laidlaw.* Why are you going?

LAIDLAW: I'm afraid of the government.

REPORTER: May I quote you?

LAIDLAW: *With a sigh.* Why not?

Blackout.

Scene vi An imported doctor and the Sisters of Charity

The reception desk of a hospital. A nun sits behind the desk. Dr. Fisher enters.

DR. FISHER: Sister?

SISTER: *Startled.* Oh, I'm sorry. I wasn't expecting anyone. I hope you don't need a doctor.

DR. FISHER: Not exactly.

SISTER: Because we haven't any. Now if you'll come back later today . . .

DR. FISHER: No, I'm sorry. You don't understand . . .

SISTER: If it's an emergency can you get to Saskatoon?

DR. FISHER: I've just come from there.

SISTER: They have the emergency system all set up in Saskatoon. There aren't any problems in getting all the help you need. Just go to the University Hospital or . . .

DR. FISHER: No, just a second . . .

SISTER: Now we do have a doctor, mind you . . .

DR. FISHER: You do?

SISTER: But he hasn't come yet.

DR. FISHER: Oh.

SISTER: He may be here this afternoon if you can wait that long . . . but if I were you I'd go to Saskatoon. It's not far.

DR. FISHER: Why?

SISTER: *Confidentially.* We don't know what he'll be like.

DR. FISHER: Oh.

SISTER: He's one of the British imports, you see.

DR. FISHER: What's wrong with them? *Suddenly embarrassed.* Excuse me. I'm sorry. I'm the doctor.

SISTER: I beg your pardon?

DR. FISHER: I'm the new doctor. My name is Fisher.

She stretches out her hand. Sister is not pleased.

SISTER: Oh. *Getting up.* If you'll come this way, I'll take you to the director.

As they exit the reporter enters and addresses the audience. The sister and the doctor pause to hear what he has to say.

REPORTER: *As newscaster.* Dr. Ida Fisher, a 45 year old British physician who left her practice and her family in London last week to serve residents of a Saskatchewan town deserted by its doctors has been forced by the doctors to move to a new location. Dr. Fisher packed her bags and left the town of Biggar last night after a charge she failed to meet medical standards was made by the local College of Physicians and Surgeons. The College forced the government to transfer her to an unnamed location.

DR. FISHER: *Furious.* These doctors have tried to blacken my reputation. I demand an immediate investigation by the College of Physicians and Surgeons into these scurrilous allegations made against me. I have never seen people so ill-informed and vindictive. They made statements without ever talking to me. This just doesn't happen in a civilized community. I am not the world's best doctor but I am as competent as the average and as conscientious. I am prepared to go before my peers and defend myself. From the moment I arrived I never felt the slightest welcome. I felt the sisters didn't believe I was anything but a housewife masquerading as a doctor.

SISTER: Are you a Catholic?

DR. FISHER: No!

Sister nods as if this explains everything.

A doctor enters and points accusingly at Fisher.

DOCTOR: British physicians are not trained the way we are. They don't have the hospital experience the average GP needs in this country.

As the lights fade we hear the voice of Pere Murray speaking at the K.O.D. rally in Saskatoon.

246

Scene vii   Pere Murray

The famous priest has taken the cause of the doctors as his own. We catch him in full flight under a large sign reading "Keep our Doctors! Welcome Pere Murray". Murray is a rough old firebrand given to extremes.

MURRAY: *Addressing the masses.* She's a card carrying Communist! I've been told she can't thread a needle—she can't take an x-ray—she's never performed an operation! I say kick her out of here—all the way back to where she came from!

Applause.

The government says we need medicare so the poor can pay their doctor bills. Well, I have known a good many people who have received medical help absolutely free of charge. In thirty-five years of running Notre Dame College with boys getting hurt all the time and having to see a doctor—I have never received a bill. If the government is allowed to control the doctors they will continue and finally they'll control every one of us and Saskatchewan will lose her democracy. This is a crisis! A grave crisis! There have been deaths, there will be violence and there could be bloodshed!

He rips off his clerical collar and his coat to reveal a plaid short sleeve shirt underneath.

The medical care programs in Europe are alright—but this is Communism! There are three Reds here. I can't see them; I can smell them. You Commies may think we're naive and hollow chested but we gave 100,000 boys fighting for the freedom you're fighting against. You Reds, I want you to know that we're as proud as hell to be Canadians! These people must understand that 100,000 of our boys died over there for our freedom and we should be ready to die too. Tell those bloody Commies to go to hell when it comes to Canada. I loath the welfare state and I love the free swinging freedoms. I've got my collar off tonight so I can tell you exactly what I think. I'm 70 and I'll never ask for an old-age pension. To hell with it. I want to be free.

I know Woodrow Lloyd and he's a great guy except that he's so damn stubborn. I know Tommy Douglas and he's a great friend except I hate his—well not his guts—his thinking. They're both great guys but they're wrong now and we've got to do something about it. They say we've got to wait two years if we want them out of office. I say let's not wait two years. I'm not afraid to stop a bullet. I had two brothers who died fighting for freedom and I think that's the greatest thing that could happen to anyone—I'm not afraid to die for freedom.

We've got to get off the fence and make our views know. This thing may break out into violence and bloodshed any day now, and God help us if it doesn't or if something else isn't done to stop it. This is an issue that is beyond religious boundaries. It doesn't matter if you're a Catholic or what you are. Did you see those Catholic women on television the other night? They were in favour of this rotten plan and I was pretty ashamed of them. *Pause.* I wouldn't be a darn bit surprised if someone put a bullet in me—I'm as likely to get it as Woodrow Lloyd . . .

A voice thunders down from over head.

VOICE: Father Murray.

MURRAY: Yes?

VOICE: This is Archbishop O'Neill.

MURRAY: Yes, your Grace?

VOICE: It's been a long time since you've seen your brother in New York, hasn't it?

MURRAY: Yes, it has but . . .

VOICE: Isn't he sick?

MURRAY: Well, he has been . . .

VOICE: I think you ought to pay him a visit, don't you?

MURRAY: Yes, but . . .

VOICE: Perhaps tomorrow morning.

MURRAY: Oh, no. I have all these speeches to make.

VOICE: I think he needs to see you.

MURRAY: But I haven't packed. My things are in Wilcox.

VOICE: We've taken care of that for you.

A suitcase lands at Murray's feet.

MURRAY: But I haven't got a ticket.

A ticket flies in.

MURRAY: *Wandering off—a little stunned.* Thank you.

VOICE: Thank God.

Cross fade to Lloyd in a spot.

LLOYD: Does Father Murray speak for the Keep Our Doctors leadership? Tonight I call upon them to publicly repudiate and repudiate absolutely Father Murray and his statements. If they do not they must accept responsibility.

In addition it seems to me imperative that the leaders of the medical profession both in Saskatchewan and in Canada likewise repudiate such statements in the strongest possible terms. And I direct a similar request to our newspaper editors. They should make clear—and quickly—their responsible opinions on this attempt to inject violence into the medical care issue.

A telephone rings harshly. Light on Mrs. Lloyd reaching for the receiver.

MRS. LLOYD: Hello?

CALLER: *Rough voice, threatening tone.* Mrs. Lloyd?

MRS. LLOYD: Yes?

CALLER: You get your husband to back off medicare . . .

MRS. LLOYD: Who is this please?

CALLER: Do you know where your kids are, right now?

MRS. LLOYD: Who is this?*Pause.* What do you mean?

A phone is hung up and we hear the dial tone. Mrs. Lloyd is frozen with fear while another phone rings. Lights up on a doctor's wife.

DOCTOR'S WIFE: *Answering.* Hello?

VOICE: Is this the good doctor's wife?

WIFE: Who is this?

VOICE: Just tell him to get back to work. I've been in the army. I know how to use a gun.

Click. Dial tone. Lights fade out on the two women.

Scene viii   The first community clinic

Dr. Hjertaas appears in a spotlight.

HJERTAAS: *To audience.* I'm Orville Hjertaas. *He pronounces it "Jerdus".* I was, at first, the only doctor practising in Prince Albert under the Medical Care Act. Our community clinic went into operation on July 1, which made it the first community sponsored clinic in the province. During the strike, since I had no anaesthetist, and was not allowed to both do the surgery and supervise an anaesthetist, I was forced to turn all surgical patients over to the opposition. I was attending two young women who were having miscarriages. Both were bleeding with placental tissues presenting from dilated cervices. Both needed to be scraped. I turned them over to the emergency staff—who changed every day, and refused to do the necessary D and C's as part of their teaching of the dangers of Medicare to the population at large. This went on for about a week while these women continued to flow and to grow more frantic every day. It is hard to forget the sight of a husband sitting at his wife's bedside, weeping over his inability to get help for her. The nurses were not even allowed to tell him which doctor was on duty.

Meanwhile I obtained an anaesthetist with a British diploma.

Therefore, on a Sunday morning, both patients transferred themselves back to my care—and with a couple of hefty fellows standing guard in the corridors we took them both to the O.R. and did the necessary surgery. You can imagine the uproar. There was a concerted effort by the medical staff to remove my hospital privileges.

Blackout.

Scene ix   Heard about town

The following scenes create a quick montage which builds to the K.O.D. mass rally of scene 9.

MAN: *Addressing a K.O.D. audience in Weyburn.* There will be 50,000 of us from all over Saskatchewan marching on Premier Lloyd's doorstep. We want Lloyd to realize his Communism isn't for Saskatchewan. But I warn you not to go in with clubs and guns. Try to avoid violence.

LISTENER: *Yelling from the audience.* Why not violence? We'll drag Lloyd out, burn down the "Lege", blow up the buildings. On to Regina!

Exit.

WOMAN: *At lunch counter.* How's the apple pie, Jeanie?

WAITRESS: Poisoned.

WOMAN: Okay, but if my doctor won't see me and I die, I'm holding you responsible!

Giggles. Exit.

CUTE ELEVATOR OPERATOR: Going up.

MAN: Top floor, please.

CUTE ELEVATOR OPERATOR: Sure. *She starts the elevator on its way.* Are you from out of town?

MAN: From Toronto.

CUTE ELEVATOR OPERATOR: Oh! Staying at this hotel?

MAN: Yes, I am. What do you think about medicare?

CUTE ELEVATOR OPERATOR: *Disappointed.* Used to be guys asked me what time I get off from work.

Exit.

Man enters wearing a National Farmers Union cap.

NFU MAN: After Athol Murray—the tension in the town? You could feel. You could almost tell as you walked down the street—you could almost tell who was for medicare and who was against it. You could feel it!

A socialite lady enters with a flower vase.

LADY: It was very touchy. We got to the point with some of our friends that we didn't entertain them any more. It became so emotional.

An office secretary enters.

SECRETARY: I remember at work, you didn't talk about medicare. You couldn't convince anybody—they just got mad and you got mad. And if they agreed with you that seemed kind of futile too.

The three of them leave.

REPORTER: *To farmer.* What would you do if your daughter was seriously ill and your doctor refused to treat her?

FARMER: *A moment and then grimly.* I'd kill him.

Exeunt—comedians rush on in the style of a vaudeville crossover—each pretending to be the other's ventriloquist dummy.

COMEDIAN 1: Have you heard about the doctor doll?

COMEDIAN 2: No, tell me about the doctor doll.

COMEDIAN 1: You wind it up and it goes on strike.

TOGETHER: Hahahahahah.

COMEDIAN 2: Well, have you heard about the medicare doll?

COMEDIAN 1: Tell me about the medicare doll.

COMEDIAN 2: Wind it up and it—

COMEDIAN 1: Yeah?

COMEDIAN 2: Issues a press release!!!

Exeunt.

OLD NURSE: *To reporter—very meaningfully.* Of course you know who the people are behind medicare. I don't have to tell you.

REPORTER: Who are you thinking of?

OLD NURSE: The people who are behind all the trouble in Canada—every big strike. You know who I mean.

REPORTER: Not exactly.

OLD NURSE: Yes you do.

REPORTER: No, I don't.

OLD NURSE: You do.

REPORTER: Do you want to spell it out for me?

No reply—Exeunt.

TEXAS DOCTOR: *Entering.* The doctors here are doing as great a thing for medicare as the heroes of the Alamo did for the independence of Texas. Doctors in Texas consider the Saskatchewan doctor's stand one of the most epic fights in modern times. My main interest in coming here is that we in Texas feel the finest doctors on the North American continent are in Saskatchewan and we understand some of them are looking for opportunities elsewhere. Texas needs these doctors. *Exit.*

WOMAN: *Entering.* Dear Editor: The crux of the matter is that Mr. Douglas has imposed socialist philosophy—from each according to his ability to each according to his need—on a profession which has increasingly abandoned internal rewards for monetary rewards in accordance with the shifts of values in our society. Yours sincerely, A Doctor's Wife. *Exit.*

K.O.D. CHORUS: *Around the edge of the playing area.* We the people of Saskatchewan want our doctors. We do not want doctors that you or the Commission can find in distant lands. We do not want card carrying communist doctors or doctors with questionable pasts.

The man and the listener from the beginning of the scene cross the stage with K.O.D. signs.

MAN: There will be 50,000 of us from all over Saskatchewan marching on Premier Lloyd's doorstep!

LISTENER: On to Regina!

Cross fade to the next scene.

Scene x   Premier's office

SECRETARY: *Intercom.* Mr. Lloyd, the party secretary, Mr. Benjamin is on the line.

LLOYD: Thanks, Betty. *Picks up phone.* Hello, Les.

BENJAMIN: *In another office.* Woodrow? Listen—the party has been getting thousands of calls and letters over this K.O.D. thing. There are a lot of people ready to demonstrate in favour of Medicare. The troops want to march. They're mad!

LLOYD: That's understandable.

BENJAMIN: You just say the word. In 96 hours we can have a mob in here you wouldn't believe.

LLOYD: *Pause—it is a tempting proposal.* No. If we're going to have democratic government according to who can get the biggest mob out, then we're all in trouble, aren't we? No, Les.

Scene xi   The great K.O.D. rally

The lawn in front of the legislative building. There is a large crowd of supporters bearing effigies of Premier Lloyd and signs such as: "Plan must satisfy all" and "Democracy is threatened."

CROWD: *Singing.* Hurrah the Doctors, hurrah the Doctors.

Someone in the crowd is yelling.

Hurrah the Doctors, hurrah the Doctors,
You can have your Medicare,
We don't want it anywhere,
Hurrah the Doctors, hurrah the Doctors!

REPORTER: The Committee to Keep our Doctors is having its much publicized rally here today in front of the Legislature. However, the 50,000 or 60,000 predicted turnout seems to have been over-optimistic on the part of the organizers. The crowd here appears only about 5,000 strong. The atmosphere is like that of a country fair.

HARRADENCE: *On the speaker's platform.* You are being punished by a group of power hungry politicians and I suggest we are not going to put up with it much longer.

REPORTER: That is Cline Harradence, a lawyer from Prince Albert addressing the crowd.

HARRADENCE: Who is going to be next? The plan is first to control the hospitals. They've done that already. Then to control the doctors, then to control the farmers and then the unions and their members. They are chipping us off a bit at a time. Is this what our fathers came to this country for? Is this what many fought and died for?

CROWD: No!

HARRADENCE: Now is the hour, this is the last stand and the last chance. Let us work, seek and actively protect our democratic rights!

Cheers.

REPORTER: Meanwhile, inside the Legislative Building, Mr. Thatcher is leading his party members from door to door of the Legislative Chamber.

Ross Thatcher and a group of Liberals enter—the followers carrying chairs. Thatcher is shaking door handles.

THATCHER: This one's definitely locked.

REPORTER: Try it again, Ross.

THATCHER: *Trying once more.* How's that?

The reporter takes a flash picture.

Want another one?

He kicks and shakes the door several times for the benefit of the press.

Alright, sit down boys.

Everyone sits down and Thatcher holds a press conference.

We think this is one of the most autocratic steps taken in the history of Saskatchewan. We have continually asked for a special session. We don't live in Russia yet, but many think conditions under this government are worse then Krushchev would have done. This group has been elected by the people of Saskatchewan and here we are locked out from our own desks. Premier Lloyd is acting like some of the petty dictators from Communist and Fascist countries.

K.O.D. MEMBER: *Rushing in, gasping for breath.* I have just come from the vast throng outside! There are thousands out there and they will be wild if you are locked out.

THATCHER: *Waving an arm grandly.* Yes, we're locked out and on direct orders of Premier Lloyd.

REPORTER: Mr. Lloyd received Mr. Thatcher's request for a special session two hours ago and sent him a reply which stated: "The Leader of the Opposition is well aware that a special session of the legislature with two hours notice is impossible. He is equally aware that the calling of a session is not his prerogative."

THATCHER: You're all invited back to our committee room for coffee. Unless you want some more pictures?

The Liberals leave.

REPORTER: The Lieutenant-Governor was rumoured to be considering dissolving the house and calling an election—but it

Linda Huffman as Ross Thatcher

Ross Thatcher

doesn't look like the government is planning to fall. We now return to our studio and regularly scheduled programming.

He leaves in the direction of the Liberal committee room. The stage is empty for a moment and then the N.F.U. man enters.

Scene xii   Turn around

NFU MAN: *Addressing the audience.* Well, we figured that practically everybody was against it and we were the only people that were for Medicare. But anyways, we had a meeting and by golly we found that there were more for it than against it. And then you felt okay about walking down the street—because then you knew who your friends were—although there were some you walked around.

We started taking up a collection—well, we weren't sure what we were going to do with the money—except that it was to set up a community clinic in Biggar. We were taking things into our own hands.

He knocks on a door and is answered by a farm wife.

WIFE: *Scowling.* What do you want?

NFU MAN: We're taking up a collection.

WIFE: Yeah?

NFU MAN: Well, it's about medical services.

WIFE: Are you for the doctors or against them?

NFU MAN: I wouldn't like to put it that way, just exactly. We're thinking about setting up some kind of co-operative clinic.

WIFE: Well, you've sure come to the right place. Come in.

NFU MAN: There and then they gave us a check for 500 dollars. In forty-eight hours we managed to raise 38,000 dollars. And you know—Biggar was Premier Lloyd's riding. We let him know what we were doing—and maybe it helped him stick to his guns.

Scene xiii   The Saskatoon agreement

REPORTER: This is the third week of the doctors' strike. The atmosphere was tense Wednesday afternoon as over a thousand people waited in the ballroom of Saskatoon's Bessborough Hotel to hear Dr. H. D. Dalgleish address the CCF Provincial Convention.

Lights up on Dalgleish.

DALGLEISH: The Council of the College has authorized me to put forward a new proposal which, in essence, involves prompt amendment of the Act and simultaneous action of the College in urging members to return to private practice.

REPORTER: The doctors have dropped their demand that the government repeal the Act. The door is open for new negotiations!

Lights fade on Dalgleish. Lord Taylor appears, a tall theatrical gentleman with an air of grandeur. He enters from behind the audience talking all the way.

TAYLOR: I will come, you shall pay my expenses and I'm going to have a fishing trip out of it. But I must not have any money. If I'm being paid by the government, the doctors just won't trust me, so I can't be paid. But you can blooming well give me some fishing.

REPORTER: *Watching his progress down the aisle.* Enter Lord Taylor . . .

TAYLOR: That was how we fixed it.

REPORTER: . . . British psychiatrist, a peer to the House of Lords appointed by the Labour government and one who had a hand in setting up the British National Health Plan.

When he reaches the stage he is met by a file of the various figures involved in the dispute. It is a little like a royal reception.

TAYLOR: So I met with Premier Lloyd and I met with some of the doctors and I began for the first time to get a feeling for what was worrying them. I thought they were decent fellows who were puzzled and worried, worried beyond measure about their freedom and all sorts of things.

I thought that once we could think of ourselves as medical colleagues, we had a hope. We met in the Medical Arts Building in Saskatoon. I sat in front of them all, it was a big group, with Dr. Dalgleish beside me. We sat together always on the sofa. Dr. Barootes was there and many more mates, people who became my friends as the battle went on. There was the Registrar of the College. A very nice big old fat chap. I was always pinching his tobacco. When I got tired they used to take me out into another room and they'd have some liquor for me or some Coca Cola or some sort of fizzy drink. (One thing they hadn't got in that place is any tea, but we still got along all right.)

Well, the process began to define itself. The doctors had already made some big concessions and so had the government. I was determined there was going to be a written agreement between these two and that this was not going to end in a fizzle. We worked on it paragraph after paragraph. Back and forth between the Cabinet and the College. I was determined to keep the two groups separate until it came to signing the agreement.

Taylor walks into the scene with the doctors he has just described and explodes. It is obvious everyone is at the end of their respective tethers.

TAYLOR: No, damn it! Bloody Hell!!!!

DOCTOR A: It has to be out of there!

TAYLOR: It does not! You have to leave it to the legal boys—we don't know anything about this! Don't you trust anybody?

DOCTOR B: No! It says they can *reading* "make regulations respecting the improvement of quality of services."

TAYLOR: Pursuant to the Act! "pursuant the Act." And the Act restricts them to being an insurance plan.

DOCTOR B: Get rid of it. We don't know what regulations they might pass.

TAYLOR: *Taking out a handkerchief.* I tell you I can't take any more of this. I can't! *He stuffs it in his mouth.* I'm fed up with this. I'm utterly fed to the teeth. Either you agree or I'm off!

DOCTOR A: Why should we make all the concessions?

TAYLOR: You aren't!

DOCTOR A: Break it off! Pull out the emergency services. Let them stew in their own juices!

DOCTOR B: Don't be a fool. Just who's stewing? We have 42 hospitals with the emergency plan working. As of today you know how many other hospitals are staffed and operating?

DOCTOR A: How many?

DOCTOR B: Fifty-five. Everybody is going back to work. We pull out the emergency service and I know for a fact the government can set up their own in two or three days. And we've got communities organizing clinics on their own all over the place . . .

DOCTOR C: It's over. It's over. They've promised to call a special session to amend the Act. We aren't going to be in any better position three weeks from now. We could be a hell of a lot worse off.

DOCTOR B: *To Taylor.* Stay. We'll work this out somehow.

TAYLOR: *Turning to the audience.* They begged me to stay. The cabinet agreed to delete the clause referring to improvement of services. The compromises came from both sides. Finally we had a document finished and it was a lovely document, too . . .

REPORTER: Lord Taylor, would you tell us who was the winner?

TAYLOR: The winner? That is a question that ought not to be asked for the moment. This province has been sick and I prescribe complete rest.

Lights fade.

258

Afterword

The company assembles one by one on the stage.

ACTOR: Doing a play on Medicare? Well, don't forget that the doctors were the underdogs.

ACTOR: So you're putting together a play about Medicare are you? Better be careful. It's still a touchy issue.

ACTOR: A play about Medicare? Are you going to tell how between the government and the doctors they put the boots to the Community Clinics? That's the real drama.

ACTOR: Medicare? Well, I remember the real issue was that they were going to put everying on a computer, see. Well, would you want the government to have a record that you had piles in 1973?

ACTOR: Medicare? We expected we were getting a complete system of health that would improve the whole level of health in the province. What we got was a way to pay the doctors. Put that in.

ACTOR: A play about Medicare, eh? Is it going to be for the government or for the doctors or for the people?

ACTOR: You know the government lost out on that fee for service business. You pay the doctor by piece work and he just runs you through like a sausage factory.

ACTOR: Well, you know, it was a rough time—but somebody had to be the first—and if we had backed down—well, the whole country would have lost out. We'd be in the same predicament as the States!

The actor who played Hjertaas steps forward.

HJERTAAS: In 1980 there are only four co-operative community clinics left in the province. In Prince Albert we have nurses working in the community, we have paramedical people, we even have a nutritionist on staff. We can concentrate on prevention as well as curing. We save the government money—we have to hospitalize about 25% less than the provincial average—and you know something? We still have to argue with the government to justify our staff nutritionist.

Lights fade to black.

259

Credits:

Cover photo: Mark Schoenberg
Cover and book design: May Chung
Typesetting: Mary Albert
Printing: Friesen Printers, Altona, Manitoba